Born in the Netherlands, Niek Sch
since 1979 and has trained as a prof
master. He has made extensiv
Anthroposophy and Theosophy
and has been working with esoteric Astrology since 1958.

THE TRUTINE OF HERMES

A GUIDE TO CALCULATING
AND
INTERPRETING THE TRUE ASCENDANT

Niek Scheps

Series Editor: Steve Eddy

ELEMENT BOOKS

© Niek Scheps 1990

First published 1990 by
Element Books Limited
Longmead, Shaftesbury, Dorset

Designed by Jenny Liddle
Cover illustration by Johtra
Cover design by Max Fairbrother
Typeset by Burns & Smith Ltd, Derby
Printed and bound by
Billings Ltd, Hylton Road, Worcester

British Library Cataloguing in Publication Data
Scheps, Niek
The trutine of Hermes: a guide to calculating and
interpreting the true ascendant.
1. Astrology
I. Title
133.5

ISBN 1-85230-131-7

For Nola, a bell of gold.

The Cup

This is the cup, the cup assigned to you
from the beginning.
I know, My child, how much of this dark
drink is your own brew
of fault or passion, ages long ago
in the deep years of yesterday, I know.

This is your road, a painful road and drear.
I made the stones that never give you rest;
And he, like you, shall come unto My breast,
but you, My child, must travel here.

This is your task, it has no joy or grace,
but it cannot be wrought by any other hand;
take it, I do not bid you understand.
I bid you close your eyes and see My face.

Swami Vivekananda

Contents

Acknowledgements

This manual has been written at the request of Helene Koppejan to accompany *The Zodiac Image Handbook*,[5] and she also supplied the basic data I needed to calculate the natal charts and the conception corrections exemplified. She also kindly allowed me to quote her descriptions of the relevant degree images.

The calculations in this book, have been carried out with the use of the *Planetentafeln für Jedermann* (Astronomical Tables) of Karl Schoch[38] for 4000 BC to AD 2000, the White ephemeris for 1801–50, Otto Barth's ephemerides for 1850–1970, and the *Concise Planetary Ephemeris* for AD 1950–2000. In about May 1988 the PCA (Personal Computer Astrology) computer program Electric Ephemeris (ver 2.3.3.) for 4000 BC to AD 2000, devised by Laurids Pedersen and Ananda Bagley, became available, enabling me to check and correct all the calculations. The format of the charts in this book is adapted with permission, from the PCA print-out.

I have to say, however, that I don't know how reliable the computerised planetary positions are, because there are some noticeable differences when compared with the results obtained from Schoch or Tuckermann. In the case of Schoch's tables the accepted margin of six minutes is appreciably more when using the PCA, although when using Neugebauer's tables[40] it is possible to calculate almost exact positions, which include a margin of only 0.01 degree. However, it is not easy to use or even to obtain these tables. Tuckermann's computerised ephemeris gives the positions with intervals of five and ten days, which is, particularly with regards to the positions of the Moon, insufficient for the calculation of a conception correction.

For the positions of Pluto before 1850, I used Kuno Foelsch's Pluto tables for 1 BC to AD 2500, as well as those of Heinz Noesselt, which are to be used in relationship with those of Schoch. The positions of Pluto before 1600, calculated with the PCA program, often show a difference of more than one degree and so we have to be careful about this. I was told that nobody really knows exactly where Pluto was, in, for instance AD 1200 or 400 BC. For the positions of Persephone, Hermes and Demeter, I used the ephemeris published in *Astrology*, by Ir C. J. Snijders.[27,42]

The Trutine of Hermes

For calculating planetary positions back to 4000 BC, Robert Hand's software programs 'Astrolabe' and 'Nova', and also a program called CCRS, are available, though I am not personally familiar with them.

The charts in this book, which are uncorrected, are based on PCA/Electric Ephemeris' print-outs. I sincerely thank Nonie for constantly encouraging me to write this book and for carefully checking the wording of the English, without which I couldn't possibly have managed.

Finally, I wish to thank the Real Israel Press for sponsoring this book.

Introduction

With the wealth of information and insights obtained from a natal chart, one might be forgiven for asking why we should in the first place want to use any correction method, why we should want to know the moment of conception and why we should want to use the degree symbols of Janduz and Jones. Why are those images so important? Why do we need to become conscious of spiritual backgrounds in order to obtain insights when examining and processing the available astrological material? These are the questions I have endeavoured to answer in this essay about the conception correction method, based on E. H. Bailey's 'Prenatal Epoch' and called the 'Trutine (or Rule) of Hermes'. The *Trutina Hermetis*, which says that 'the sign in which the Moon was found at the conception would be in the Ascendant at the nativity', was ascribed to the Egyptian priest-king-philosopher Hermes Trismegistos, Hermes the 'Thrice Greatest', and part of the forty-two books which disappeared in the burning of Alexandria, although some volumes were saved and secretly preserved (according to Manley Palmer Hall in *The Secret Teachings of All Ages*).

Although this particular Rule was discussed by Ptolemy[26] in Book III par. 1–2, the text of the Rule itself was given in No. 51 of his *Centilogue* (100 proverbs, see J. M. Ashmand's comments[26] on the *Tetrabiblos*), and was quoted by Alan Leo.[29b] In Robbins' translation,[26] p. 227 (see also pp. 91 and 270) it is said that the Rule was attributed to the mythical Egyptian King Nechepso and his priest Petosiris in a major work, from which only some fragments,[50] dated approximately 150 BC, are preserved, quoting from *Hermes and Asklepios*.

Boll[31b] (p. 154, cf. Bouché-Leclercq,[31c] pp. 376–9) writes that Achinapolus taught his astrological theories and rules about the conception at the astrology school founded by Berossos, a Chaldean priest-astrologer-historian, in 300 BC on the Greek island of Kos. At that time the conception chart seems to have been of much more importance than the birthchart.[31b] We know that for instance the birth of at least one child was deliberately delayed because of dangerous planetary positions; the name of that child was Alexander the Great.[31b] We also know that even the conception was orchestrated by astrologers in order to be sure of the right constellations.[31b] Kos was also the seat of one of the temples, dedicated to the mythical Asklepios, the son of Apollo, and was also the seat of a medical school founded by Hippocrates, who was born on this island.

The name 'trutine' (Latin *trutina*, Greek *trutenei*) means a pair of scales, or more exactly the pivot which measures the equilibrium. An Old Egyptian papyrus (1450 BC) shows the scene in the Hall of Judgment, described in the Egyptian Book of the Dead. The ibis-headed Thoth is standing beside a pair of weighing scales, measuring with a ruler the outcome of the weighing of the heart, the Egyptian symbol of the soul, of the newly dead and announcing it to Osiris, the god of death and resurrection, who was equivalent to the Grecian Hades. The dog-headed Anubis is in charge of the actual weighing. A heart is in the left scale (Old English *scealu*, meaning shell or cup, which is of Cancer, from Old Norse *skall*), and in the other scale the feather of Ma-a-t, goddess of truth and justice. Other pictures show that in fact it is Thoth-Hermes who is in charge of the actual weighing, for which reasons I have chosen the beautiful painting of the sign of Libra by the well-known Dutch painter Johfra for the cover of this book, and the title *The Trutine of Hermes*. To me it has become clear that the symbol of a pair of scales was deliberately chosen to express the idea of a perfect equilibrium between the position of the conception Moon in the scale at the left-hand side, equal to the position of the natal Ascendant (or the Descendant) at the right-hand side, and also the position of the Ascendant (or the Descendant) of the moment of conception at the left, matching exactly the position of the Moon at birth in the scale on the right. The second image of for instance the 29th degree of Cancer, as part of a very important set of 29th degrees, might give some food for thought.

The Greek Hermes-Psychopompos, who corresponds to the Egyptian Thoth, conducts the dead souls to the Underworld, and sometimes back to this world (as, for instance, in the case of Persephone), using his magic staff with the lemniscate at the top, but is not known to weigh the souls. It is said that Thoth is identified with the Hebrew patriarch Enoch, with Cadmus, the inventor of the Phoenician/Hebrew alphabet, with the Roman Mercury and the Scandinavian Odin, etc. In Christianity it is the archangel Michael who is charged with the weighing of dead souls.

'Weighing', in the Hebrew language, has the root *sheqèl*, also recognised in the name of a coin, 'shekel', and we will return later on to this subject. It is fascinating to discover that the numerical value of *sheqèl* (300 + 100 + 30) 430, is equal to the word for soul, *nephèsch* (50 + 80 + 300) 430. It is as we know the etheric Moon-soul body which is tied to the physical body, by which life-experiences and actions, recorded in the soul, are weighed after death by that which in the Egyptian imagination was called the Moongod Thoth. I am convinced this judgment is linked with the Ascendant degree images corrected by the 'Rule of Hermes'.

Solomon in *Proverbs* 16:2 refers to Jahweh weighing the spirit (Hebrew *roe'ach*). Of course, we have to know that behind the imagined shapes of gods, angelic forces are operating, which are symbolised in astrology by the planet forces.

I came across the Rule of Hermes in September 1958 while studying my first astrology book by C. Aq. Libra,[14] and struggling with the insufficient instructions on how to use this rule. It was some time before I was able to go into more detail with the help of Gorter's *Technique of Astrology*,[11] at that time only available in antiquarian bookshops. Gorter published the full text of the Four Orders of Bailey's Prenatal Epoch, demonstrated by an example. Unfortunately he calculated only the first 'regular' date and as the result did not confirm the Ascendant degree which he had already corrected in another way he left it at that and decided the Rule was not worth using. It is amazing to discover how many people think that all babies are born after a pregnancy of 273 days and therefore do not think to calculate either the extended count or the shorter gravidities, which I call the 'reduced' count. On checking Gorter's example I noticed also that he was mistaken in subtracting from instead of adding to the Moon position, which result indeed led to nothing. Furthermore, by calculating the short gravidity of 253 days, which is absolutely within the bounds of possibility, I actually found the desired Ascendant degree! Finally, he made the calculations unnecessarily hard by taking not the 13° of the average progression of the Moon, but dividing the distance in degrees between the natal Moon and (in this case) the Descendant, by the *true* speed of the Moon on the 'index date'.

I had to wait till the autumn of 1959 when I met astrologer Wim Koppejan, and came to understand his approach to calculating the conception correction before I got much further. Because of his knowledge of my chart, Koppejan, my friend for many years, always emphasised that I must make my own spiritual journey, and for this reason never consented to be my teacher, although he was always generous in his encouragement. In particular his book on the degrees has been a great source of inspiration for which I am deeply grateful.

The difference between his method and that of Bailey is that Koppejan, along with Thierens[8] (page 41), meticulously adhered to the Rule exactly as it was given, a possibility which Bailey did mention, but never put into practice, which is probably why it was never used by Libra and Gorter either. This seems to be why so many other astrologers also gave up, assuming that this part of the Rule was not to be used. The aspect in question of the Rule of Hermes states that the position of the conception Moon could indicate *either* the Ascendant or the Descendant in the natal chart, and that the position of the natal Moon could indicate *either* the Ascendant or the Descendant of the conception chart in all four of the orders given by Bailey. This means that on each possible conception date the opposite of the natal Moon position also has to be taken and calculated. Although Bailey included 'variations' in certain cases, Koppejan was able to extend the rule given in the fourth column of Bailey's scheme (to calculate not only the 'regular' conception date, but also the date fourteen days earlier or later in time, to include a longer or shorter gestation period), and to further extend or reduce it by yet another fortnight. Following his example, I always calculate all six or eight possibilities thus obtained, believing, with him, that those astrologers who regard the Rule of Hermes as 'incomplete and not useful' have been misled by the somewhat limiting four orders given by Bailey. For almost thirty years I have satisfactorily used my adaptation of this excellent method, based on the original Rule of Hermes, in thousands of charts, at the same time using the degree symbols as interpreted by Koppejan.

It is clear that Koppejan was fully justified in altering some details of the four limiting orders and these alterations in fact entailed a return to the original rule as given by Hermes, Nechepso and Ptolemy, and this will be confirmed by looking at the original texts and translations.

The Latin translation of the Greek text in the *Centilogue* of Ptolemy by Argoli Andreas (1659) reads:

> quod locus Lunae in natinitatis, est ascendans in conception; et locus ascendans Lunae in conceptione, est ascendans natinitatis; vel locus *oppositus*.

Ashmand's translation of Ptolemy's *Centilogue*, as published by Alan Leo, gives the following:

> Make the sign occupied by the Moon at the time of birth the sign ascending at the time of the conception and consider that (sign) in which she may be posited at the conception, *or the opposite one*, as the sign ascending at birth.

The English translation of van Solt's Dutch translation of the original Greek text reads:

> There where the Moon is at the moment of birth, there the sperm had determined the time at the moment of seminal discharge. And there where the Moon is during the impregnation, *or the opposite*, she has indicated the moment of birth.

Bailey on page 20 formulates this rule as follows:

> Astrologically considered, the pre-Natal epoch is a certain specific moment of time, occurring at a certain number of days earlier or later than 273 days before birth, when the degree ascending on the eastern horizon, and the longitude of the Moon thereat, interchange with the longitude of the Moon and the degree ascending at birth, *or their respective opposite points.*
> ... when the ascending degree at such time is the place held by the moon at birth, *or its opposite point*, and the Moon at such time is the place of the ascending degree at birth, *or its opposite point.*

In Chapter 3 page 25, Bailey says 'the Trutine of Hermes ... consists of the somewhat vague and incomplete dictum that the place of the Moon at conception was the Ascendant of the birth figure or its opposite point.' Furthermore, he says 'it was only half of a very important law'. He decided that 'additional investigation settled the point as to when the Moon's place and Ascendant, or the Moon's place and Descendant, should interchange, and the main postulate for the epoch was put forward in four clearly defined laws.' These I have included in chapter 6. Their limitations were ignored, and the rule was restored by Koppejan, as I have explained.

In his book *The Correction of the Birthchart* Drs Wim van Dam[1] gives a complete conception correction calculation of a fictitious birthtime. Unfortunately, he mistakenly supposed that the natal Moon was waxing instead of waning, and this assumption led him to a wrong starting-point. Because of this error, he counted the distance from the Moon to the *Ascendant* instead of the *Descendant*, which is 94 degrees and not 85. This is fortunately not disastrous in the case given, because of the position of the natal Moon, which happens to be more or less half-way between the Ascendant and the Descendant although, bearing in mind what is said in chapter 2 (about the position of the natal Moon) it would have led to a misinterpretation of the value of the incarnation impulse. The final result of his efforts was that an incorrect regular date was taken, which date, as we know, is preferable to other dates of shorter or longer gravidities. Also, his method is more complicated and it is not necessary to work with an indexdate. In spite of these drawbacks, however, he managed to calculate an excellent result, matching exactly the fictitious birthtime, which makes it all the more sad that in the end he concluded, 'the Rule of Hermes is total chaos', and therefore to be rejected. His argument that too many conception possibilities have to be considered can be resolved by using the degree symbols of Janduz and Jones, as demonstrated clearly through this book.

Perhaps I should declare my interest at the outset of this treatise and make clear that my concern is with the path and destiny of the human being, and his relationship with his Maker. To this end I have spent thirty years seeking to discover the deep significance of every degree in the zodiac, and in particular, of the one illustrating the corrected Ascendant degree which is demonstrably connected with the moment of conception. I hold that to be the time of high drama and resolve, when the incarnating soul bravely accepts its blueprint for the coming life.

I should explain, too, that I share with a number of other Dutch astrologers the unfashionable belief that Pluto is the higher ruler of Aries, and that there are three 'hypothetical' planets, Persephone, Hermes and Demeter, which are the higher rulers of, respectively, Taurus, Gemini and Cancer. The three hypothetical planets are described in an article about Dutch astrology in the *Astrological Journal*[27] and an ephemeris for them was published in the same magazine in the spring of 1973.

Koppejan's concept of the 'circuit' is a system by which the path of the solar energy symbolised by the Sun can be traced as it flows through the natal chart. We consider the Sun, symbol of the spiritual centre of consciousness, to define the starting-point of a source of illumination, which starts beaming through the chart from one ruler to another like a cosmic relay race (Gemini), the baton being passed from ruler to ruler. This is achieved by locating and contacting the ruler of the sign in which the Sun is found in the given chart, and from there the current moves on to 'induce' the ruler of the sign in which that particular planet is found, and so on from ruler to ruler. The positions and aspects of the planets along this 'heartline' observed in any chart are essential for drawing the contours of an interpretation of any individual person.

The expression 'inducing' (from the Latin *inducere*, to lead) was used by Koppejan in the electrical sense, suggesting the production of an electrical current by induction. The solar energy (Leo) is regarded as an electromagnetic current (Aquarius) to be switched on, and the whole process can be compared with the nervous system. Hopefully, but this is somewhat rarely the case, at the conclusion of the circuit, the solar energy will reach the solar source again, which means that all the planets included in the circuit can be controlled by the will's centre represented by the Sun. This return to the Sun in a chart only happens if the native has a planet in Leo, which is ruled by the Sun, or has Uranus in Aquarius, which is a 'stillstand' (another concept used by Koppejan, when the ruler of a sign is positioned within its own sign), requiring the flow to leap into the opposite sign, shaping an invisible, beautifully arched bridge. We recognise the meanings of Saturn and Uranus, rulers of Aquarius, equal to the meaning of the aspect of the opposition. A Higher Self, however, needs to have achieved a certain spiritual and solar level before this leaping into an opposite sign is possible. There are some other cases where we can see this happening, for instance if an individual lives up to his chart at an optimal level of spiritual consciousness and is determined to reach for the qualities of the opposite sign. In fact it is true that any desired leap into the opposite sign can be made possible if such is required in order to spark off a solar flow through the chart, assembling all the planet functions into a unified co-operation. I have given examples of the use of the circuit in several chapters in this manual, for instance the rather short circuit of Kruger (Chapter 13), compared with the extensive and complicated circuits of Bacon (Chapter 11) and Rodin (Chapter 8).

I believe that cosmic and spiritual life is nourished by the wisdom and knowledge (Gemini), revealed and expressed in the numerology of the biblical Hebrew and Greek languages, and drawn from Hebraic-Jewish tradition, rather than the sterile teachings of dogmatic ecclesiastical belief. For this reason only I quote from the Bible and illustrate in particular with Hebrew examples. In this context I wish to express my deep and affectionate gratitude to my Jewish teacher, Prof. Friedrich Weinreb,[16] from whose profound insights and wisdom I have often quoted.

If, in my attempt to make things clear, I have oversimplified the instructions for calculating the conception correction, I apologise, but I do know that many people have found it difficult to master the complexities of this method, and I hope that at least I have not added to their confusion.

Abbreviations used in Calculations and Chart Data

Asc.	= Ascendant	Node	= Moon's North Node
Conc.	= Conception		
CC	= Conception Correction	Part ft/PF	= Part of Fortune
		R	= Radix
Desc.	= Descendant	RLT	= Real Local Time
GMT	= Greenwich Mean Time	SR	= Solar Return
		ST	= Sidereal Time
LT	= Local Time	WAK	= W. A. Koppejan
MC	= Medium Coeli (Midheaven)		

Ari	= Aries	Lib	= Libra
Tau	= Taurus	Sco	= Scorpio
Gem	= Gemini	Sag	= Sagittarius
Can	= Cancer	Cap	= Capricornus
Leo	= Leo	Aqu	= Aquarius
Vir	= Virgo	Pis	= Pisces

Sun	= Sun	Ura	= Uranus
Moo	= Moon	Nep	= Neptune
Mer	= Mercury	Plu	= Pluto
Ven	= Venus	P	= Persephone
Mar	= Mars	H	= Hermes
Jup	= Jupiter	D	= Demeter
Sat	= Saturn		

Cnj	= conjunction of 0°	Sqr	= square of 90°
ssx	= semi sextile of 30°	Tri	= triangle of 120°
Sxt	= sextile of 60°	qcx	= quincunx (or inconjunction) of 150°
ssq	= semi square of 45°		
		opp	= opposition of 180°

The charts are based on given times, not on conception corrected times. House cusps will differ slightly.

CHAPTER ONE

The Degree Symbols of
Janduz and Jones

Out of several other sets of degree symbols, the 360 symbols of the French Janduz (J. Duzèa),[2] intended as 'a new procedure to rectify the time of birth', and the 360 Sabian symbols of the Canadian astrologer Dr Marc Edmond Jones,[3] have been selected by the Dutch astrologer Willem Koppejan as the two sets of images most reliably expressing the true astral or Akashic contents of Cancer, which rules conception. They are reflected by the Moon (the Janduz images) and by Demeter (the 'Sabian symbols' of Jones), both planetery functions having been identified by Koppejan as the two soul mirrors ruling Cancer. In his opinion these two planets manifest respectively the etheric (Moon) and astral (Demeter) levels of Life. Therefore he regarded both sets of 360 symbols as unbreakably connected, showing the Demetrian interior and the lunar exterior of everything created on earth.

Dr Marc Edmond Jones considered the Sabian symbols which were clairvoyantly seen by the medium Elsie Wheeler, to be 'for the sole purpose of dramatising the nature of the *Ascendant*' in the first place, and also for 'rectification of the birth time' (*The Sabian Symbols in Astrology*', page 126). Dane Rudhyar[4] interpreted the Sabian symbols as 'a cyclic and structured series which formalizes and reveals the archetypal meaning of 360 basic phases of human experience'. Wim Koppejan, gifted with a rarely found and refined intuition which unlocked his inner knowledge, ignored the other existing sets of symbols, such as those of Charubel (John Thomas) and Sepharial/La Volasfera, as being 'unreliable and unsound'. He regarded the Janduz and Jones images as exclusively essential for interpretation on a real spiritual level.

He joined the two sets together because he recognised the Sabian symbols as illustrating a more profound, and at the same time more elevated level than the Janduz pictures, and the combined images were brilliantly interpreted by him in his 'Book of Degree Symbols',[5] which has been circulating in manuscript among his circle of friends since 9 June 1956. The entire set, reworked by his wife Drs. Helene Koppejan, is to be published by Element Books.

Although the images of Janduz have been used fragmentarily by several other Dutch astrologers,[30],[31] the double set of degree symbols were used by Koppejan in the first place to identify and to interpret the Ascendant degree symbol as a personality symbol, or in Jungian terms the persona (which will be discussed in Chapter 3), the summarising principle covering the entire natal chart and containing all the characteristics of the native. In other words, all the contents of the natal chart as expressed in the positions of planets in signs, houses and aspects, are condensed, substantiated and made recognisable by the contents of the first image of Janduz and the second symbol of Jones for that particular Ascendant degree.

To determine the relevant Ascendant degree, it was essential to find a reliable method to check this calculation, and Koppejan was fortunate to find such a method in the 'Prenatal Epoch', a conception correction method, introduced in 1890 by the English astrologer Sepharial[6] and re-presented in 1916 (republished in 1973) in a refined form by the nowadays often belittled English astrologer E. H. Bailey, DA, FAS.[7] This was discussed and reviewed in the thirties by Dutch astrologers such as Thierens,[8] Knegt[9] and, on behalf of the Netherlands Astrological Society, van Solt.[1]

As we have discussed in the Introduction, Koppejan restored the original rule in such a way that we obtain two options, instead of one, on each calculated conception date. When we also apply Bailey's 'extended count', and repeatedly extend it as far as possible, we obtain three dates for each two options. By assuming the time of pregnancy to have been longer than normal, we also obtain the long gestation periods of over 290 days, which have been medically demonstrated and are therefore justifiably included. In many cases we find that even four conception dates are possible, for instance 256, 270, 284 and 298 days prior to birth. This makes eight options altogether, and with the fast rising signs it is actually possible to obtain even more, as we will see in Baden Powell's conception correction in Chapter 14.

Koppejan spent a lifetime carefully calculating thousands of natal charts of famous and well known people of all times, including royalty, prime ministers, politicians, artists, poets and writers, actors, composers and musicians. He started a vast data bank in 1942 with reliable birthtimes, painstakingly checked over and over again, collecting at the same time a large amount of biographical information. He regarded the Bailey method as 'sound and sane as can be'. So many questions and doubts, he used to say, about interpretations which seemingly didn't fit or suit the native, which is so often the case, could satisfactorily be answered by the contents of the Ascendant degree symbols calculated with Bailey's method. This is something I can wholeheartedly support, having calculated hundreds of charts of composers and other musicians from all over the world, and having recalculated and checked a great deal of Koppejan's life work.

The so-called 'Trutine of Hermes' is always said to be attributed to the Greek Ptolemy in his *Tetrabiblos*, but the truth seems to be that he only mentioned a 'rule' which was originally stated by the Egyptian Nechepso and his Priest Petosiris,[26] who in turn based their knowledge on the ancient wisdom of the Egyptian priest, king and philosopher Hermes Tresmegistos (Hermes, the Thrice Greatest). Although Bailey originally meant his method to locate in the first place the sex of a native and secondly to be able to correct or even to identify an unknown birthtime, Koppejan used his method in the first place to correct the given birthtime of a natal chart in order to unmask the precise Ascendant degree and its symbols, and secondly, to be able to calculate the conception chart. This chart he considered to be the counterpart of another important moment in time, the moment of the burial or cremation of the physical body.

Bailey, having found the sex, discarded all other possibilities, and by doing so in fact limited his horizon. The way the original rule was used by Koppejan, eight or even more possibilities are found. By doing this and by disconnecting it from Bailey's 'Law of Sex', he created much more space, widening the horizon and allowing more light to shine in. Thus released from the narrower view, intuition is allowed free play and spontaneous insights can 'spring to life', so to speak. Koppejan looked at it from a spiritual point of view.

It is unjustifiable to say, as some of his modern critics do, that with six or even more possibilities, one is always able to find a satisfactory answer. On the contrary, as I said, the more calculated possibilities we have, the wider is our view, though the choice is much more complicated and difficult. Of course it also has to be said that we are looking at the spiritual or the psychological meanings of the degree symbols and not only at the correction of a birthtime. It is surely unnecessary to say that it is rather irresponsible to calculate fictitious birthtimes instead of real ones,[13] and to base one's views on these results. It is unfortunate, too, that the value of this method was completely overlooked by most other astrologers,[6] who stopped after having calculated only the first possibility, subsequently to condemn the value of the entire method.

I hope that my reference to spiritual matters will not trouble those whose approach is exclusively pragmatic and whose *modus operandi* relies heavily on computerised data, valuable as I know this to be, and I plead with them not to repudiate the work of those pioneering theosophical astrologers who were inspired by the esoteric teachings of the past. In this connection I would just remind them of the lasting harm done by those who, in the eighteenth century, brought about the separation of astronomy and astrology when they embraced science exclusively, thus limiting their field of vision. These days it is again permissible to raise one's hat to both the left brain and the right brain equally!

Examining all the calculated conception corrections of a natal chart, it is not an easy job to decide which will be the true one. Intuition, astrological insight and biographical information are required in order to be able to locate the correct Ascendant degree. Koppejan's interpretations enable us to find which calculated degree symbol fits a given chart like the lid to a jar, as we Dutch Cancerian people like to say, a metaphor incorporating the idea of Saturn (lid) and the Moon/Demeter (jar), planets which are the rulers of respectively Capricorn and Cancer square Aries, the natural Ascendant.

In the same context, it is interesting to note that it has been the Dutch (Cancer) people, who have taken up the challenge given by the English (Aries) astrologer Bailey to sort out this business of the conception correction calculation method properly, reiterating the idea that the conception is symbolised by the sign of Cancer. Amazingly, this system has never found champions in England, and it seems that nowadays only a very few people are familiar with this method. Apparently there are some in the USA,[11] although it is hard to understand how each of six astrologers using this method came up with a different result.

> *You are a distinct portion of the essence of God;*
> *and contain part of him in yourself.*
>
> *Why, then, are you ignorant of your noble birth?*
> *Why do you not consider whence you came?*
> *Why do you not remember,*
> *when you are eating,*
> *who you are who eats*
> *and whom you feed?*

Do you not know that it is the Divine you feed;
the Divine you exercise?
You carry a God about with you, poor wretch, and know nothing of it.

Epictetus (AD 50)

CHAPTER TWO

The Position of the Natal Moon

Ode: Intimations of Immortality

Our birth is but a sleep and a forgetting:
The Soul that rises with us, our life's Star,
Hath had elsewhere its setting,
And cometh from afar;
Not in entire forgetfulness,
and not in utter nakedness,
But trailing clouds of glory do we come
From God, who is our home:
Heaven lies about us in our infancy!

William Wordsworth

Let us now consider how we can possibly find a clue as to which degree symbol out of the calculated possibilities is the right one. We wondered whether perhaps the position of the Moon in the natal chart would give an indication of why an incarnating soul had chosen a particular degree symbol for its Ascendant.

The 'Trutine of Hermes' mentions four 'Orders' operating:

1. Moon below the horizon and waxing;
2. Moon above the horizon and waxing;
3. Moon above the horizon and waning;
4. Moon below the horizon and waning.

What is the particular significance of the Moon being above or below the horizon and also in its being either waxing or waning?

In the *2nd order* where we find the natal Moon *above* the horizon and *waxing* in relation to the Sun, the first image of Janduz is implied, expressing itself in the outside world of the Moon or Maya. *Above* means in the upper half of the chart, marked by Capricorn ruled by Saturn, and Cancer ruled by the Moon, the 'day shell' of life.

And this also is the significance of a waxing natal Moon, positioned in the outgoing arch which has a lunar etheric significance, in relation to the Sun, and which is the symbol of the spiritual nucleus in a human being. The Moon is the reflecting, summarising principle of the five sensory (or 'material') planet functions of Mercury, Venus, Mars, Jupiter and Saturn. A waxing Moon is still growing in experience, and is expressing a young, extrovert soul, seeking experience in establishing itself or seeking opportunities to outcrystallise spiritual matter on the material levels of earthly life.

Also, the *quality* of the outgoing aspect of the Moon in relation to the Sun (the conjunction to the opposition) will give further detail about the phase this soul has already established in previous incarnations. For instance, a Moon in an outgoing conjunction with the Sun, a New Moon in fact, is in the beginning phase of a new cycle of experience, wherein it will learn how to reflect spiritual matters, while a Moon in an outgoing opposition with the Sun, Full Moon in fact, which has reached the phase of a maximal ability to reflect spiritual matters in the outside world, has reached a turning-point and is approaching the gate leading into the ingoing phase. All the meanings of the various aspects in between have to be interpreted in a similar way.

In the *4th order* we find the Moon radix *below* and *waning* is marked by the second image of Jones, expressing the inside or astral world of Demeter, the higher ruler of Cancer. *Below* means the Moon is positioned under the horizon, in the 'night shell' of the chart, marked by Cancer, Demeter.

So this is the significance of waning, when the Moon is positioned in the ingoing arch (astral Demeter significance) in relation to the Sun, both showing a mature, old, introvert soul whose ability to reflect the Moon is coloured by the phase it has reached, interpreted in the light of the position in sign and also the quality of the aspect it is shaping with the Sun. Positioned on the ingoing astral Demeter arch, it is much more bound to reflect the Demeter function, which summarises the planetary functions of the five extrasensory (or 'mystical') planets, namely Uranus, Neptune, Pluto, Persephone, and Hermes, 'overarched' as they are by Demeter. A waning Moon is on its way to rejoin the solar spiritual source, the Sun, and is gradually becoming more and more immersed in that source – which means that another cycle of experience is coming to completion. Much of what we said in the first paragraph can be adjusted for this case. But what are the meanings of the

1st order: Moon *below* the horizon and *waxing*, and the
3rd order: Moon *above* the horizon and *waning*?

The *1st order* shows the natal Moon *below* the horizon and *waxing*:

Although positioned in the Demeterian night shell of the natal chart, below the horizon, at the same time the Moon has the marks of the outgoing arch, reflecting towards the mirroring surface of the earth and establishing phenomena in matter with the support of the material, or lower planets, mentioned above.

The *3rd order* shows the Moon *above* the horizon and *waning*:

This is the same situation as the 2nd order (see above) but because waning, the need or the ability for outcrystallising (above) those material phenomena is decreasing, vanishing, fading away; perhaps showing the inability of the soul to achieve those experiences it needs, however desperately they are wanted.

Th˙ next train of thought was inspired when I was calculating the conception correction of the blind Braille, and might be worth considering as well. I envisioned that crucial moment, when the incarnating soul (the astral body) in 'space' was at the edge of taking off into incarnation and I was wondering if this was entirely its own independent decision or whether possibly the angels were 'pushing' it. Is there in 'space' something like free will or co-operation with 'heavenly' forces? Is there a free choice or even the possibility of a refusal?

If the natal Moon is *waxing* we have to calculate the distance to the *Ascendant* in order to know how long the time of gestation was and also to locate the date of conception. The Ascendant, as the rising point of the chart, is symbolised by Aries and has the quality of *acting independently*. In this case I am inclined to say, this soul was allowed to make a free and independent decision to incarnate. Because the Moon will be in an outgoing aspect to the Sun, this soul wants to incarnate in order to experience exclusively the physical world of matter, reflecting knowledge of spirituality found in matter. But with heavy afflictions we can also imagine this soul being forced after repeated refusals to incarnate.

With a *waning* natal Moon we count the distance to the *Descendant* which shows the *co-operation* with the outside surrounding world, symbolised by Libra. This soul is co-operating with heavenly entities or angels, even with 'God', and only wants to function in the spiritual world, because the Moon is in an ingoing aspect to the Sun and has lost its drive to operate on purely material levels. This does not mean any ignorance of matter, but rather an operating in matter with a total dedication to it in the light of the spirit. Its decision is carefully weighed; it knows it will be sent out into incarnation, into matter, with a particular divine task. Because the Moon will be on the ingoing arch, its background is more on Demeter's level, faced towards the Sun (waning) and therefore more spiritually evolved. These souls have in former lives developed a great capacity to reflect spiritual truths.

Is it possible that the soul at the time of conception knew whether the Ascendant of that moment would turn out to be the position of the natal Moon or its opposite point? How does the soul know all this? Is it because 'space' in fact is not as far away as we imagine heaven to be? Is it because all souls are still dwelling around us, and just as we are on earth, they too are within the atmosphere of the Moon – that is, on or within the atmosphere of the earth? Or are they in the valley of Avalon, said to be similar to the Egyptian 'Amenti', the dwelling-place of dead souls in the Isles in the West? It may be that these souls are simply in another dimension and invisible to most of us.

If they are indeed still bound by earth's gravity and the pull of Saturn, this could go some way towards explaining why transits to their charts continue to operate significantly even after death, when they are strongly in the minds of friends, family or admirers (see the case of Koppejan himself, page 89); why 'telepathy' seems to be an accessible mode of communication; why legendary souls like King Arthur are said to be 'only sleeping' until the call for action comes; and why the messages channelled by mediums so often indicate a soul preoccupied with earthly matters. Is it possible that it is not in fact the Akashic records that are being tapped but the Higher Self of the relevant being, whether inherent in one personality, or a series, each one enshrined in the relevant chart? That the re-clothing of the 'dry bones', as prophesied by Ezekiel, and the promised ecstasy in the air (the so-called 'rapture') might refer to a time when all souls actually may be released from this heavy time-cycle, and move on to bigger, better, brighter adventures in the future?

Aspects to the Natal Moon

The next thing to examine is the way the natal Moon is aspected, in other words how far and in which way the etheric lunar soul body is supported by other planetary functions, in performing what it set out to reflect. A poorly or a richly aspected Moon will certainly be expressed in a poor or a rich quality in the degree image operating. Therefore the aspects between the Ascendant and the planets as well as the relationship between the Ascendant and the Moon have to be considered as well.

Taking into account the Anthroposophical concepts, introduced by Dr Rudolf Steiner[17] (but see also Blavatsky[18]), of an etheric soul body, tied firmly and unbreakably to the physical body, and reflecting the contents of an astral body, Koppejan, who regarded Steiner's as the best and most advanced ideas currently circulating, has made it clear in his essays 'The Etheric Moon Body' and 'The Sevenfold Man' why the etheric soul body is ruled by the Moon and the astral body by Demeter, and why the etheric Moon body is so totally involved in the shaping of the physical body during ten lunar revolutions or approximately 273 days, confirmed by the Rule of Hermes. Ten lunar revolutions or sidereal months × 27·321661 is 273·21661 or 273 days 5h and 12m.

Infant Sorrow

My mother groan'd! my father wept.
Into the dangerous world I leapt:
Helpless, naked, piping loud:
Like a fiend hid in a cloud.

Struggling in my father's hands,
Striving against my swadling bands,
Bound and weary I thought best
To sulk upon my mother's breast.

William Blake

CHAPTER THREE

The Ascendant, Symbol of the Persona

The Ascendant represents the persona, literally meaning a mask as worn by the ancient Greek actors, not only to amplify the voice, but also to emphasise the expression of emotions and feelings. In the Jungian sense, the persona conceals a person's true thoughts and feelings, especially in his adaptation to the outside world: 'The Ascendant can act like a wall or a façade that an individual erects around himself. It is often like a mask that he hides behind, it is simply concerned with survival issues.'[22] The English word 'countenance' (meaning 'face', 'to allow') is related to the French 'contenance', which means behaviour, control, and both words are derived from the Latin *continentia*, 'to control'. And as Arroyo[25] said, 'since the Ascendant in a natural chart correlates with the sign Aries, the Ascendant is always indicative of a way of expressing one's individuality and thus — in a sense — one's ego' although I should rather choose the word 'personality' instead of 'individuality'.

The face is said to be 'the mirror of the Soul, reflecting the divine image and radiating the divine fire'.[20] The soul itself, imprinted with that divine image, should reflect this in the face. But now so many faces have lost their freedom to reflect the soul and its divine image and have become the controlled mask of the modern human who knows only too well how to behave and how to control and who now needs to unmask the face and this untrue behaviour in order to be reborn like a phoenix, rising renewed from his own ashes.

To identify one's exact rising degree and the contents of its images as the symbols of the personality represents a step forward in this process of unmasking the potential condensed from the entire natal chart. The fascinating thing about Bailey's conception correction method is that it provides us with a way of unmasking the persona the Higher Self has chosen to put on (unmasking the persona can be seen as one of the functions of Pluto, higher ruler of Aries), allowing us to uncover that which is concealed under the mask in and by the human face. All planetary functions are revealed in the parts of the human face,[20] which as a part of the head is considered to be ruled by Aries.

Although a small excursion, I like to point towards the meaning of the word 'consider' ('think carefully'), which is derived from the Latin *sider* meaning star, and was used for 'watching the stars'. How appropriate! Watch the stars as they are shining bright, and observe the light radiating from the human face, generated by the indwelling angel.[20]

The human face is the symbol of the divine unity, as we can learn from the Hebrew word for face, *paniem* (see also Chapter 8). In Kabbalistic numerology (gematria), each letter of the Hebrew alphabet is given a numerical value. The root of *paniem*, *pan*, is written with the letters *peh* (80) and *nun* (50). These values add up to 130 or 10 times the value of 13, and this in Hebrew is *echad* (1+8+4) or unity. The 13 of course redirects us to the thirteen planetary functions recognised by us, as well as the implications of the twelve sons of Jacob, the twelve tribes of Israel and the twelve disciples, surrounding the One. Although this is not the place to go too deeply into this subject, it is worth noting that the whole subject of numerology, or gematria, is a rich field to explore in conjunction with astrology, since the numbers revealed in the various planetary aspects, and also in the conception correction calculations, can indicate the 'level' of the incarnating soul. For a more detailed study of this subject, see Weinreb's *Roots of the Bible*, Bullinger, Curtiss and other Kabbalistic studies.[16]

It is essential to know that the correct position for both the biblical and modern 'Israelite', and of anyone wishing to re-enter into a true relationship with his Maker, is to stand *'upright'* and to *face* God (*Jahweh*, meaning 'I am'). The Hebrew word for 'facing' is the same word as that used for the human face. One can only really express fully what one originally wanted to be (Leo, Sun), as shown in one's natal chart and in the presonality symbols of one's corrected Ascendant degree, if one has unmasked one's face to see what lies beyond it. In order to do this, we must discover the exact Ascendant degree.

We should realise that Bailey's conception correction method is not in the first place intended to prove that the given birthtime was right. We are given a method to show the moment in which a double of the Higher Self descends in a flash and enters the physical body at the very moment this body is pushed out through the gate into the world of matter. Having wings like an angel, this double comes flying in, along the coloured segment of that particular degree and its symbols, the images we mentioned, to join the physical body being born. This is beautifully expressed by van Solt on page 74 of his booklet: 'The ecliptic or the zodiac is an auric girdle or belt and every degree of this is like a segment of a particular colour, stretching from the North pole to the South pole of the ecliptic.'

This very moment of the descent of the Higher Self into the physical body does not necessarily have to be the same as the moment of the first cry of the baby or the moment the cord is cut; it may be that the descent can take place just before or just after the actual moment of birth. However, the conception correction method proves in most cases that the descent synchronises with the birth. This, of course, can only be considered to be true if we have been able to recognise the right Ascendant degree symbol for the given natal chart.

The physical body is symbolised by the Ascendant and correlated to Aries, the sign of the East, where the Sun rises daily. It feels right to look a little closer at what is known about these items from traditional Hebrew sources.

In Hebrew the East is called *qedem*. Numerologically this gives us *qoph* (100), *dalleth* (4), *mem* (40), which adds up to the astonishing value of 144 about which so much has been written already. Immediately one thinks of the 144,000 elected ones, 'singing the new song of the Lamb', as recorded in the Revelation of St John. Through generations since Adam those 144,000 elected ones have carried in the bloodstream of their future 'chariot-of-fire body', (visualise that extraordinary event of the prophet Elijah flying up into heaven!), a spark of light to be ignited by Christ, thus transmuting the physical body in the 'twinkling of an eye' into the divine fire of the Resurrection body, symbolised by Pluto, considered to be the higher ruler of Aries. This future body will be the carrier of the same – albeit perfected – Ascendant degree symbol.

According to Nicodemus, when Christ descended into hell after his sacrifice at Golgotha (Gulgoleth, meaning 'the place of the skull', also 'the head', ascribed to Aries) a fiery ray of royal purple beamed out from His head into the depths of the infernal regions, as He reclaimed the souls of the long-dead saints, who were then seen on the streets of Jerusalem, and later with Jesus and the disciples in Galilee (Matt. 27: 52, 53). By means of this Plutonic energy, the death-forces of Scorpio ('death, where is thy sting?') were lifted up to activate the mighty powers of Resurrection. Thereafter the spiritual representative of the physical body was able to appear as a permanent presence instead of only a temporary one.

Scorpio knows nothing of resurrection, only the change of life into death and vice versa, the means by which the birth of a temporary physical body is made possible. Pluto/Aries is transfiguration and transmutation of life-forms, and in particular, the physical body. This is the process made manifest by Christ on Mount Tabor (Matt. 17: 2). At the last supper, He described His *physical* body as 'bread and wine' leading to Eternal life (Matt. 26: 26), and by this I understand the permanent appearance on *earth* of the entire Higher Self in a transfigured physical body. Hebrew tradition teaches us how bread and wine are symbolically linked to the impulse which was given at Easter. Consider for a moment the phenomenon of light and fire in connection with the divine physical body. Through their long years in the wilderness, and on Mount Sinai, the Israelites were accompanied by a pillar of fire; Jahweh spoke to Moses from the burning bush (Exod. 3: 2, 3) and Shadrach, Meshach and Abed-nego walked, with the Son of God, in the burning fiery furnace (Dan. 3: 20, 21); tongues of flame hovered over the heads of the disciples and others at Pentecost (the fiftieth day after Easter, Acts 2), and so on.

Mars, the ruler of Scorpio, only burns to ashes. Pluto, the higher ruler of Aries, burns, and lives, risen. The Plutonic forces manifested by Christ are similar to those demonstrated by Moses (Num. 21: 9) when he saved the mortally stung Israelites in the desert by raising a fiery serpent of brass on a pole for them to look upon it. From the Hebrew language and Jewish tradition we learn that in this symbol of a brass serpent, the presence of the Messiah is doubly incorporated, and the New Testament tells us who this Messiah is. The Hebrew name for man and woman, created by God, is similar to the word for divine fire. In Old Scandinavian languages the word for a physical body is *lic-haam*, literally meaning a 'house of light'.

The discovery of Pluto in 1930 made it clear that the time of change foretold by St Paul had drawn near. Now that Pluto is in Scorpio, its own sign, the time has come for it to be faced and understood more clearly.

Calculating the conception chart (emphasised by Ptolemy and practised in Chinese astrology) is also important for another reason: it can shed light on what developed during the ten lunar revolutions of the pregnancy, helping us to understand what might have caused, for instance, severe damage to the physical body – since this may not be fully apparent in the natal chart. And this chart also can be compared with another moment in time when the same body is buried or cremated after death, contributing to our knowledge of what the individual has achieved in this life in the physical sense.

In the 21st week of the pregnancy, and felt clearly by the mother, the moment of the so-called quickening of the embryo occurs. This can be recognised as the moment the spiritual body (and not the Higher Self), symbolised by the Sun, descends and enters the embryo, and initiates (Pluto) its life in this world. The 21st week is approximately 150 days or 5 solar months, and 5 is the number of the fifth sign, Leo, ruled by the Sun, the spirit, giver of life.

Supported by the available calculated material, it seems to me possible to show that the acceptance by the Higher Self of a certain degree symbol, selected from the 360 conception 'gates' before the moment of its actual incarnation, was a free choice (Libra) and a free (Aquarius) decision (Leo). I imagine these symbols will have been reflected (Cancer) to and imprinted (Capricorn) in the Higher Self and its soul representatives, the astral and etheric bodies, and were freely accepted as the symbols of its forthcoming physical body, as the summarised concept of its entire being, condensed into both Ascendant degree symbols. All the possibilities already existing and contained in the Higher Self may be in fact the sum of all the potential the Higher Self has achieved in previous lives, its spiritual capital (Taurus), to use a financial metaphor, to be processed (Scorpio) in its coming life (Leo), summarised and expressed in the two images for that particular Ascendant degree.

The 360 degrees of the zodiac have been identified by Koppejan as the 360 'zodiacal pores of the earth aura through which the cosmic forces enter, coming from atmospheres outside the zodiac, where the Higher Self is at "home" '.

In my opinion each Higher Self takes part in one of those 360 sequences, each of them involving a particular aspect of life, and was willing to undertake the inherent demands before incarnation, although it might well have subsequently forgotten what had been promised. According to Jewish lore, one of the angels in charge made a fingersnap under the nose of the soul, moments before it incarnated, and as a result it immediately forgot where it came from. This, it is said, is why we have our upperlip divided into two halves, with a tiny dent under the nose. The nose, ruled as it is by Jupiter, symbolises the aims we have forgotten by the time we arrive in life. We have good reason to be grateful that we have such a thing as the conception correction method to remind us of the aims and tasks we have to perform within our physical body.

The 360 degrees can be divided into thirty sets of 12 degrees, one of the same number from each consecutive sign – that is, sets of twelve first degrees, of twelve second degrees and so on. In Koppejan's view, each set of 12 degrees embodies a particular basic problem, which the divine impulse has set out in the first image of the first sign, Aries, and then gradually unfolded in the following degrees of the same number in every sign. In each of the second images of each degree is shown the way in which this problem can be resolved (see Chapter 8).

In fact these thirty sets, each containing twelve related degrees of the same number, can be seen as the twelve parts of an enormous task, expressed by 'heaven' in the degree images, a task to be undertaken in each individual life, in order that what is known as the Kingdom of Heaven on Earth, which is within us, might be manifested. This task requires a sincere dedication to, and a Christ-centred meditation on, performing revolutionary deeds within a balanced personality, symbolised and made possible by the power of Pluto, and thus invoking the entire cardinal cross.

This concept of Pluto as the higher ruler of Aries will probably give the right answers as to how one can perform 'even greater deeds than I', as promised by Christ. This heavenly task cannot possibly be accomplished by the muscled Mars, the 'lower' ruler of Aries and of Scorpio, acting alone. Only when Mars is acting under the control of Pluto is a human being equipped to perform the deeds required by heaven. Such a person will go 'from strength to strength'.

By truly demonstrating physically both Ascendant degree symbols, we initiate the strength of Pluto in ourselves, unmasking the strength of our entire being and, finally, initiating that hidden spark of Light in our physical body which allows us to be transmuted in a 'Chariot of Fire',[13] or a 'Diamond Vehicle'. Recalling the words of Blake's 'Jerusalem', one can feel quivers running over the spine.

Van Solt, on page 25 of his essay,[1] summarised all the possibilities of the 'Trutine of Hermes' in that beautiful symbol of the caduceus of Hermes. Contemplating this high spiritual symbol, he considers the 'Trutine of Hermes' to be the 'Caduceus, becoming the symbol of the Seer and the Healer who supplies comfort and relief through his insights, but only in the hands of initiated astrologers/priests', a symbol which should not be used by profane people, who view things superficially instead of going deep into the individual's personality in order to understand fully why he is what he is, or has been in the past.

I see something of God each hour of the
twenty-four, and each moment then,
in the faces of men and women
I see God, and in my own face in the glass,
I find letters from God dropt in the street
and every one is signed by God's name,
and I leave them where they are,
for I know that where so'ere I go,
others will punctually come for ever and ever.

Walt Whitman

CHAPTER FOUR

The Conception

The Hebrew word for conception or becoming pregnant is derived from the root *abar*, in numbers *ayin* (70) *beth* (2) *resj* (200) which brings us to 272, very close to the 273 days of the average time of pregnancy. Impregnation is seen as the passing of seed, but there is more to say.

We find *abar* in the very name of *Heber*, the great-grandson of Shem, said to be the ancestor of the Hebrew race. *Abar* literally means crossing – crossing or passing a sea or a river, coming from an area on the other side. Heber and the Hebrews therefore are said to have come 'from the other side of the fourth river, the Euphrates, one of the four subsidiary rivers which sprang from the river in the garden of Eden, and this fourth river forms the uttermost boundary of this world'.[16] Originating from the other world means that the Hebrew, or anyone who wants to be an *Ibri*, is taking a position on 'the other side' which is opposed to this material world.

Abar is the word used for the golden chains locking the Holy of Holies in the temple in Jerusalem (the physical body as the temple of God) and it is related to the Passover, which is the name of the Hebrew sacrificial lamb, prepared in the night Israel left Egypt and therefore it is also the name for Christ, *Agnus Dei*, whose agony began the moment he crossed the brook Kidron. Significantly, it is also used for a ferryboat, and we remember how, in Greek mythology, dead souls had to be ferried across the River Styx by Charon, the ferryman.

Surprisingly, the English word 'aberration' is literally taken from this same word *abar*, which also meant an aberration of the laws given by Moses, literally crossing the border of what was allowed because aberration results in being sent into captivity, crossing the River Euphrates into Babylon. The same word is used for floods (the Nile overflowing for instance) and also for a suffering soul, overflowing with tears.

Is all this really significant for an incarnating soul? Is it really suffering on its journey into incarnation, coming from afar?

We know for instance from the grail stories how Lohengrin was brought to this world by a swan. And we know how often the incarnating soul is thought to be brought by a swan or a stork. It is interesting to know that in Dutch folklore the baby is delivered by a stork, or a swan and a reference to this still appears on the roofs of farms in Friesland, which are decorated with a number of carved wooden swans equal to the number of babies born under that roof. In Dutch nursery rhymes one sings about 'white swans and green swans, which are floating into the land of the angels', and vice versa. In this connection it is worthwhile to know that the Hebrew word for a swan is *theneshameth*, carrying the word *neshama*, which means 'heavenly soul'. Legends all over the world contain similar material. The Vedas tell about the Hamsa, in this case a pair of swans, the vehicle of Brahma, the radiating universal spirit (Leo, Sun) and the self. In Greek mythology the Sun god Apollo was born from the offspring of Leda and the Swan (Zeus); in Egypt, Osiris was born from an ibis egg, and in Hindu mythology the god Vishnu was parented by a garoeda, a mythological bird akin to the phoenix. In Scandinavian legends a duck is associated with childbirth, elsewhere a goose. The seven rishis (analogous to the seven stars of the Great Bear, which in India is called the Swan), were the original seven perfect souls, selected out of Atlantis. In Christianity the swan is dedicated to the Virgin Mary. In Jewish tradition the *neshama* is the heavenly soul, a light body, created in the image of God. Oval-shaped it carries two centres which house the spirit and the Holy Ghost. It has the ability to 'see' visions, mirrored by the angels during sleep, and it is the bearer of wisdom. By means of the *neshama* one is able to return to God, unless it is cut off by impurity, uncleanness or defilement and pollution in every aspect of life. The swan is one of the so-called 'unclean' birds and not to be eaten, but according to some authors this is because it is holy.

Let us put all this together in relation to the 273 days of the average time of pregnancy. After 272 days of gestation, the infant, the incarnated soul, is ready to be born. This seems to be the minimum period needed by the soul, to grow and to develop its physical vehicle in the womb, then literally to be born while the embryonic waters, which protected and symbolically 'nourished' it for 10 lunar months, are overflowing! But what about a premature birth of less than 273 days, or one more than 273 days? Both cases have their own significance and can be easily interpreted.

One way to arrive at the number 272 is to multiply 16 by 17. The number 16 is connected with the number 160 for silver, in Hebrew *kesseph*, made up of the letters *kaph* (20), *sammig* (60) and *peh* (80), which also means 'to become pale' like the eclipsed Sun or Moon, 'to desire', and it is the metal used for a coin called a

sheqel (*sjin* (300), *qoph* (100) *lammed* (30)), which has the value of
430. This number equates to the number 430 of *nephesh* (*nun* (50)
peh (80), *sjin* (300)), identified as the etheric Moon-body-soul. The
number 17 signifies completion and perfection.

At the time I was writing this chapter, I had a significant dream,
related to this subject. As so often, I was flying home across a
wide river, with, funnily enough, windmills on either side. In this
dream I was taught: 'Usually, karmic debts have to be paid off by
the soul in silver shekels'. Combining the meanings of the
numbers 16 and 17, with the message in the dream we can
discover that in a period of 272 days the soul, identified by the
Moon and Demeter, the rulers of Cancer, the very sign which
rules silver, has been refined like silver, and is completed and
perfected, ready to be born and is prepared to pay off in its
coming lifetime, any karmic debts, with which the soul is
burdened life after life. Knowing this, the soul may indeed be
suffering.

The number 272 of *abar* carries more secrets in it. Reversed, the
letters of the word spell *raba*, which means 'a raven, hunger, a
stranger, to be still in fear, to rest, and to dwell quietly'. I don't
think it is that easy for a soul to incarnate, being like a raven,
threatened and frightened in its flight, being hungry and thirsty,
desiring to be quiet and restful, while at the same time safely
dwelling within the womb, symbolically having been quenched
by the cosmic waters. I don't think it is too difficult to see the
incarnating Soul carrying these characteristics. After 272 days or
10 (Capricorn, Saturn) lunar (Cancer, Moon) months, the Soul
(Cancer) is harmonised and stabilised (Libra, Venus) and ready to
be born, and the very next day, is pushed through the gate of Life
(Aries, Mars and Pluto). So in this process we see an activation of
all four cardinal signs.

Mother and Son

It is not yours, O mother, to complain,
Not, mother, yours to weep,
Though nevermore your son again
Shall to your bosom creep,
Though nevermore again you watch your baby sleep.

Though in the greener paths of earth
Mother and child, no more
We wander; and no more the birth
Of me, whom once you bore,
Seems still the brave reward that once it seemed of yore;

Though as all passes, day and night,
the seasons and the years,
From you, O mother, this delight,
This also disappears,
Some profit yet survives all your pangs and tears.

The child, the seed, the grain of corn,
The acorn on the hill,
Each for some separate end is born
In season fit, and still,
Each must in strength arise to work the Almighty will.

Robert Louis Stevenson (1850–1894)

CHAPTER FIVE

The Julian and Gregorian Calendar

Before the calendar which is in use nowadays (the Gregorian calendar, named after Pope Gregory XIII), another calendar was used, the so-called Julian or Medieval calendar. This Julian calendar, designed by the Alexandrian astronomer Sosigenes, was introduced by the Roman Emperor Julius Caesar. He declared the year 709 of the Roman calendar, (commemorating the foundation of Rome), to be the first Julian year, which in our modern calendar equates to the year 44 BC (astronomically 45 BC) and it came into function on 1 January of that year.

The Julian calendar is based on the course of the Sun through the ecliptic, and is known as a solar calendar. The ancient Babylonian and Hebrew calendars in use for thousands of years before that were fixed according to the phases of the Moon and were therefore known as lunar calendars. Although the Hebrew, Israelite and Jewish New Year and the new months (synodical months of approximately 29·5306 days), were determined by the phase of the New Moon, such a year at the same time observed the four seasons, and so was a luni-solar year comprising 354 days. To match with the solar year of 365 days it was necessary to insert a leap year seven times in nineteen years – every two or three years. In each of those seven leap years, a thirteenth month was inserted, and that month was called Adar-Sjeni. The Christian calendar in use nowadays is seen as a fixed luni-solar calendar within a fixed solar calendar.

The introduction of the Julian calendar, which was entirely based on the revolution of the Sun and on a tropic year of 365·25 days, represented an important shift in human consciousness with regard to the phenomenon of time. The same thing was reflected in the field of religion, which had for thousands of years been largely Moon-based. This was certainly true in the religion of the Hebrews and Israelites and is true to this day for the Jewish race. More precisely, human consciousness (Sun, ruler of Leo) originally focused on the Father/Mother divinity, expressed by the axis of Capricorn/Cancer, then gradually responded to the teachings of Christ (called the Sun of Righteousness by Malachi), which emphasised the ideas of service and sacrifice inherent in the following axis of Virgo and Pisces. Thus our mind is drawn to Leo, the central sign between these two axes, unbreakably connected with the opposite sign of Aquarius, the heavenly waterbearer.

Of course there is much more that could be said about calendars, and we should investigate Hebrew chronology, which started to count from the creation of Adam (said to be 4000 BC), and in this connection we should look at the meanings of the Hebrew names for the thirteen months, but unfortunately they cannot be included in this small volume. Suffice it to say that with the appearance of Christ a shift towards a Sun consciousness took place, and this was strongly emphasised by a Roman emperor with the introduction of a new calendar in 45 BC. This expansion of solar consciousness doesn't mean an exclusion of the ancient Hebrew cosmic laws and festivals, given by Moses and based on lunar conditions. It should rather be seen as an inclusion, but at a raised spiritual level.

Although every four years a leap year was introduced into the Julian calendar, from then on an astronomical error, of which Ptolemy was already aware, gradually slipped in, because the average length of the solar year was erroneously assumed to be 365·25 days. In modern times this has been corrected to 365·24219647 days. This solar year is the length in time, measured from the spring equinox or 0 degrees of Aries, needed by the Sun to move along the ecliptic until the same point is reached again. And it involved another error also, because the true date of the spring equinox was not exactly known at that time. Several scientists such as Beda (eighth century), and astronomers such as Roger Bacon (thirteenth century), Campanus, and Regiomontanus (fifteenth century), were fully aware of this error and reported the calendar to be slow of the true astronomical dates. Bacon especially was very upset that according to the untrue calendar 'Christian believers were consuming meat in Lent when it should have been fish in a time of fasting' as he wrote to Pope Clemens IV, but the time was not yet ripe for an adjustment.

By the sixteenth century the difference in the calendar had increased up to 10 days and more and more often the need to adjust these errors was stressed. It was the medical doctor Lilius (Aloigi Giglio, born in 1552 in Spain) who proposed an ingenious calendar reform, which was presented to the Pope ten years after his death by his brother. Advised by a council of experts, scientists and clergy, Pope Gregory XIII in his Bull 'Inter

Gravissimas', dated 24.2.1582, rescinded the Julian calendar, declaring that 5 October 1582 was to be 15 October, the first date of the new Gregorian calendar, an advance of ten days.

As we mentioned earlier on, the entire matter came about because of the upsetting fact that the feasts of Lent and Easter were no longer celebrated on the right date, a matter of great concern because of the importance of Easter being celebrated on the Sunday following the first Full Moon after the spring equinox. Pope Gregory also put right the true date of the spring equinox, which was again fixed on 21 March, so that Easter from now on could be celebrated on the right day.

According to Davidson,[30] on Good Friday 7 April AD 30 (Julian calendar), the Full Moon was in Libra, opposite the Sun in Aries. The Sunday following was the third day, the day of the Resurrection, from then on to be celebrated as Easter. Accidentally (but how fascinating!), we have found a very important clue as to why Pluto, despite popular current opinion, *has* to be assigned to Aries, the sign of the East and also the symbol of the Ascendant, the physical body, perfected in Christ who was the first one in history to be resurrected. This is also expressed in German as *Ostern*, meaning East. The Dutch language uses *Pasen* for Easter, after the Hebrew word *pesach*, which in its numerical values is similar to bread and wine, a concept of considerable interest.

With a shock I realised what an extraordinary impact Christ has had in connection with the human calendar, in fact with history, a word cleverly seen by some as His Story. Not only because of the date of the resurrection, but also because of a much less well-known fact (although it was familiar until the fourth century), that 5 October, the start of the new calendar, was in fact the birthday of Jesus Christ in the year 4 BC, as recorded in the Great Pyramid.[30]

Until 1582 it was impossible to celebrate this birthdate properly, because 5 October according to the Julian calendar was in fact 12, 13, 14 or 15 October, varying each century. Now we are able to sense on the right day with the Sun in the same position as it was in 4 BC, in 11 degrees Libra, His solar return from year to year. This birthday was for ages commonly believed by the early Christians to be the correct one, until the Romans, to please the German tribes, changed the date to 25 December, the date of the German Midwinter celebrations and the Roman Saturnalia.

I am convinced that the significance of the celebrations in Lent and Easter and consequently Whitsun, as well as the birthday of Jesus, have to be seen in the light of not only astronomical but also astro-cosmic facts. Is it not because of the extremely important recognition, that the Christ has been given all power in heaven and on earth, that He should be seen as the key figure? In fact, Christ literally has to be considered as the key unlocking heaven and the heavenly constellations. Christ, the Son of Man (Aquarius), rules all that lies within the care of the cosmos, in heavenly love for all men and all things, and this is inherent in the vessel of the divine waterbearer, expressed in the sign of Aquarius, the sign of heavenly times, of Oeranos/Uranus and Saturn. And it is St Peter, the Rock (Saturn) who holds the key of the Kingdom. It is Christ, the Lord of the Constellations, who with healing wings invisibly hovers over any birthchart.

Having recognised this fact, it is easy to see how significant human calendars are. If the calendar had not been put right in the sixteenth century, we should never have been able to celebrate properly, cosmically, all the dates so important for all of us.

With reference to what was said earlier about the 'lunar' and the 'solar' years, I would like to stress a few significant differences between the two calendars.

The lunar year showed an awareness of the phases of the Moon as it circled around the earth and in particular the phases of the New and of the Full Moon, which occurred thirteen times each year. Some of them marked the feasts celebrated in Hebrew times, and which are still observed in Judaism. Nowadays we are accustomed to the New Moon and Full Moon meditations (Capricorn) observed by 'New Age' people and although these are worthwhile in themselves, one wonders whether these people are in fact aware of the original cosmic significance of their practices. Originally those phases of the Moon were recognised as moments of religious renewal in time, and this is something which certainly should be fully included in those meditations. The New Moon marks the renewal of the outer life-experiences of a solar and spiritual quality, and the Full Moon marks the renewal of inner Demeter experiences, from a divine overarching umbrella reflected in and directed towards everyday circumstances and experiences.

In spite of the errors we have mentioned, the concept of the solar year, introduced with the Julian calendar, indicates a consciousness of the Sun 'illuminating the ecliptic pathway'. Since the introduction of the Julian calendar, the new year and the new month are marked by the entry of a particular zodiacal sign which was not the case in earlier times. In fact from then on, theoretically speaking, humans were able to develop a consciousness of cosmically determined conditions, something which was only finally made practicable by the introduction of the Gregorian calendar in 1582. At the same time the cosmic or spiritual meanings of those lunar events have been completely lost. Even in Christian Church circles, where for instance Easter is celebrated the Sunday after the first Full Moon in Aries, it should be celebrated on the exact day this occurs and not on the more convenient Sunday afterwards. Of course modern Full Moon meditations should be separated from mother and fertility goddesses, derived from the religions of Assyria, Asia Minor and India. This would be backsliding from the real Demeter quality of the central divinity, known to the Hebrews and the Israelites as Jahweh/I am, and still fundamental for genuinely spiritual, as opposed to psychic, life.

In the Great Pyramid of Gizeh, we find that the measurements of the fundamental structures are based on 365·4 'Pyramidal inches', the number which as we know measures the solar year. All the measurements in this structure were consciously chosen to 'engrave' in stone a history of 6,000 years, based on a vast body of exact astronomical and astrological knowledge. Most fascinating with regards to our subject, all the dates incorporated in the stone of this pyramid can be checked astrologically and the results show extraordinary links with certain sets of twelve degree symbols. These results not only show how ancient and exact these degree symbols are, but also provide a vast amount of factual evidence, to demonstrate the unshakable truth about this structure and all it contains.

In this connection it is also claimed that for thousands of years the Mayans, and their forefathers, who are said to be the sun-worshipping remnants of the lost Empire of Atlantis, but practising their religion in a corrupt, bestial way, possessed a calendar, based on the true solar year, which is said to have been even more precise than our Gregorian calendar.

Finally, it is known that early Chinese astronomy divided the zodiacal circle of 360 degrees into 36,524 parts, 6087⅓ parts per sign of 60 degrees, which shaped a zodiac of six signs. This indicates that the Chinese also knew about the true length of the solar year.

For one or another reason all this ancient knowledge was lost to European culture and had to be regained in order to restore the calendars used.

*　*　*

Internationally the new Gregorian calendar was not easily accepted, and it took quite a long time before all the local disagreements were definitely settled. Therefore we can't simply say, the date of 5/15 October 1582 is the basic date; it is safer to consult the various studies about this subject. In order to work responsibly, however, as far as I know, a little information can be found in *1001 Nativities* by Alan Leo, and more, but only for USA and Canada, in *Time Changes in the USA* by Doris Chase Doane. In 1955 a most comprehensive and detailed study written by the Dutch librarian W. E. van Wijk, *De Gregoriaanse kalender* ('The Gregorian calendar'), was republished in Holland by Kluwers١ Academic Publishers, Dordrecht, having been originally published by Nijhoff, The Hague, in 1932. Unfortunately this has not been translated into English. Neugebauer[40] refers to Schramm,[39] who published a precise overview of the dates on which the Gregorian calendar was accepted in the various countries affected.

In 1937 the German Ed. Koppenstätter published *Zonen und Sommerzeiten* ('Zones and Summer Times'), and sadly, this has not been translated into English either. It should be noted, however, that his dates for starting the Gregorian calendar in the various parts of the world do not always correspond to those given by van Wijk.

It is astonishing to see how little importance or care has been given to this subject in *The International Atlas* by Thomas G. Shanks, ACS Publ. San Diego CA (USA), 1985, see Table II, which merely states: 'Western countries not listed here changed to the Gregorian calendar before the nineteenth century'. This is totally inaccurate. Also, the dates given for the other countries are different from van Wijk's dates. By 'Western countries', the countries of Western Europe, including Britain, are meant. Studying van Wijk, we will notice the entire matter of changing the calendar was not so easy and there was much more than only 'before the nineteenth century'. The following (incomplete) list of dates when the calendar was changed into the Gregorian form is quoted from van Wijk:

Bulgaria	1.4.1916 first Gregorian date.
China	1.1.1929 first Gregorian date.
Denmark	18.2.1699 = 1.3.1700.
France	10.12.1582 Julian = 20.12.1582 Gregorian date.
Germany	5.10.1583 = 15.10.1583, only accepted slowly in the various parts of Germany, and not until 1631 in Hildesheim. Although the Elzas originally accepted the new calendar 16.2.1682, it was banned and again accepted on 18.2.1699 = 1.3.1699.
Greece	23.3.1924 first Gregorian date.

England	3.9.1752 = 14.9.1752. We also have to be aware that before 1752 the New Year in England began on 25 March (see note 6, below).
Holland	15.12.1582 = 25.12.1582, but in the provinces of Holland and Zeeland: 2.1.1583 = 12.1.1583. Among the various parts of the Netherlands confusion reigned until the Gregorian calendar was definitely accepted in 1701.[47] Cf.Chandu.[45]
Italy	5.10.1582 = 15.10.1582.
Japan	1.1.1873 first Gregorian date.
Norway	similar to Denmark.
Poland	5.10.1582 = 15.10.1582 but with severe local difficulties everywhere, only 21.3.1915 definitely accepted.
Portugal	5.10.1582 = 15.10.1582.
Russia	31.1.1918 = 14.2.1918.
Spain	5.10.1582 = 15.10.1582.
Sweden	17.2.1753 = 1.3.1753, chaotic before this date, so be careful.
Switzerland	Several dates: from 22.1.1584 to 1811!
Turkey	1.1.1927 first Gregorian date.

Knowing that for the sixteenth century the calendar was ten days slow, we are able to work out how many days' difference there was for other centuries between the two calendars, one day for each century.

Notes

1. Make sure in which calendar date the birthdate has been recorded. In most encyclopedias the Julian date is recorded, but not always.
2. Using Schoch's tables: after 1.1.1600 the Gregorian date is needed and before this date the Julian date.
3. Using the Tuckermann ephemeris: the Julian date is needed until 31.12.1649.
4. Using the PCA electric ephemeris computer program: till 16.10.1582 the Julian date has to be entered.
5. In medieval Italy the new day began at sunset, as it did in

Hebrew times. So for instance a birthtime recorded as 'the third hour in the night' has to be considered as three hours after sunset. The time of sunset and sunrise has to be calculated and the result of the difference between the two has to be divided by twelve in order to find the length of a day hour and a night hour.[19] This information is essential for calculating the charts of, for instance Da Vinci and Machiavelli. Dates must be checked on the true astronomical date, for instance a date recorded as 14 April 1461 and 3 hrs in the night, is astronomically 13 April, 3 night hours after sunset.

6. In England, till 1752 the official new year began around Greg. 23 March. A date recorded as 22 January (Julian) 1560 is astronomically 1 February (Gregorian) 1561 which can be demonstrated in the case of Bacon.[24] How to calculate a conception corrected birthtime for Julian dates will be shown in Chapter 11 (Bacon).

An article in the Astrological Association *Newsletter*, November 1987, gives a complete conversion table from Julian to Gregorian dates and other worthwhile information. This material was derived from Chapter 4 of *Astronomy for Astrologers* by John and Peter Filbey (Aquarian Press, 1984).

CHAPTER SIX

The Trutine of Hermes

The following scheme contains the basic facts given by Bailey, and can be used to calculate a conception correction if the two alterations mentioned are included.

The Four Orders of Bailey's Prenatal Epoch

Moon Position (natal chart)	Moon Asc/Desc (distance in degrees)	Longer/Shorter (than 273 days)	Forwards/Backwards (14 days)
Below the horizon and waxing	Moon/Asc. Moon Conc. = Asc. R. M/R = Desc. Conc.	longer	forwards
Above the horizon and waxing	Moon/Asc. Moon Conc. = Asc. R. M/R = Asc. Conc.	shorter	backwards
Above the horizon and waning	Moon/Desc. Moon Conc. = Desc. R. M/R = Desc. Conc.	longer	forwards
Below the horizon and waning	Moon/Desc. Moon Conc. = Desc. R. M/R = Asc. Conc.	shorter	backwards

Bailey's Prenatal Epoch is extended by Koppejan. He meticulously adhered to the Rule exactly as it was given, but with the proviso that 'Moon radix = *Descendant* conception' as given by Bailey in the 1st and 3rd order, can also be 'Moon radix = *Ascendant* conception', and that in the 2nd and the 4th order, 'Moon radix = *Ascendant* conception' can also be 'Moon radix = *Descendant* conception'. As a result of this we obtain a 2nd option for the same conception date. This matter is discussed in detail in the Introduction.

Koppejan also discovered that 'Moon conception = *Ascendant* radix', as given by Bailey in the 1st and 2nd order, can also be 'Moon conception = *Descendant* radix' and in the 3rd and 4th order 'Moon conception = *Descendant* radix' can also be 'Moon conception = *Ascendant* radix'.

Secondly, Koppejan went a step further than Bailey's 'extended count' ('14 days added to the regular conception date') by also *subtracting* 14 days from the calculated 'regular' conception date, to include a shorter gestation period. If necessary this can be further extended by calculating another fortnight later or earlier. These alternative dates are medically within normal limits.

The following calculations can be used for a birth in northern latitudes, either for western or eastern longitudes, but for the calculation in southern latitudes an example will be given in Chapter 13, where the conception correction of Paul Kruger is discussed. The abbreviations used here and elsewhere in the book are as follows:

Asc. = Ascendant   PF = Part of Fortune
Conc. = Conception   R   = Radix
CC   = Conception Correction   RLT = Real Local Time
Desc. = Descendant   RST = Real Sidereal Time
GMT   = Greenwich Mean Time   ST = Sidereal Time
LMT   = Local Mean Time

To calculate the conception correction stage by stage, using the Placidus house system, we have to take the following seven steps:

1. In the natal chart we check whether the natal Moon is below or above the horizon (1st column).
2. Decide whether the natal Moon is waxing (ahead of the Sun) or waning (behind the Sun) (1st column). This is easy to locate if we imagine a line rising from the Sun to its opposite point. We will find a waxing Moon at the right-hand side of the line and a waning Moon at the left-hand side.
3. Count the distance in degrees between the natal Moon and the Ascendant or the Descendant (2nd column), ignoring the minutes in length.
4. Divide the number of degrees by 13° (the average daily speed of the Moon), to discover the number of days shorter or longer than 273 days (3rd column).
5. The resultant number of days is added to or subtracted from 273 days, which is the average time of pregnancy.
6. Subtract this result from the date of birth to find the first possible day of conception, the so called 'regular' date.
7. By adding to or subtracting from the regular date in units of 14 days, we find the 'extended count' of plus 14 days up to approx. 300 days, or the 'reduced count' even to 5/6 months, if necessary. For 'normal' births the time of pregnancy fluctuates from 254 days to 298 days although

occasionally and presumably more than 300 days, as exemplified in the case of HRH Prince-Willem Alexander of Orange (see Chapter 16). The above steps from 1 to 7 are summarised in the following scheme, which will be given in each of the examples:

Moon *above/below* the horizon and *waxing/waning*
Moon conception = Descendant or Ascendant radix v.v.
Moon radix = Descendant or Ascendant conception v.v.
Distance between the Moon (xx°xx′)
and the *Descendant/Ascendant* (xx°xx′)
= xx° : 13°
= x days *longer/shorter* than 273 days
= x days before the birthdate
= *1st conception date* = '*regular*'

We now proceed with the calculation as follows:

8. From the ephemeris we take the ST at noon (or midnight) of the conception day, and

9. we take the position of the Moon at noon (or midnight) of the conception date. Before 1850, Nos. 8 and 9 have to be calculated with a computer program or with the Schoch tables. See the examples given for Bacon and Novalis.

10. Locate the *ST of the Ascendant which is equal to the position of the natal Moon* (needed for calculating the 1st option) and its *opposite point* (needed for calculating the 2nd option of the same date), to be found in the tables of houses for northern or southern latitudes, of the town where the conception presumably took place, or to be calculated with a computer program, as exemplified by Novalis. In all examples the following scheme will be given:

Interpolated ST of the Ascendant equal to the
position of the natal Moon (sign) xx°xx′ = ST xxh xxm
and its opposite point (sign) xx°xx′ = ST xxh xxm

11. The calculated difference in time between the ST at noon and the ST of the Ascendant of the natal Moon (or its opposite position) gives us the RLT am or pm in each example given thus:

'From the ephemeris we take the ST at noon and from the table of houses of the latitude of the birthplace (or the town of conception if this is known), we take the interpolated ST of the Ascendant equal to the position of the natal Moon and also, for the 2nd possibility of the same date, the ST of its opposite point. The difference between the two STs supplies the RLT, as follows':

ST (date) at noon	xxh xxm
RLT	−/+ xxh xxm
ST natal Moon (sign) xx°xx′	xxh xxm

In order to calculate this difference, it will sometimes be necessary to add 24 hours to each of these two sidereal times.

12. The conversion of the RLT into GMT, necessary for calculating the progression of the Moon, can be tricky. Always make sure whether the GMT is later or earlier than the RLT. Also, there is a difference in case of western or eastern longitudes. In the given examples we find the following sentence:

'We have to convert the RLT into GMT by adding to or subtracting from it xx minutes which gives the GMT +/− and we calculate the progression of the conception Moon in +/− GMT xxh xxm, by using diurnal proportional logarithms, to be found in the ephemeris, as follows':

RLT	−/+ xxhxxm	
Difference from GMT	−/+ xxhxxm	
GMT	−/+ xxhxxm	= Log.
Daily speed of the Moon	xx°xx′	= Log.
Progression of the Moon		Log. = −/+ xx°xx′

13. 'Checking the ephemeris of the consecutive dates, we take the position of the Moon at noon and calculate the progression of the Moon the day before or the day after the calculated conception date, and we adjust this position by adding to or subtracting from, the progression of the Moon in xxh xxm, at a daily speed of xx° xx′, as follows':

Moon at noon	(sign) xx° xx′
Progression in xxhxxm	xx° xx′
Corrected Ascendant radix	(sign) xx° xx′

14. The difference in time between the ST of the corrected Ascendant degree and the ST of the uncorrected Ascendant allows us to adjust the position of the natal Moon, necessary for calculating the corrected position of the Part of Fortune.

In case the computer does not present a ST, to avoid extra work one could take the GMT calculated with a computer, to be compared with the uncorrected GMT.

> *Ascendant (sign) xx° xx' is rising at xx° xx' (birthplace)*
> at approx. ST xxh xxm
> approx. xxm earlier or later
> than the official time
> corrected LMT xxh xxm
> corrected natal Moon (sign) xx° xx'
> corrected PF (sign) xx° xx'

15. In the same way we calculate the 2nd option for the same date, taking the interpolated ST of the opposite point of the position of the natal Moon.
16. We calculate the other conception dates by counting backwards or forwards in units of 14 days (see 4th column).

About the habit of calculating with painful accuracy, even in seconds, I would like to make some remarks. Firstly, in cities such as London, New York and so on, we rarely know exactly where in the city the birth took place. Secondly, we don't really know the exact speed of the Moon; we assume this speed increases or decreases with a sudden shock in time from day to day, but of course this stepping up of speed is a steady one, though the detailed information about this is not generally available. Therefore, only in cases where we know the exact geographical position of the town of birth, does it make sense to interpolate accurately the exact position of the rise of the natal Moon. If not, it is sufficient to calculate in degrees and minutes, ignoring the seconds. In the final results it will make only a small difference, perhaps of 1 or 2 minutes. For the same reasons the correction of the daily ST could be ignored. However, it does no harm to insert these corrections, as is demonstrated in several examples.

When calculating the first conception date we occasionally find the Moon in the 'wrong' position, for example in the sign previous to the one expected. This in my experience shows that we are dealing with a premature birth. In that case one is required to calculate also the shorter gestation times. It also gives us a clue that the given birthtime might be totally wrong and should perhaps be adjusted to one hour earlier. Recalculating the natal chart one hour earlier than the given birthtime will often lead to the desired results. I can quote cases where the mother was sure about the day on which her child was conceived, and my adjusted calculations for an hour earlier confirmed her statement.

Bailey claimed that his method could be used for this kind of correction to the birthtime, and even to find an unknown birthtime.

Obstetric statistics of durations of pregnancy in percentages, as given by Bailey:

Week	Duration in days	% of Total Births
36th	246–52	3
37th	253–9	11
38th	260–6	12
39th	267–73	29
40th	274–80	19
41st	281–7	14
42nd	288–94	9
43rd	295–301	3

In special cases, up-to-date statistics should be consulted, because of the steady advance of medical science which is ensuring the survival of infants born at an ever-earlier stage in the pregnancy. Nowadays the normal time of pregnancy is considered to be 280 days, and it is said that 95 per cent of births occur between 266 and 294 days.

CHAPTER SEVEN

Dali and the Wheelbarrow

Name	Salvador Dali
Birthdate	11 May 1904
Birthplace	Figueras, Gerona, Spain, 42°N16' and 2°E57'
LMT	8h 45m am
GMT	8h 45m am (since 1901 WET)
RLT	8h 57m am
RST	0h 11m 52s: Ascendant 22°14' Cancer (uncorrected) Sun Taurus 20°13', Moon 2°28' Aries (uncorrected)
Houses	Placidus.

The conception correction of this chart is indeed remarkable because all three conception correction possibilities not only point to the same Ascendant degree, but also to almost the same minute, and all three at the very end of the degree (56, 58 and 59 minutes). In cases like this, on the edge of the next degree, the inherent symbols of both can be perceived shining through the personality, and so we have in fact a double Ascendant degree symbol, of not only the 21st degree but also the 22nd. The four pictures of both degrees are clearly visible in his life-style and creativity, as we will discuss later on.

In this connection it is interesting to note that Dali often composed his paintings as a double image, two images in one. For example we have the watch (Saturn/time) in an eye (Leo with Hermes), and he did the same with other creations. We know Dali has his Part of Fortune conjunct Pluto in Gemini and Saturn in the 21st degree of Aquarius opposite Hermes (ruler of the dualistic sign of Gemini) in a sparking, ingoing arch, and this is very noticeable in his character (the Uranian quality of the ingoing opposition). The 'ingoing' quality of an aspect is also called 'approaching', and the 'outgoing' quality 'departing'.

Calculating the conception correction of this Cancer Ascendant in the old-fashioned way 'by hand', we will help to save a lot of grateful braincells and circuits from total atrophy (justifiably feared by many!). Hopefully we have not yet forgotten how to do

SALVADOR DALI

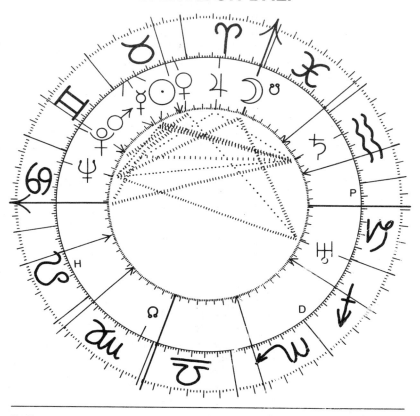

Radix			
	MC	1 27 Ari	Sun	20 13 Tau	11
SALVADOR DALI	ASC	20 58 Can	Moon	2 25 Ari	10
		Plac	Mercury	23 29 Tau	R 11
	11.	8 9 Tau	Venus	4 36 Tau	10
Date: 11 5 1904	12.	17 27 Gem	Mars	25 11 Tau	11
Time: 8 45 0 E O	2.	10 8 Leo	Jupiter	16 53 Ari	10
Latitude: 42 16 N	3.	2 37 Vir	Saturn	20 40 Aqu	8
Longitude: 2 57 E			Uranus	29 24 Sag	R 6
	Node	24 53 Vir 3	Neptune	4 2 Can	12
	Part ft	3 10 Gem 11	Pluto	19 29 Gem	12
			Perseph	27 36 Cap	7
Aspects: Radix/Radix Orb: 8 0			Hermes	17 11 Leo	2
			Demeter	1 45 Sag	5

MC Cnj Moo 0 58	MC Sqr Ura 2 3	MC Sqr Nep 2 34	ASC Sxt Sun 0 45
ASC Sxt Mer 2 31	ASC qcx Sat 0 18	ASC ssx Plu 1 29	Sun Cnj Mer 3 16
Sun Cnj Mar 4 58	Sun Sqr Sat 0 27	Sun ssq Nep 1 11	Sun ssx Plu 0 44
Moo Sqr Ura 3 1	Moo Sqr Nep 1 37	Mer Cnj Mar 1 43	Mer Sqr Sat 2 49
Ven Tri Ura 5 12	Ven Sxt Nep 0 34	Ven ssq Plu 0 7	Mar Sqr Sat 4 31
Jup Sxt Sat 3 47	Jup Sxt Plu 2 36	Sat ses Nep 1 38	Sat Tri Plu 1 11
Ura Opp Nep 4 38	Nod Tri Mer 1 25	Nod Tri Mar 0 18	

this without a computer program. During any calculation we first
try to lift our spiritual consciousness high above the centre of the
chart in an attempt to contact the Higher Self, asking for support
in sorting out the real Ascendant degree symbol. In this case, if
performed in the right way, we immediately sense a shower of
shooting sparks, initiating a whirl of thoughts and intuitive
insights.

Looking at his natal chart, we notice the positions of four
planets in Taurus, which is the sign of the artist, the painter,
wrestling with and creating in matter. These include the Sun
(creativity), Mercury (expression), Venus (artistic balance) and
Mars (technical abilities), all together showing a rich creative
versatility and all of them sharing the squares with Saturn.

Flying along the lines of this circuit (see the Introduction), we
start with the Sun, the symbol of the radiating centre, in the 21st
of Taurus in an exact outgoing square with Saturn in Aquarius in
the 8th house. It is clear this dangerous position points towards a
creative force threatened by automatisms and prone to spiritual
poverty and therefore mental illness. As we know he always had
to battle for mental stability. We look for the ruler of his Sun in
Taurus, Venus, which is positioned in its own sign. This position
of Venus threatens to stop the flow of his circuit, since the
creative solar energy, by locking itself in matter, is obstructing the
flow while at the same time piling up the material. Therefore the
forces of the opposite sign of Scorpio urgently need to be
invoked, symbolising as they do the skills and techniques
required to transform and process matter.

When Scorpio is involved, the flow of energy surprisingly
beams back to Mars, the ruler of Scorpio, positioned in Taurus.
This flow is remarkable because one could wonder why it was
needed. In my view it was only required to force the energy to
reach out exclusively for the higher function of Taurus, for
Persephone, whose force enables him to receive visions of forms
and shapes as they occur in art. We notice Mars in conjunction
with the Sun, and it is interesting to remember that Dali watched
sunsets over and over again (see the first image of 22nd Cancer)
receiving 'dream photographs' as he called them, to inspire his
creativity.

By doing so he directed the flow to Persephone in Capricorn,
reaching out for more and even better visions to be given form
(Capricorn) in matter. Only if this really happens, can the
outgoing square of the Sun with the ruler of Capricorn and
Aquarius, Saturn, be adequately activated. Only then will forms
start snowing down from 'heaven', because we find Saturn in

Aquarius, inducing Uranus in Sagittarius (*Oeranos* in Greek literally means heaven). This is in a very wide outgoing conjunction with the reflector of astral images, Demeter, ruler of Cancer and the ruler of his Ascendant. Because Jupiter, ruler of Sagittarius, is positioned in Aries, the flow is then able to contact the Moon (ingoing conjunct Jupiter in Aries) in an ingoing square with Neptune in the 5th of Cancer.

This Neptune, ruler of Pisces, in the 5th of Cancer in the 12th house, and his Ascendant are unfortunately not included in the circuit. Thus there is a curious split in his personality which, however, enables him to outcrystallise his dream photographs, welling up from the astral imaginative spheres. 'Snowing down' and at the same time 'welling up' sounds almost 'Dali-istic'!

Pisces is untenanted in Dali's chart, except for the north node, pointing towards a certain karmically caused 'lack' of *pure* inspiration and fantasy, and the need to immerse himself in the conditions expressed in the 21st degree of Cancer. The Higher Self needed to experience and achieve this degree symbol in order to be 'filled' with the function of Neptune.

We have also noticed that the Sun in the 21st of Taurus is in an ongoing battle to establish stability in time and conscience, because it shapes an outgoing square with Saturn in the 21st Aquarius. Twice we find a 21st degree, of planets which are themselves the rulers of the fixed cross, and in the signs thereof, remarkable in itself (to be compared with Novalis, Chapter 10). The Aquarian eccentricity of Dali is well known, as are the three-dimensional perspectives he achieved in his paintings. He is a surrealistic artist who painted unrelated and/or distorted objects with meticulous accuracy, linking them in such a way that a reality is suggested which in fact does not exist.

His entire being seems to be obsessed by the phenomenon of time (Saturn) expressed, for example, in *The Immersion of Time*, in his jewellery designs such as the watch called *The Eye of Time*, a clockface within an eye, and also in another design of a watch in an eye held on either side by human hands. Clearly his Saturn in the 21st Aquarius opposite Hermes in the 18th Leo (eyes) is functioning in those creations, and also in the way he links objects to form another reality. The same Saturn in ingoing square to the Sun is responsible for his terrifying fears, and we are not surprised to read in his autobiography that he regards a wheelbarrow as the symbol of fear. This will be discussed later on.

Although much more could be said as to how the energy flow of this circuit continues, for the moment it is sufficient to have some basic understanding of the human being delineated by this chart, Dali. With this in mind, we are ready to begin the calculation of the conception correction.

Reminding ourselves of what is said in the Trutine of Hermes, we first establish the following basic facts:

1. With the 23rd of Cancer rising, the natal Moon is in the 3rd of Aries and the natal Sun in the 21st of Taurus. We draw a line from the Sun to the same degree of the opposite sign and locate the Moon at the right side at the ingoing arch which means the Moon is waning. The Moon is positioned above the horizontal Ascendant–Descendant axis, which means it is above the horizon. The scheme in Chapter 6 shows this to be the 3rd order of Bailey, which says, 'Moon/Descendant, longer and forwards'.

2. We count the distance between the Moon in the 3rd of Aries and the *Descendant* in the 23rd of Capricorn as 70°, ignoring the minutes.

3. We divide this distance of 70° by 13° (which is the average distance covered by the Moon in a day) = 5/6 days.

4. 5 days longer than 273 days (the average time of pregnancy) = 278 days

5. 278 days subtracted from the birthdate 11.5.1904 = 6.8.1903, which is the first possible, regular date of conception. Another way of calculating is by subtracting a full year from the birthdate 11.5.1904, giving 11.5.1903; subtract 278 days (see 4) from 365 days = 87 days to be added to the date of 11.5.1903 to find the date of 6.8.1903.

6. According to the 3rd order of Bailey, see the 1st paragraph, '*Moon Radix is Descendant Conception*', we need to know the ST of the position of the opposite of the natal Moon (3rd of Libra) and also (because according to the 3rd order '*or Ascendant Conception*') for the true position of the Moon, the 3rd of Aries, which can be found in the table of houses for 42°16′ North). Both sidereal times have to be interpolated in order to be accurate:

Interpolated ST of the Ascendant equal to the
position of the natal Moon
2°28′ Aries at ST 18h 05m
and its opposite position, 2°28′ Libra at ST 6h 13m

Moon *above* the horizon and *waning*

Scheme for Calculating the 3rd Order
Moon conception = Descendant or Ascendant radix
Moon radix = Descendant or Ascendant conception

Distance between the Moon (2°28′ Aries)
and the *Descendant* (22°14′ Capricorn)
= 70°:13
= 5 days *longer* than 273 days
= 278 days before the birthday 11.5.1904
= 'regular' *6.8.1903*

Possibility (1)
The calculation of this first, 'regular', conception date is carried
out as follows:

From the ephemeris we take the ST at noon at 6.8.1903 and we
take the interpolated ST of the Ascendant equal to the position of
the natal Moon and also for the second possibility of the same
date, the ST of its opposite point. In both cases the difference
between the two sidereal times supplies the RLT. In this case we
will find we need only the second possibility, as follows:

ST 6.8.1903 (278) at noon	8h 55
RLT	−2h 42m
ST 2°28′ Libra	6h 13m

We convert the RLT −2h 42m (which in fact is 9h 18m am) into
GMT by adding 12m to it = −2h 54m and we calculate the
progression of the conception Moon in GMT −2h 54m by using
diurnal proportional logarithms, to be found in the ephemeris:

RLT	−2h 42m (= 9h 18m am)	
Difference from GMT	+0h 12m	
GMT	−2h 54m	= Log. 9178
Daily motion of the Moon	11°53′	= Log. 3053
Progression of the Moon		Log. 12231 = −1°26′

Checking the ephemeris for 6.8.1903, we take the position of the
Moon at noon and we adjust this position by subtracting the
progression in −2h 54m at a daily motion of 11°53′, which is the
motion of the Moon between 5 and 6 August = −1°26′, as
follows:

6.8.1903 Moon at noon	22°25′ Capricorn
Progression in −2h 54m	−1°26′
Corrected Descendant radix	20°59′ Capricorn
Corrected Ascendant radix	20°59′ Cancer

Ascendant 20°59' Cancer is rising at 42°N16' at
approx. ST 0h 06m
approx. 6m earlier
than the official time
corrected LMT 8h 39m a.m.
corrected natal Moon 2°26' Aries
corrected PF 3°12' Gemini

A birthtime only 6m earlier than was recorded could well have been right.

We have calculated only the second option of this first date because the first one results in approximately the 28th of Cancer, which means a birth much later than estimated which can therefore be safely ignored.

By now, those who are familiar with the degree images may have in mind the images of the 21st and 22nd degrees of Cancer and we will begin to consider how far those symbols fit the chart, recalling what we found before beginning the calculations:

21st CANCER

Janduz: 'A waning moon amidst clouds gives a feeble glow on the sea,
where a dismasted ship is floating.
At the left is an abandoned cart
which is about to sink into the coastal sand.'

Rudhyar: 'A prima donna sings to a glittering audience.'

22nd CANCER

Janduz: 'At the right a man is standing on the top of a hill,
with a staff of "authority" in his hand.
His face is lit up by the setting sun at his left,
he does not notice the torrent of turbulent water raging below him.'

Rudhyar: 'A young woman dreamily awaits a sailing boat.'

Thinking about the 'cart', we remember with a shock from his autobiography, that Dali was extremely frightened of wheelbarrows. In an interview he called them '*the* symbol of fear, an alarming symbol full of erotica'. Speaking of his painting of a structure of wheelbarrows in the shape of a dome (which is symbolised by Demeter, ruler of Cancer), he says: 'they obstruct the spirit from floating into higher realms and therefore one finds in the top of the dome only fragments of wheelbarrows.' And there was also his film called *La carretilla de carne*, a story about a woman in love with a wheelbarrow which became alive. He used this symbol also in his ballet *Tristan*, and there was even a huge wheelbarrow in his garden! This evidence is almost too much, and it seems sufficient to say that 21st Cancer is indeed the right Ascendant degree. Let us have a look at his chart to find some more clues.

On a spiritual level, we find the Sun and three other planets in Taurus, and Persephone in Capricorn, all earth signs, but on a soul level we find the Moon in the 3rd of Aries ingoing conjunct Jupiter 17th Aries, both in the 10th house and though in fire signs, they are in an ingoing square with Neptune (water) in the 5th of Cancer (a water sign) (in the 12th house). All that we were looking for we find in this chart, and expressed in the Janduz symbol of the 21st degree of Cancer. Interestingly, we find a *waning* Moon in his chart as well.

His personal and emotional circumstances, as well as his talent for the etheric reflection (lunar soul body) of the images, mirrored by the angels into his Demeter astral soul body, despite the ingoing conjunction with Jupiter which gives direction and purpose, are actually demonstrating a leak, an inability to reflect inspired, *pure* (Neptune) images (Cancer). This obviously needed to be experienced and developed in this life, and so it would seem that the conditions of the 21st and 22nd degrees of Cancer were deliberately chosen by his Higher Self, in order to further his spiritual development. We recall our thoughts about the squares of the Moon and Jupiter. We will now pause in our consideration of his chart in order to calculate the other possibilities.

Possibility (2)
We continue our calculations and move a *fortnight forwards to 264 days*. We take the ST at noon at 20.8.1903 and take the same ST of the Ascendant equal to the position of the opposite of the natal Moon. The difference between the two sidereal times supplies the RLT, as follows:

20.8.1903 noon ST	9h 50m
RLT	−3h 37m
ST of 2°28' Libra	6h 13m

We convert the RLT −3h 37m into GMT by adding 12m to it = −3h 49m, and we calculate the progression of the conception Moon in GMT −3h 49m:

RLT	−3h 37m (= 8h 23m am)		
Difference from GMT	+0h 12m		
GMT	−3h 49m	= Log.	7985
Daily motion of the Moon	14°54'	= Log.	+2070
Progression of the Moon		Log.	10055 = −2°22'

Checking the ephemeris for 20.8.1903, we take the position of the Moon at noon and adjust this position by subtracting from it the progression in −3h 49m, at a daily speed of 14°54′ which is the speed between 19 and 20 August 1903 = −2°22′, as follows:

20.8.1903 Moon at noon	23°20′ Cancer
Progression in −3h 49m	−2°22′
Corrected Ascendant radix	20°58′ Cancer

Ascendant 20°58′ Cancer is rising at 42°N16′
at approx. ST 0h 06m
approx. 6m earlier
than the official time
corrected LMT 8h 39m am
corrected natal Moon 2°25′ Aries
corrected PF 3°10′ Gemini

This result is almost similar to the previous correction, and again, a birthtime only 6m earlier than was recorded.

We have calculated only the second option of this date because the first one results in approximately 14th Cancer which means a birth much earlier than estimated, which can therefore be safely ignored.

Surprisingly, again we have found the same 21st degree of Cancer and again we experience with Dali the loneliness, the helplessness and the emptiness of its corresponding image. In our thoughts we again move around his natal Neptune in the 5th of Cancer in the 12th house and by now we perhaps begin to understand why his Part of Fortune, his task in this life, as we see it, is in Gemini, in the 11th house, conjunct Pluto in Gemini, meaning the unmasking of self-knowledge (Gemini, ruled by Hermes), but also initiating the wisdom symbolised by the key in the Janduz image of 18th Leo. This is the position of his Hermes, which hopefully will supply him with that so needed firm grip on the solar helm which steers his life's boat, stabilising his existence and avoiding shipwrecks, finding direction only if the suffering essences of Pisces, of Neptune, of the 12th house, are fully experienced and integrated into his entire being. If he indeed managed to achieve all this, only the story of his life can tell. From his autobiography we know that at one time he experienced a major crisis threatening him with complete madness. He suffered endless convulsions of laughter (Saturn in Aquarius! square the Sun and so on) but he was miraculously cured by his wife Gala who successfully managed to transform his anguish into creativity, saving his sanity.

Possibility (3)
But we still have to calculate the last possibility: perhaps we will be able to find another degree. We turn to the possibility of *292 days of 23.7.1903*:
We take the ST at noon at 23.7.1903 and take the same ST of the Ascendant equal to the position of the natal Moon. The difference between the two sidereal times supplies the RLT, as follows:

23.7.1903 (292) noon ST		8h 00m
RLT		+10h 04m
ST Aries 2°28'		18h 04m

Ignoring the correction of the ST in +10h 04m, we convert the RLT +10h 04m pm. into GMT by subtracting 12m from it = +9h 52m and calculate the progression of the conception Moon in GMT +9h 52m:

RLT	+10h 04m	
Difference from GMT	−0h 12m	
GMT	+9h 52m	= Log. 3860
Daily motion of the Moon	15°18'	= Log. 1955
Progression of the Moon		Log. 5815 = +6°17'

Checking the ephemeris for 23.7.1903, we take the position of the Moon at noon and adjust this position by adding to it the progression in +9h 52m at a daily speed of 15°18' which is the speed from 23 to 24 July 1903, as follows:

23.7.1903 Moon at noon	14°39' Cancer
Progression in +9h 52m	+6°17'
Corrected Ascendant radix	20°56' Cancer

Ascendant 20°56' Cancer is rising at 42°N16' at
approx. ST 0h 06m
approx. 6m earlier
than the official time
corrected LMT 8h 39m am
corrected natal Moon 2°25' Aries
corrected PF 3°09' Gemini

In this case we have calculated only the first option because the second one results in approximately 13th Cancer, which means a birth much earlier than estimated and to be ignored.
This final result, surprisingly exactly the same as the two previous corrections, is indeed extraordinary. It really is fairly rare to find not only the same degree three times, but almost

exactly the same minute also. In my opinion, it can only mean that the Higher Self was determined to have this particular degree symbol as his personality mask. Also, if it was, and I believe it was, a solar plan, to make sure of the timing (Saturn) in order to have the 21st degree of Cancer, and if indeed that particular degree symbol was right, it gives us clear insights into his natal Sun square Saturn.

To be able to aim (Jupiter) well at sea (Neptune, Pisces), in maritime navigation, abandoned as one is to the often unpredictable elements, one needs to be very well equipped. One needs reliable charts, sextants and compasses, but above all, one needs to steer a course that accords with God's will. In my view, all the conditions required by the first image of 21st Cancer can be fulfilled by Gemini, enforced by Saturn in Aquarius opposite Hermes in Leo, square the Sun and the other planets in Taurus, including the Moon in Aries conjunct Jupiter, both ingoing square Neptune in Cancer. Of course, more than merely physical navigation is implied here, and we have to adjust our views to the fact that Dali has proved to be in many ways a brilliant and gifted artist. Incidentally, while making these calculations I was unaware that transiting Jupiter was in 21st Scorpio, but this gave the right aims and purposes, to direct the way I (with the Sun in the 21st of Leo!) worked through the material for this example. Moreover, Jupiter square his 21st Aquarius Saturn urged me to sort out once and for all the often insufficient and contradictory information about time changes and zones!

In introducing the use of transits to check the appropriateness of the calculated Ascendant degree and its symbols, I nevertheless have to warn very strongly against trying to 'prove' any calculated possibility by referring to transits. On the other hand, the transit of a particular planet, such as Jupiter in this case, pointing to particular features in the natal chart, does seem to be significant, and has to be taken cautiously into account.

Taking a last glimpse at Dali's chart, we find our conclusions reinforced by the idea that only when Scorpio, the opposite sign to Taurus, is reached, can the solar energy flow include all the planets of this chart, with the significant exception of Neptune in the 5th degree of Cancer in the 12th house, conjunct the Ascendant, and for this particular reason I believe the symbols of the 21st degree of Cancer have been chosen by this Higher Self as the right mask for his persona, his Ascendant degree, calculated according to the method given by Bailey.

Other remarkable conception corrections with similar results can be found by calculating the conception correction of Thomas Mann (all three corrections the same 1st Virgo), John Addey (three times 9th Leo), Robert Louis Stevenson (according to Koppejan an extremely difficult correction although definitely pointing towards 19th Aquarius), R. Peynet (constructive correction with only one possibility of 30th Scorpio), Frederick Polak (three times 26th Pisces) and Jules B. Schurmann, a poet who wrote refined verses (all three corrections 29th Libra). For details see the information given in *The Zodiac Image Handbook* for the relevant above-mentioned degrees.

* * *

Dali died on the morning of 23 January 1989, some time between 10 am and 12 noon. We find the transiting Sun in the 4th degree of Aquarius (a rich and noble man ascends the steps of a 'heavenly' palace). The Sun shapes a perfect ingoing trine with his Part of Fortune radix in the 4th of Gemini. In this light we may assume that Dali's spirit has gained strength in understanding and self-knowledge which will have contributed much towards a stronger life- and will-centre.

It is almost certain that the transiting Moon would be found in the 21st of Leo, in an exact opposition with the radix Saturn in the 21st of Aquarius in the 8th house, and also an exact outgoing (activating) square with his 21st Taurus natal Sun. This could mean that on an astral level his etheric soul body will have to face, and painfully digest, the artistic but often dreadful forms and shapes he created in his life.

His progressed Moon is in the 5th of Taurus, in exact conjunction with his natal Venus. This etheric soul body has therefore reached a stage of harmonious stability or equilibrium but will also be laden with an enormous quantity of material, piled up and to be sorted out. The first image of this degree conveys the idea of a 'memento mori', the need to work through and transform spiritual possessions and property (Taurus/ Scorpio).

The progressed Jupiter is in the 30th of Aries and in an exact outgoing trine with Uranus in Sagittarius: that which was purposefully established will bring a rich profit for his entire being, a new impulse for the discovery and achievement of new goals in life.

It is important that his progressed Part of Fortune is to be found in the 20th of Gemini, right on his natal Pluto in the 12th house, in the same sign as it was in his natal chart. Again the need to face the unmasking of self-knowledge and ways of expression, and to find new impulses in order to be able to advance along his life's path. We wonder if the impulse to learn how to express himself in his life was answered positively; the 20th degree of Gemini doesn't show much beauty.

CHAPTER EIGHT

Auguste Rodin and the Hand of God

Birthdate	12.11.1840
Birthplace	Paris (France) 48°N50′ and 2°E20″
LMT	12h 00m noon (uncorrected)
GMT	11h 50m 39s am
RLT	12h 00m noon
RST	15h 26m: Ascendant 23°05′ Capricorn (uncorrected) Sun 20°13′ Scorpio, Moon 28°44′ Gemini (uncorrected)
House system	Placidus.

Although this chart is calculated by using the White ephemeris (1800–1850), to check the positions and to obtain the required sidereal time, I used the PCA Electric Ephemeris, an astrological software program suitable for Amstrad's Locoscript 2. How to use this program in order to calculate a conception correction for dates before 1850 is demonstrated in Chapter 11 (Francis Bacon). Unfortunately the PCA doesn't give a sidereal time, which is a problem because for the conception correction calculation the sidereal time is vital. We obtain the sidereal time thus:

1. By using a printed ephemeris, such as the *Barth* or the *Concise Planetary Ephemeris* for any year. This is not entirely accurate because the daily ST differs from year to year (although it has to be said, the final result will only be slightly changed, up to a maximum of 2 minutes which can effectively be ignored).

2. By calculating the ST using Schoch's tables, although, as mentioned before, they are neither easy to obtain nor simple to use.

3. By calculating with a computer program:
   Because we prefer to calculate for GMT 12h 00m (noon), we enter the date, 12h 00m at noon and the positions for Greenwich, to obtain the Ascendant and the position of the Moon at noon. Reading the position of the Ascendant in the tables of houses for Greenwich, we find the

AUGUSTE RODIN

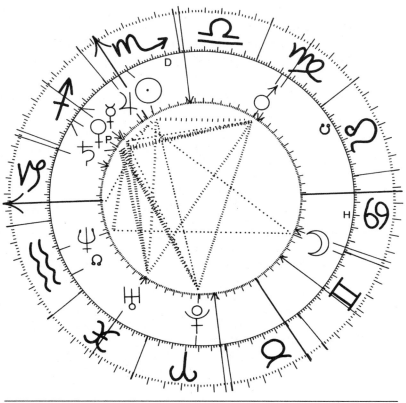

Radix				Sun	20	13	Sco	9
	MC	24 3 Sco		Moon	28	44	Gem	5
	ASC	23 3 Cap						
AUGUSTE RODIN		Plac		Mercury	12	44	Sag	10
	11.	13 38 Sag		Venus	18	44	Sag	11
Date:	12 11 1840	12.	1 41 Cap	Mars	19	17	Vir	8
Time:	11 50 39 E O	2.	16 30 Pis	Jupiter	27	27	Sco	10
Latitude:	48 51 N	3.	27 49 Ari	Saturn	20	20	Sag	11
Longitude:	2 20 E			Uranus	16	31	Pis	R 2
				Neptune	12	10	Aqu	1
		Node	22 53 Aqu 1	Pluto	18	19	Ari	R 2
		Part it	1 34 Vir 7	Perseph	19	30	Sag	11
Aspects: Radix/Radix		Orb: 8 0		Hermes	15	15	Can	7
				Demeter	6	10	Sco	9

MC Sqr Nod 1 10	ASC Sxt Sun 2 50	ASC ssx Nod 0 10	Sun ssx Ven 1 29
Sun Sxt Mar 0 56	Sun Cnj Jup 7 14	Sun ssx Sat 0 6	Sun Tri Ura 3 42
Sun qcx Plu 1 54	Moo qcx Jup 1 17	Moo ses Nep 1 34	Mer Cnj Ven 6 1
Mer Sqr Mar 6 33	Mer Cnj Sat 7 36	Mer Sqr Ura 3 47	Mer Sxt Nep 0 34
Mer Tri Plu 5 35	Ven Sqr Mar 0 32	Ven Cnj Sat 1 35	Ven Sqr Ura 2 13
Ven Tri Plu 0 25	Mar Sqr Sat 1 3	Mar Opp Ura 2 45	Mar qcx Plu 0 57
Sat Sqr Ura 3 48	Sat Tri Plu 2 0	Ura ssx Plu 1 48	Nod Sqr Sun 2 40
Nod Sxt Sat 2 33			

interpolated ST at noon. See also the examples given for
Bacon and Novalis.

4. By using the annual ephemerides of Raphael from 1800 to
    1850, sometimes obtainable from antiquarian bookshops,
    although rarely.

From Rodin's birthchart we take the following basic data, needed
in order to calculate the conception correction:

1. The natal 29th Gemini Moon is *below the horizon and
    waning* (which is the fourth option of the four orders:
    'Moon/Descendant shorter/backwards'), and we find the
    distance between the Moon and the 24th Cancer
    Descendant to be 25°, ignoring the minutes.
2. Divide these 25° by 13°, which is the average daily
    motion of the Moon = 2 (days),
3. 2 days 'shorter' than 273 days (the average time of
    pregnancy) = 271 days,
4. 271 days subtracted from the birthdate 12.11.1840 =
    14.2.1840, which is the first possible date of conception.
    Another way of calculating is by subtracting a full year
    from the birthdate (12.11.1840) giving 12.11.1839; subtract
    271 days from 365 days = 94 days to be added to the date
    of 12.11.1839 to find the date of 14.2.1840.
5. For any conception date we normally have two
    possibilities to be calculated, but in the case of the fast
    rising signs, there are sometimes three.

The date of 14.2.1840 shows the Moon at 15°29' Cancer and the
next day (15.2.1840) at 29°32' Cancer, which is needed to
calculate both possibilities of the same date and also the daily
progression of the Moon.

According to the 4th order of Bailey, see the 1st paragraph,
'Moon Radix is Asc. or Desc. Conception', we need to know the
sidereal time of the natal moon (28°44' Gemini), and also
(because according to the 4th order *'or Descendant Conception'*) for
the opposite point of 28°44' Sagittarius, which can be found in
the tables of houses for Paris (48°N 50'). This sidereal time has to
be interpolated in order to be accurate.

Interpolated ST of the Ascendant equal to the
position of the natal Moon
28°44' Gemini at ST approx. 21h 55m
and also its opposite point 28°44' Sagittarius
at ST approx. 13h 54m
Moon *below* the horizon and *waning*

Scheme for Calculating the 4th Order
Moon conception = Descendant or Ascendant radix
Moon radix = Ascendant or Descendant conception
Distance between the Moon (28°44' Gemini)
and the *Descendant* (23°05' Cancer)
= 25°:13
= 2 days *shorter* than 273 days
= 271 days before the birthdate 12.11.1840
= *14.2.1840*

The calculation of this first, so-called 'regular' conception date is carried out as follows:
14.2.1840 (271 days) ST at noon 21h 36m, Moon at noon 15°29' Cancer
15.2.1840 (270 days) ST at noon 21h 40m, Moon at noon 29°32' Cancer

Possibility (1)
We take the ST at noon at 14.2.1840 and find in the tables of houses for Paris (48°N50') the ST of the Ascendant equal to the position of the natal Moon and also for the second possibility of the same date, the ST of its opposite point. In both cases the difference between the two sidereal times supplies the RLT, as follows:

14.2.1840 (271) ST at noon	21h 36m
RLT	+0h 19m
ST 28°44' Gemini	21h 55m

We convert the RLT +0h 19m into GMT by subtracting 9m (20 seconds to be ignored) from it = +0h 10m and we calculate the progression of the conception Moon in GMT +0h 10m.

RLT	+0h 19m	
Difference from GMT	−0h 09m	
GMT	+0h 10m	= Log. 21584
Daily motion of the Moon	14°03'	= Log. 2325
Progression of the Moon		Log. 23909 = +0°06'

We take the position of the Moon at noon and we adjust this position by adding to it the progression in GMT +0h 10m at a daily motion of 14°03', which is the progression we previously calculated from 14 to 15 February, as follows:

14.2.1840 Moon at noon	15°29' Cancer
Progression in +0h 10m	+0°06'
Corrected Descendant radix	15°35' Cancer
Corrected Ascendant radix	15°35' Capricorn

Ascendant 15°35' Capricorn is rising at 48°N50'
at approx. ST 15h 01m
approx. 25m earlier
than the official time
corrected LMT 11h 35m am
corrected natal Moon 28°31' Gemini
corrected PF 23°53' Leo

Possibility (2)
We already have from the ephemeris the necessary information
for calculating the second possibility of the same date. Therefore
we repeat:

14.2.1840 (271 days) ST at noon 21h 36m, Moon at noon 15°29'
Cancer
15.2.1840 (270 days) ST at noon 21h 40m, Moon at noon 29°32'
Cancer

We take the ST at noon at 15.2.1840 but now we take the ST of the
Ascendant equal to the *opposite* position of the natal Moon, that is
28°44' Sagittarius. The difference between the two sidereal times
supplies the RLT, as follows:

15.2.1840 (270) noon ST	21h 40m	
RLT	−7h 46m	
ST 28°44' Sagittarius	13h 54m	

Converting the RLT = −7h 46m (which in fact is 4h 14m am) into
GMT by adding 9m to it = −7h 55m and we calculate the
progression of the conception Moon in GMT −7h 55m:

RLT	−7h 46m		
Difference from GMT	+0h 09m		
GMT	−7h 55m	= Log.	4817
Daily motion of the Moon	14°03'	= Log.	+2325
Progression of the Moon		Log.	7142 = −4°38'

We take the position of the Moon at noon and we adjust this
position by subtracting the progression in −7h 55m at a daily
motion of 14°03' which is the motion from 14 to 15 February =
−4°38', as follows:

15.2.1840 Moon at noon	29°32' Cancer
Progression in −7h 55m	−4°38'
Corrected Descendant radix	24°54' Cancer
Corrected Ascendant radix	24°54' Capricorn

Ascendant 24°54' Capricorn is rising at 48°N50'
at approx. ST 15h 33m
approx. 7m later
than the official time
corrected LMT 12h 07m
Corrected natal Moon 28°49' Gemini
Corrected PF 3°30' Virgo

Possibility (3)
According to the 4th order we calculate the next possibility of 14
days back in time, which is 1.2.1840, holding two possibilities to
calculate:

From the ephemeris we take the following items:

1.2.1840 (285 days) ST at noon 20h 45m, Moon at noon 17°16'
Capricorn
2.2.1840 (284 days) ST at noon 20h 49m, Moon at noon 29°55'
Capricorn

We take the ST at noon on 1.2.1840 and as before the same ST of
the Ascendant equal to the position of the natal Moon and for the
second possibility of the same date, the ST of its opposite point.
The difference between the two sidereal times supplies the RLT,
as follows:

1.2.1840 (285) ST at noon	20h 45m
RLT	+1h 10m
ST 28°44' Gemini	21h 55m

We convert the RLT +1h 10m to GMT by subtracting 9m from it
= +1h 01m and we calculate the progression of the conception
Moon in GMT +1h 01m:

RLT	+1h 10m		
Difference from GMT	−0h 09m		
GMT	+1h 01m	= Log.	13730
Daily motion of the Moon	12°39'	= Log.	+2781
Progression of the Moon		Log.	16511 = +0°32'

We take the position of the Moon at noon and we adjust this
position by adding the progression in +1h 01m at a daily motion
of 12°39' (which is the motion from 1 to 2 February) = +0°32', as
follows:

1.2.1840 Moon at noon	17°16' Capricorn
Progression in +1h 01m	+0°32'
Corrected Ascendant radix	17°48' Capricorn

Ascendant 17°48' Capricorn is rising at 48°N50'
approx. ST 15h 08m
approx. 18m earlier than the official time
corrected LMT 11h 42m am
corrected natal Moon 28°35' Gemini
corrected PF 26°10' Leo

Possibility (4)
For the second possibility of the same date we adapt the same
items but now for 2.2.1840:

1.2.1840 (285 days) ST at noon 20h 45m, Moon at noon 17°16'
Capricorn
2.2.1840 (284 days) ST at noon 20h 49m, Moon at noon 29°55'
Capricorn

2.2.1840 (284) ST at noon	20h 49m
RLT	−6h 55m
ST 28°44' Sagittarius	13h 54m

We convert the RLT −6h 55m (which in fact is 5h 05m am) to
GMT by adding 9m to it = −7h 04m and we calculate the
progression of the conception Moon in GMT −7h 04m:

RLT	−6h 55m		
Difference from GMT	+0h 09m		
GMT	−7h 04m	= Log.	5310
Daily motion of the Moon	12°39'	= Log.	+2781
Progression of the Moon		Log.	8091 = −3°43'

We take the position of the Moon at noon for 2.2.1840, and adjust
this position by subtracting the progression in −7h 04m at a daily
motion of 12°39' = −3°43', as follows:

2.2.1840 Moon at noon	29°55' Capricorn
Progression in −7h 04m	−3°43'
Corrected Ascendant radix	26°12' Capricorn

Ascendant 26°12' Capricorn is rising at 48°N50'
at approx. ST 15h 37m
approx. 11m later
than the official time
corrected LMT 12h 11m
corrected natal Moon 28°50' Gemini
corrected PF 4°49' Virgo

Having calculated the possibilities for 271 and 285 days, we also
have to consider the possibility of an even longer period of
pregnancy, in this case 285 plus 14 is 299 days. Although this is

fairly rare, a pregnancy of about 300 days is still within the limit. Subtracting 14 days from 1.2.1840 = 18.1.1840 = 299 days, we calculate thus:

18.1.1840 (299 days) ST at noon 19h 49m, Moon at noon 20°33' Cancer
19.1.1840 (298 days) ST at noon 19h 53m, Moon at noon 4°51' Leo

Possibility (5)
We take the ST at noon on 18.1.1840 and as before we take the same ST of the Ascendant equal to the position of the natal Moon and also for the second possibility of the same date, the ST of its opposite point. In both cases the difference between the two sidereal times supplies the RLT, as follows:

18.1.1840 (299) ST at noon	19h 49m
RLT	+2h 06m
ST 28°44' Gemini	21h 55m

We convert the RLT +2h 06m to GMT by subtracting 9m from it = +1h 57m and we calculate the progression of the conception Moon in GMT +1h 57m:

RLT	+2h 06m		
Difference from GMT	−0h 09m		
GMT	+1h 57m	= Log.	10902
Daily motion of the Moon	14°18'	= Log.	+2249
Progression of the Moon		Log.	13151 = +1°10'

We take the position of the Moon at noon and adjust this position by adding to it the progression in +1h 57m at a daily motion of 14°18', which is the motion from 18 to 19 January = +1°10' as calculated, as follows:

18/1 Moon at noon	20°33' Cancer
Progression +1h 57m	+1°10'
Corrected Descendant	21°43' Cancer
Corrected Ascendant	21°43' Capricorn

21°43' Capricorn is rising at 48°N50'
at approx. ST 15h 22m
approx. 4m earlier
than the official birthtime
corrected LMT 11h 56m
corrected natal Moon 28°43' Gemini
corrected PF 0°13' Virgo

Possibility (6)
The second possibility of the same date must actually be

calculated for the next day, 19.1.1840, in order to be able to subtract from the Moon position.

18.1.1840 (299 days) ST at noon 19h 49m — Moon at noon 20°33′ Cancer
19.1.1840 (298 days) ST at noon 19h 53m — Moon at noon 4°51′ Leo

19.1.1840 (298) ST at noon	19h 53m
RLT	−5h 59m
ST 28°44′ Sagittarius	13h 54m

We convert the RLT = −5h 59m into GMT by adding 9m to it = −6h 08m and we calculate the progression of the conception Moon in GMT −6h 08m, as follows:

RLT	−5h 59m (which in fact is 6h 01m am)	
Difference from GMT	+0h 09m	
GMT	−6h 08m = Log.	5925
Daily motion of the Moon	14°18′ = Log.	+2249
Progression of the Moon	Log.	8174 = −3°39′

We take the position of the Moon at noon for 19 January and adjust this position by subtracting the progression in −6h 08m at a daily speed of 14°18′, which is the motion from 18 to 19 January = −3°39′, as follows:

19.1.1840 Moon at noon	4°51′ Leo
Progression in −6h 08m	−3°39′
Corrected Descendant radix	1°12′ Leo
Corrected Ascendant radix	1°12′ Aquarius

Ascendant 1°12′ Aquarius is rising at 48°N50′
at approx. ST 15h 51m
approx. 25m later
than the official time
corrected LMT 00h 25m pm

A birth of 25m later than stated can be ignored.

Possibility (7)
Finally we also calculate the possibility of a pregnancy of minus 14 days and although 256 days of pregnancy is indeed pretty short, it is not impossible: statistically, 256 days is proved to be possible in 11 per cent of all cases.

We take the ST at noon for 28 and 29.2.1840 and as before the ST of the Ascendant equal to the position of the natal Moon and also for the second possibility of the same date, the ST of its opposite point. The difference between the two sidereal times supplies the RLT, as follows:

28.2.1840 (256 days) ST at noon 22h 29m, Moon at noon 12°42' Capricorn
29.2.1840 (255 days) ST at noon 22h 33m, Moon at noon 25°11' Capricorn

29.2.1840 ST at noon	22h 33m
RLT	−8h 39m
ST 28°44' Sagittarius	13h 54m

We convert the RLT −8h 39m (which in fact is RLT 3h 21m am) to GMT by adding 9m to it = −8h 48m and we calculate the progression of the conception Moon in GMT −8h 48m, as follows:

RLT	−8h 39m		
Difference from GMT	+0h 09m		
GMT	−8h 48m	= Log.	4357
Daily motion of the Moon	12°29'	= Log.	+2839
Progression of the Moon		Log.	7196 = −4°35'

We take the position of the Moon at 29.2.1840 at noon and adjust this position by subtracting the progression of the Moon in −8h 48m at a daily motion of 12°29' (which is the motion from 28 to 29 February) = −4° 35', as follows:

29.2.1840 Moon at noon	25°11' Capricorn
Progression in −8h 48m	−4°35'
Corrected Ascendant radix	20°36' Capricorn

Ascendant 20°36' Capricorn is rising at 48°N50'
at approx. ST 15h 18m
approx. 8m earlier
than the official time
corrected LMT 11h 52m
corrected natal Moon 28°40' Gemini
corrected PF 29°03' Leo

The other possibility of the same date can to be ignored, because of finishing up too far before the given birthtime.

Summary of Possibilities

Date	No. days	CC	PF	ST	Time difference	☽
14/2	271	15°35' ♑	23°53' ♌	15h 01m	25' earlier	28°31' ♊
		24°54' ♑	3°30' ♍	15h 33m	7' later	28°49' ♊
1/2	285	17°48' ♑	26°10' ♌	15h 08m	18' earlier	28°35' ♊
2/2	284	26°12' ♑	4°49' ♍	15h 37m	11' earlier	28°50' ♊
18/1	299	21°43' ♑	0°13' ♍	15h 22m	4' earlier	28°43' ♊
		1°12' ♑	0°57' ♍	15h 51m	25' later	28°58' ♊
28/2	256	20°36' ♑	29°03' ♌	15h 18m	6' earlier	28°40' ♊

Rodin, creator of *Man and his Thought*, was one of the giants among artists, known as the thinker in art, and the 'Father of modern Sculpture'. He was both technically and artistically skilled, and his work showed extreme contrasts between rough and smooth textures, portraying the male and female in their most intimate human interplay. He was born with the Sun at 20°13' Scorpio (transformation) in an outgoing conjunction (awareness) with Demeter (inner sight) at 6°10' Scorpio, and in an ingoing (spiritual) conjunction with Jupiter (philosophical thinking) at 27°27' Scorpio, all three in the 10th house. For a great deal of his life, Rodin was the subject of the most controversial argument and criticism, always having to fight for public and official recognition.

Looking at his chart, we notice a short but powerful circuit, moving from the Sun in Scorpio to its ruler Mars, at 19°17' Virgo, in the processing and transforming 8th house. From there we progress to Mercury (expression), the ruler of Virgo (virginal purity), which is found at 12°44' Sagittarius in the 11th house, in conjunction with Venus at 18°44' and Persephone at 19°30', joint rulers of Taurus (materialising visions) and both in an ingoing, spiritual conjunction; and there we also find Saturn (form-giving), the ruler of both his Capricorn Ascendant and of Aquarius at 20°16'. From this position in Sagittarius, we locate Jupiter (faith and belief), ruler of Pisces (natural environment) and Sagittarius (philosophy) at 27°26' Scorpio in the 10th house, which we find in an ingoing conjunction with the Sun at 20°13'. We notice that in this circuit the functions of all the sensory planets except the Moon have been included, and this errant Moon (experiences and feelings), is found at 28°44' Gemini in the 5th house (creation). A sculptor of Rodin's calibre was able to use the inner eye of his astral body to conceptualise visions of beauty, captured in matter, knowing exactly which parts of the stone had to be removed in order to make his perceptions of purity visible, releasing the figure from its prison (see Mercury in the 13th of Sagittarius!) and bringing it into the light. Rodin added great thoughts to these materialised visions in stone.

Secondly, all the sensory planets are positioned in the upper half (Moon and Saturn significance) of the chart, and are mainly concentrated in the 10th and 11th house. The extrasensory planets, apart from Persephone (visionary ability), and the Ascendant, are not included in the circuit, and those planets are positioned in the under half (Demeter significance) of the chart.

Thirdly, because of the foregoing, and most significantly, this chart is split into two halves, a division between the sensory planet functions and the extrasensory planet functions. The significance of this split, running straight over the axis between Capricorn and Cancer, and symbolising the physical body, the Ascendant and the Descendant, has provided an essential indication for our final conclusions about the corrected Ascendant degree of 18th Capricorn. The planets are spread out over the chart and, with exception of the Moon, strongly connected with the Sun.

I would like to introduce here the concept of the 'art cross' in a natal chart, originally noted by the Dutch astrologer Ram.[41] This cross is shaped by the houses which are analogous to the signs of the fixed cross – that is, the 2nd, 5th, 8th and 11th houses, and essential for an artist. In Rodin's chart it is visible in a significant way; and most extraordinary (but how could it be otherwise?), we find that the rulers of these art houses in his chart are the rulers of the mutual or 'philosopher's' cross:

— Jupiter (philosophical thinking, faith), ruler of the 2nd house (envisioning images in matter) is in the 10th house in Scorpio (transformation, processes);
— Mercury (expression), ruler of the 5th house (creativity) and ruler of the 8th house (processing materials) is in the 11th house in Sagittarius;
— and again Jupiter, which is also the ruler of the 11th house (the public opinion, friends) is in the 10th house (officials of State departments and art salons as in his case).

For these reasons we are able to recognise Rodin for the great thinker he was, and the thoughts he invested in his art in, for instance, *The Thinker*, and in *Man and his Thought*. If one thinks for a minute about his Jupiter in that horrible 28th degree of Scorpio in the 10th house, it becomes clear why his art caused such storms of anger and disbelief, with critics tearing his works apart, both figuratively, and literally; some of his statues were actually hacked to pieces with an axe.

Notice the positions found in his art cross, in the 10th (official status) and 11th (public opinion) houses and in particular of Mercury and Jupiter, the rulers of the Gemini–Sagittarius axis (and of Virgo); and immediately our attention is drawn to the idea of a message (Mercury and Jupiter): a message, which Rodin enthusiastically (Jupiter) projected (Mercury) into his creations, to be recognised (Gemini, Mercury)) and evaluated (Sagittarius, Jupiter) by the public. In my opinion, that message expressed in marble, said that human beings, separated into male and female, are in some way also separated in the spiritual side of their being. Physically, a human is divided by the diaphragm into an underpart and an upperpart. We notice that Rodin often made the upperpart visible, bringing it into light and life, but leaving the underpart invisible, 'imprisoned in matter', in marble, as if they were waiting to be released and lifted into the Light. This not only points to the planets in Sagittarius which are square Uranus at 16°34' Pisces in the 2nd house, but also to his Sun in the ingoing square with Neptune in the 13th of Aquarius. This last degree strongly expresses the idea of being imprisoned (the lion in a cage) and the idea that the way out is only to be found in a vertical way, by leaping straight up into the hand of what St Paul called 'the living God'.

We also notice another kind of split, which divides his sculptures into two distinct kinds. On the one hand he modelled some of his statues and busts directly, with an 'aggressive, deliberate roughness' as Myers puts it, giving them a primitive reality, and on the other hand he created some wonderful, fully spiritualised, smooth and purified forms of a beauty which is almost out of this world.

In my opinion a gap is also emphasised between man's physical and spiritual existence, but this is superbly bridged over by Rodin. A symbol of the missing link, stressing this split, was beautifully created in his masterwork the 'Hand of God', which is portrayed holding male and female as if they are cradled. I like to look at it in the sense that what is missing between the male (Sun, spirit) and the female (Moon, Soul) and causing the gap, is the lack of a unifying Christ-centred Higher Self, which is carried by the stronger spirit of the male. We notice that in his chart he had Hermes (spiritual links) in 15°15' Cancer in the 6th house and right opposite his Ascendant in 18th Capricorn, with neither included in his circuit.

By studying the chart and life-style of Auguste Rodin, we are forced to deal with the highest spiritual knowledge (Leo), carrying far-reaching and revealing (Uranus) consequences (Saturn). We are forced to look at the way a human being

(Aquarius) is constructed spiritually (Leo) in order to become aware (Sun) exactly where a division could occur. In Koppejan's concept of the sevenfold man,[5] he introduced an astro-cosmic scheme which is related to the seven bodies recognised by Blavatsky[18] and Steiner,[17] and entirely matching the bodies mentioned by St Paul in 1 Cor. 15:40–44. If all seven bodies are co-operating smoothly and perfectly, one can speak of a Higher Self presence and even of a presence transcending this, which we call the octave of the spiritual centre, or the eighth body. We will return to the number eight later.

Positioning these seven bodies in a vertical scheme, we will find under the Sun (the spiritual body) or the central fourth body, the Demeter-astral soul body (overarching the five extrasensory planet functions of Uranus, Neptune, Pluto, Persephone and Hermes), the lunar-etheric soul body (overarching the five sensory planets of Mercury, Venus, Mars, Jupiter and Saturn) and at the bottom, the Ascendant (physical body). These three bodies below the Sun are to be seen as also being under the supreme control of the Sun, that is the physical, and both soul bodies, are reflected in three bodies pertaining to the Higher Self, situated above the Sun centre. Both sections of each three bodies are to be focused in the solar spiritual body in the centre. If this does not happen, a division occurs, and of course this is the case with millions of people. This spiritual division between both parts can only be lifted by a Christ-centred Higher Self consciousness (the higher octave level of the Leo/Aquarius axis), which then crowns the spiritual solar body with what in biblical terms is called the Glory, in Hebrew *kabood*, meaning also a heavy weight. The numerical value of this word is 26 and equal to the name of God, in Hebrew *Jahweh*. But, as Jesus said 'For my yoke is easy and my burden is light' (Matt. 11: 30). In Hebrew, the name of God, *Jahweh*, is contained numerologically within the name of Jesus, *Jehoshoe'ah*, stressing 'I and the Father are One'.

Returning to the chart of Rodin and reminding ourselves of what I said about the horizontal split in it, we will now have a good look at the images of the degree which I have decided is his Ascendant degree:

18th CAPRICORN

Janduz: 'At the left a man standing upright, looks as if he has been cut in half at the waist; at the right, two men are fighting savagely.'

Rudhyar: 'The Union Jack is flying from a new British destroyer.'

The first image immediately confirms our thoughts and conclusions. Rodin's first masterwork was a nude, muscled man, standing upright, called *The Bronze Age*, which was followed by that of John the Baptist. At first sight, the second image seems confusing. What has this image to do with Rodin? But analysing the symbols expressed in this image, we indeed are able to find dazzling clues. For the moment, let us forget the idea of a British destroyer and let us look instead at the Union Jack, the flag of Great Britain. This flag comprises the upright red cross of St George of England, the white diagonal cross on a blue background of St Andrew of Scotland, and the red diagonal cross of St Patrick of Ireland.

Meditating upon this complex symbol, and at the same time, using our Hermes abilities of projection and introjection, we are inwardly, in the membrane of our astral body, drawing all the lines which are shaping squares and triangles, and we notice that by doing so, in a mysterious way those lines are linked together. Symbolically speaking, in our solar consciousness, line by line, like drips of the sweetest honey, like wisdom, the essential significance of this flag will crystallise out. This banner of England, the country which is said to be ruled by Aries, Pluto, is telling us an extraordinary story and one which is very relevant to our subject.

Recall for a minute the fact that the colour of the upright standing cross of St George is red, and that red is the colour of Aries. Add the fact that Aries in a natal chart is the symbol of the Ascendant, the physical body. The horizontal and vertical lines of the red George's cross literally represent the Ascendant and Descendant of the physical body of an upright standing man. Although the horizontal line shows the division mentioned, in this symbol it is beautifully connecting the lower and upper parts. In addition the red diagonal lines of the cross of St Patrick, together with the white diagonal lines of the cross of St Andrew, literally represent the spread-out legs and raised arms of this physical body. The spaces in between these parts are the eight blue triangles shaping four squares, each of them divided into two blue triangles. The colour blue, symbolising the overarching (Cancer) blue sky, the firmament, is of Sagittarius.

When thinking about the name of this flag, we have to know that 'Jack' in fact represents a human being, and that the name is derived from Jacob, who was the patriarch of the twelve tribes of biblical and modern Israel. 'Union' means that those twelve tribes are united in Jacob and, consequently, in the races of the United Kingdom. From the centre we draw an invisible circle around the square of this banner, because we know that a square is the result of a circle marked by four corners. Let us compare this circle with the zodiacal circle, marked by the four corners of the cardinal cross, Aries–Cancer–Libra–Capricorn. The centre in a circle of twelve, the Sun is in the centre of the solar system, in the centre of the zodiac, with the earth circling around it; and although this idea can be extended and expressed in many ways, for our present purpose it goes too far to be explored in detail. It is sufficient to say that in this flag the centre within a circle is to be seen as the elevated consciousness of the Higher Self. The important question as to why this symbol of a man representing a unity of twelve is carried by the United Kingdom unfortunately goes beyond the scope of this book.

We could explore further the colours of this flag. It is for the moment sufficient to know that the red of the cross of St George, symbol of the human physical body, ruled by Aries–Pluto, has a particular meaning. In Hebrew the name for red is *tola – thaaph* (400), *lammed* (30), *ayin* (70), which gives a total numerical value of 500. This very number is linked to the cycle of the mythological red-coloured phoenix. This bird is also assigned to Aries–Pluto, and is said to fly after 500 years from the East to Heliopolis, the city of the Sun, to burn itself on its nest. Mysteriously, a young bird rose from the ashes, renewed, it is said, by the miraculous activity of a particular worm, as the early Church fathers firmly believed. Could it be that this worm is the *tola'at*, by which the red colouring is produced, causing that phenomenon? It is interesting also to know that the Hebrew tabernacle was covered with rams' skins dyed with the red or scarlet colour produced by this worm.

The Flag of England

The dead dumb fog hath wrapped it,
the frozen dews have kissed,
the morning stars have hailed it,
a fellow-star in the mist.
What is the Flag of England?
Ye have but my breath to dare,
Ye have but my waves to conquer.
Go forth, for it is there!

Rudyard Kipling

And now we will look at the symbol of the destroyer. It is often regretted that the Jones symbols, said to originate from ancient Celtic sources, have been updated into modern images. But as we will see later on, it couldn't be better expressed. Let us forget the idea of a 'destroyer' and see it just as a ship. A ship with a mast in its centre (the spirit) and two lines on either side, symbolising the sails through which the Holy Spirit blows where it wills, and a triangle, pointing upwards, becomes visible. Even under water we can envisage another triangle, reflected in the water, as the invisible underpart of the body, the unconscious, where the mast is 'rooted'. In Hebrew a ship is called *Aniah*, composed of *aleph* (1), *waaph* (60), *nun* (50), *jod* (10), *jod* (10), *he* (5), and carries in it the word *ani:aleph* (1), *nun* (50), *jod* (10), meaning 'I', of the self conscious human being, fully aware of his spiritual centre, and crowned with his Higher Self. The centre will be the point where the mast is fixed, holding the sails. It is the place where the two triangles are connected, the under and the upper part, shaping a square. Like the horizontal line of the George cross in the Union Jack, so is the deck of this ship the horizontal line of the Ascendant and the Descendant, representing the axis of Aries and Libra. This ship, symbol of the 'I' of man, on its centred mast, is flying the Union Jack, which, as we have seen, is also a symbol, carrying three crosses, and shaping eight lines delineating the main parts of the human physical body, and uniting twelve points in a circle to indicate a spiritually evolved human being.

After these excursions, needed to explain the symbols, we return to the concept of the sevenfold man, 'crowned' with an eighth body, the Higher Self. By now we are able to understand what is expressed in the second image of the 18th degree of Capricorn. The Union Jack, having four triangles, is the completed symbol of the two main triangles of the ship, the I. It is the perfect symbol of the eighth body of the spiritually evolved man, descended into the circle of twelve, uniting the twelve tribes of Israel, uniting the twelve signs of the zodiac in the natal chart, and uniting the twelve disciples/apostles of Christ. Likewise Christ is the centre of those twelve, and Jahweh was and still is of the twelve tribes of Israel, should the human Christ-centred consciousness be in the centre of the twelve signs of his natal chart. Compare this with the structure of a cone, the top being the Higher Self spiralling down into a circle at the bottom, the natal chart. A triangle is the structure in which we find the spirit and the soul, the male and the female, positioned on opposite corners, either side of the bottom line, with the Higher Self at the apex. It is also extremely significant as the symbol of the Great Pyramid in Gizeh and its missing top-stone, Christ. For these reasons alone it should be on top of the list of subjects to be studied by humans, so that they may know and understand why the symbol of 'Israel' is the bread of life for mankind.

Considering the eight lines, projected as the upright standing man in the zodiacal circle, and focusing our mind in the sign of Cancer, we find the vertical axis Cancer–Capricorn as the head and body of a man, the following axis Leo–Aquarius as his left leg and right arm, and the previous axis of Gemini–Sagittarius as his right leg and his left arm. We find these crossing lines also in the pyramidal nerve tracts, crossing in the physical body, and connected with the left and right parts of the brain. The horizontal axis Aries–Libra we find in the horizontal arm of the George cross in the Union Jack and echoed by the diaphragm, which is seemingly missing in the man of the first image. These eight points are the eight signs found in Koppejan's concept of the astrological symbol of the Sun Grail in its twelvefold existence. For each of the twelve Sun positions this 'grail' is to be seen as substance received in the container of the astral soul body, to be reflected by the etheric lunar soul body, and to be made fully conscious by the human spirit, symbolised by the Sun. It is the holy spirit which descends as a white dove, holding in its beak the nourishing grail essence of life, referred to in the Grail stories. It is this nourishment which the astral body receives from heaven as a Christ-centred gift, providing our spirit and mind (Sun) with continuous outbursts of higher knowledge, for man to recognise consciously. It is interesting to know that only a few people are aware that the word 'conscious' is derived from two Latin words, *con*, meaning with, and *scire*, meaning to know. To become conscious means to become one who has been given the spiritual knowledge of the Sun of God by the white dove of the Holy Spirit.

Even more could be said about the number eight. It is the figure of eight which shapes the lemniscate, the well-known symbol for the connection between heaven and earth, between spirit and matter. The number eight has important connotations in Hebrew, *shemonah* which has the word *sjemen* (300 + 50 + 40) as the base, which means 'olive oil'. The number 390 is equal to the total number value of the Hebrew word for heaven, *shamajim* (*sjin* (300) *mem* (40), *jod* (10), *mem* (40)). Originally the golden eight-branched candleholder in the temple in Jerusalem was lit by olive oil, the production of which involved eight days of preparation. Olive oil is the ever-renewing substance, given by heaven. The astro-cosmic meaning of the number eight in the Grail and the Union Jack, expressed in the symbols of the 18th degree of Capricorn, is the actual substance we need to be able to discuss and to demonstrate in the chart and being of Auguste Rodin. More, the bedrock of the twelvefold problem presented by all the 18th degrees, is shown in the fundamental structures of this Capricorn stage.

Returning to the chart of Rodin, I recall the split in his chart marked by the axis of Capricorn–Cancer, and stressed by the position of his Hermes (introjection) in the 16th of Cancer, and we are reminded of the first image of 18th Capricorn, the split man. We also return to the sculptures Rodin created, so often showing only the upperpart of a body, and the underpart incarcerated in marble or bronze – see for instance, *Man and his Thought*. Didn't he want to know, to recognise or to appreciate this underpart or was he, on the contrary, fully aware, and giving the message that the underpart of humans is something they don't want to think about, suppressed in their unconscious? Put away and hidden in matter, blocked, imprisoned and waiting to be released? May we come to the conclusion that this is reaching beyond the physical, to show another, a spiritual gap? Is the human underpart missing the connective link with its Higher Self upperpart, held in the hand (Gemini) of God? Looking at his chart we find Hermes, higher ruler of Gemini, the sign where contrasts are ripped apart, in the 16th of Cancer. Cancer is the sign of the female principle, of the Chinese symbols yin and yang united in a circle, the sign of the etheric, lunar soul body and the astral, Demeterian, soul body. It is the sign where upper and under parts are divided but are also linked together. This gap emphasises Demeter, which rules the diaphragm or midriff, seat of the solar plexus, which separates the two parts of the body. Looking at the 18th degree of Capricorn, we see an upright standing man pictured, showing a gap exactly there where the diaphragm is situated and missing, not able to link the upper and lower parts of his body together. We noticed in Rodin's chart that his Sun is positioned in a wide outgoing conjunction (which on its own suggests a lack of spiritual awareness) with his Demeter. Hermes, the winged Messenger of the Gods, is the mediating link between the two worlds. Hermes is found in a tense opposition with his Ascendant and not included in his circuit. It is Hermes in Cancer which draws our attention to this fundamental problem. It is a problem still unresolved nowadays and not even recognised by humanity. This position confirms what Rodin said: 'movement and mobility is the dynamic of the physical body wherein all that lives in the soul has been expressed' and we recognise the reference to Hermes, ruler of Gemini, in Cancer, in these words.

Although it can't be done in this book, I think we should analyse the contents of all the 18th degrees, expressing between them a particular problem, unfolded in twelve parts, as we postulated in Chapter 1. By doing so, we will undoubtedly find

confirmation for our thoughts. What we *can* do is have a look at
the base of the problem of the 18th degrees, laid out in the images
of the 18th degree of Aries:

18th ARIES

Janduz: '*A man and a woman, standing upright,*
give each other their right hand,
They both have an air of goodness and gentleness.
The man makes a gesture of protection.'

Rudhyar: '*An empty hammock is hanging between two lovely trees.*'

At first sight we may well wonder, what it is that could possibly
be seen as a basic problem for humans, laid out in this picture. I
think the answer cannot be found in only that protective, 'Dutch-
Uncle' gesture. There is much more. Both the man, being a
symbol of the solar spirit, and the woman, symbol of the lunar
soul, seem to be unaware of the fact that something is missing
between them. Not aware of the fact, 'that spirit (man) and soul
(woman) are instruments, organs of their invisible Ego [Higher
Self] which directs and guides the Spirit and the Soul' .... 'the
deeper esoteric message in this degree is, that it is the Ego and
the spirit which are guiding and directing the soul'.[5a] The second
image 'shows the reconciliation between spirit and soul'. I think
it is this problem which he was struggling with, and which is
behind Rodin's sculptures of loving couples, and I think he found
an answer to it, clearly recognisable in one of his sculptures, the
'Hand of God', which shows a united couple being held in the
cradle of God's hand, which is the symbol of the Higher Self.

Looking for other 18th degrees, we found that many of them
were operating in Rodin's life, to be found in progressions,
transits and so on, confirming his corrected Ascendant degree,
but not all of them will be demonstrated and listed here.

Rodin's birthtime was published in a German magazine with a
transit of Mars in the 18th of Taurus; I worked on his chart with
transiting Venus in the 18th of Virgo; *Le Penseur* was revealed to
the public with transiting Venus in the 18th of Taurus.

In 1864 his beloved sister Marie died and this event is said to
have completely changed his life. Apparently he wanted to
become a monk, but was kindly turned away by the Abbot, who
said that it was art he was born for and not a monastic life. The
Abbot ordered a bust of himself, and this was Rodin's first
successful commission. At that time we find his progressed

Venus, ruler of the 3rd house (brothers and sisters), and the 8th house (death and transformation), in 17°13' Capricorn, in conjunction with his corrected Ascendant degree.

From now on his progressed Pluto retrogrades into the 18th degree of Aries, positioned in its own sign as I believe, fiercely driving him to work in a primitive and aggressively rough style, forced as Pluto was, to reach the opposite sign of Libra, inducing Venus (art) in that burning degree of 19th Sagittarius, in the ingoing conjunction with Persephone. These two planets are the rulers of Taurus, and in conjunction with Saturn, inevitably show the influence of Pluto, initiating a sort of hot-water geyser, which produced a continuous flow of inspiration and vision, to be realised into marble and bronze beauty. Pluto stayed in this degree till 1916, during Rodin's most productive years. In this I find granite-hard evidence for the idea that Pluto is indeed the ruler of Aries.

He worked on *The Burghers of Calais* during 1893/4 with his progressed Mars, completing the entire cardinal cross in his chart, in 18th Libra (Rudhyar: 'two men placed under arrest and brought to court'). In 1347 six civilians of Calais were taken by King Edward III as hostages, representing the surrendering town, but were later pardoned because of the joyful news that the Queen was expecting a baby. During 1893/4 Rodin also had his progressed Pluto retrograde in the 18th of Aries, inducing the 18th of Libra and his progressed Mars, and both square his Ascendant, and because of this we have to be aware that the entire cardinal cross in 18th degrees was operating through him, once more stressing the importance of this set of twelve degrees. With Mars and Pluto both square his Ascendant degree, we can imagine he had to endure a tremendously high creative pressure, which would ultimately initiate (Pluto) the world into the hidden spiritual secrets of the human being, expressed in the 18th degree of Aries. Pluto in the outgoing square with his Ascendant clearly meant to activate his physical body, unmasking its underlying problems. This statue of the Burghers was the cause of a fierce battle (Mars opposite Pluto square the Ascendant) with the authorities, because Rodin, with his already controversial insistence on realism, insisted it should be placed almost on ground level, but they wanted it placed in the traditional way, on a high plinth. Rodin lost the battle.

In his conception chart he had the Moon in the 18th of Capricorn, and Jupiter in the 18th of Scorpio. In his solar return for the year he died (on 17 November), for 13.11.1917 GMT 3h 40m 17m, we find his MC in 18th Cancer in opposition to his Ascendant. Did he indeed manage to establish his physical presence (Ascendant) harmoniously on the public stage (MC) in relation to what he had to say in stone and bronze?

* * *

By now I think we are able to say a little about the image of a destroyer in the 18th of Capricorn. A destroyer chases submarines which threaten to attack the ship. Hostile elements are to be destroyed. Let us try to translate this image. As we have seen, the ship is the symbol of the 'I', the Sun, the central spiritual body of a human being. The sea symbolises the unconscious, and the submarine symbolises hostile elements, dwelling in that unconscious, which have to be identified and destroyed, just as in psychoanalysis suppressed hostile and threatening material has to be captured, and brought to the surface in order to be processed in full awareness of the solar spirit. In this we recognise the function of Aries, Pluto square Cancer, Moon and Demeter, Pluto unmasking the unconscious. Scorpio, of course, with its transforming and processing abilities, has its own function in this process. We remember the underpart of the triangle of the ship, reflected in the water of the unconscious. We remember the horizontal physical line of the George's flag marking the division between upper- and underpart, controlling the physical appearance. The underpart holds the genitals and the root chakra, which when uncontrolled are the centre of destruction, but when controlled become the seat of the creative Kundalini serpent forces. Those forces and centre cannot be controlled by themselves, but only by a will's centre (Sun) which is lifted up by the Higher Self in the head, which is ruled by Pluto, higher ruler of Aries. Only then is the Kundalini enabled to rise through the spinal cord into the head, illuminating the entire being and allowing man access to extrasensorial powers. Is it for these reasons Rodin emphasised the human head in his creations?

One has to wonder what it was that had to be hidden in Rodin's sculptures, to be eliminated in the dense structures of stone; imprisoned but ultimately to be released? In his chart we find the Sun in Scorpio (sexuality) in a wide outgoing conjunction with his Demeter (higher ruler of Cancer) symbol of the personal and collective unconscious, also in Scorpio and it is this, though Rodin was not originally aware of it, which we have to look at.

The circuit moves to Mars in Virgo (virginal purity, service) in the 8th house (transformation) which shapes ingoing squares with Saturn (conscience, morality, stone) and Persephone (materialised visions) in Sagittarius (philosophy, the thinker, faith) and the message becomes as clear as crystal. It is this lower part, often almost overemphasised in his creations by being embedded in stone, which he wants to put high in his banner (Union Jack) to show to the world, to point out and to draw our attention to. A real thinker (Sagittarius grail) has eliminated and sublimated the hind axis of Scorpio (desires of sex and passion) and Taurus (love and possessive greed) and is able to express (Gemini) his deep thoughts, outcrystallised in stone (Capricorn), about what the unconscious (Cancer) contains, and as Rodin did, to materialise them in art in a grand way.

The problem that the 18th degrees is setting out urges one to dive deep into the uttermost depths of the unconscious and to bring the contents of it to the surface of consciousness. It is well-known that Rodin as no one else, has struggled with this basic problem. At the same time he is showing us the answers, if we look at those 'spiritualised' sculptures, *Man and his Thought*, *Aurora*, *The Farewell*, *The Dream* and others, wherein time and eternity seem to have merged, and matter, heavy and dense, has vaporised into spiritual values, like the sweet fragrance of certain burnt offerings which in ancient times reached the nostrils (Sagittarius) of the 'Living God'.

His Part of Fortune, in conjunction with the south node, was in 26°10' Leo:

27th LEO

Janduz: 'A two-edged dagger lies flat on the earth,
a scythe stands upright, planted in the bare soil.'
Rudhyar: 'In the East, light slowly increases, wiping out the stars.'

The first image shows a horizontal (the dagger) and a vertical line (the scythe), invisibly intersecting. '... what we see is a typical example of esoteric intersections by which another dimension, that of Aquarius opposite Leo, is invoked, the elevated spiritual levels of the most intense material and spiritual changes.'[5a] I am not convinced that in his individual life he was actually able to fully substantiate this individual physical and spiritual change. In his progressed chart for the year he died, 1917, he again had the Part of Fortune in Leo and again in conjunction with the south node, though in other degrees. This could mean that to a certain extent he did manage, but, because again in conjunction with the south node, the task was not yet fully realised. We assume that karmically still more had to be done. The second image he certainly created in his sculpture in marble called *Aurora*. Only a head sits on a surface of white marble, stressing the incredible thought that at the end of human evolution, the shape of a human being will be reduced, and its powers concentrated into 'only' a head and a face. Something like the Ophaniem (see also Chapter 3), the 'wheels with eyes', the highest angelic beings immanent before the throne of God, in charge of primordial matter. This of course, is the highest envisioned message he could possibly dream of and express in his art. If this is true, he has indeed been a prophet (Venus in the ingoing conjunction with Persephone) heralding (Sagittarius) the final shape (Saturn) of the human in its development (Sagittarius). Interestingly, he started his career by sculpting, almost anonymously, angels to be placed in a park in Brussels.

The word *Ophaniem* is represented by the numbers $1 + (80 + 50)$, plus the plural *mem*, or 40, and we quickly recognise the Holy One, 1, *aleph*, and the $80 + 50$ of *peh* and *nun* which is the 130 of *pan*, meaning 'face', as we discovered in Chapter 3. The name *ophan* means 'a turning wheel', and is used for time, and by extension, for the turning circle of the year. The Ophaniem are said to belong to the highest order of angelic beings (Aquarius), classified as pertaining to Chochma in the Kabbalistic system. These 'wheels' are in charge of the influx of cosmic energy, as in the pure divine impulse of dynamic creation, the primordial fire. Chochma is said to represent the experience of the vision of 'God-face-to-face', and one of the symbols for Chochma is the 'Inner Robe of Glory'. We remember that Moses experienced such a vision of God on Mount Sinai (*sammig* (60) + *jod* (10) + *nun* (50) + *jod* (10) = 130), and that afterwards he had to cover his brightly lit face with a cloth to protect people from the sight. Because the name of the force radiating from his head, is called *qeren* (*qoph* (100), *resj* (200), *nun* (50)), it was translated as 'horns', *qeren* also being the word for horn of any type, in particular a ram's horn. Michelangelo's sculpture portrays him literally with a pair of horns. The ram, which is assigned to Aries, certainly stresses the Pluto/Aries forces involved, often compared to those of nuclear power.

Rudolf Steiner, in his book *Spiritual Hierarchies*, pointed out that these Ophaniem, or 'Thrones', the so-called Spirits of Will (Leo/Aquarius), are dedicated (I have particularly chosen this word because of its Taurean connotation), to the radiation of the divine impulse (Aries) into the cosmos wherever it is needed for creation, causing the first appearance (Aries) of primordial matter (Taurus), the first stage of the realisation of the Divine Plan (Leo). The 'Thrones' have reached the stage in their human (Aquarius) development (Taurus), in which they are 'wholeheartedly' (Leo) dedicated to serve (Virgo), and to sacrifice (Pisces) the core, or substance of their being by radiating warmth into matter. Most significantly, they are said to concentrate exclusively on the shaping and the development of the human physical body.

We can locate the head, and the face, within the Kabbalistic philosophical system called *Eetz Hachajiem*, the Tree of Life, in which we are given an Order of ten mutually linked *sephiroth*, placed in a formation of triangles which are connected by twenty-two pathways. Together they give the number 32, which is, for instance, the number for the Hebrew word *leb* (*lammed* (30) + *beth* (2)), as found in the word for white, *laban* (with the *nun* (50) as suffix), meaning 'heart', assigned to Leo, and ruled by the Sun. We are, so to speak, at the heart of that of which we are striving to become spiritually conscious (Leo). The top three sephiroth, or the Supernals, at the apex of the Tree of Life, are known as the Head of the Celestial, or Archetypal Man, Adam Kadmon, and, if we observe the precept 'as above, so below', of microcosmic man also. The Hebrew name *Kadmon*, is related to another Hebrew word, *qedem* (*qoph* (100) + *dalleth* (4) + *mem* (40) = 144), meaning the East, which we mentioned in Chapter 3. The apex of this top triangle is Kether, meaning 'crown', and known as 'the Vast Countenance', with Chochma (wisdom), forming the left side of the face, and Binah (understanding), forming the right side.

* * *

At the time Koppejan calculated Rodin's chart, transiting Jupiter was in the 27th degree of Aquarius, and at certain vital times I had transiting Saturn and Uranus in the 27th of Sagittarius, Mars in the 27th of Aquarius and the Sun in the 27th of Libra, confirming the calculated Part of Fortune resulting from an Ascendant of 18° Capricorn. In his solar return for 1917 Rodin had Mercury, ruler of the 8th house, in the 27th of Scorpio. In 1880 he started an intense love affair which lasted till 1885, and his progressed chart for 1880 shows the MC in the 27th of Sagittarius (see the sculptor in the second image) and the Part of Fortune was in 26°17 Aquarius. The 27th of Sagittarius was operating between 1888 and 1898 with his progressed Saturn.

* * *

It is said that Rodin was like a 'belated' pupil of Michelangelo, demonstrating the same skills. I corrected Michelangelo's Ascendant and found it to be the 27th degree of Sagittarius (26°48 exactly, see the second image, most appropriate). Surprisingly, his conception chart shows thrice an 18th degree: Mars 18th Virgo conjunct Pluto in the same degree, and Neptune in 18th Scorpio. Could it be that Rodin was the reincarnation of Michelangelo? Anyway, he had some things in common with him, sharing not only his skills but also the problems of the 18th degrees, and also, as we said above, having touched the 27th of Sagittarius with his progressed Saturn. Added to this, in Rodin's chart we find Taurus on the cusp of the 4th house, which is not only marking his personal unconscious but also his personal deep past, previous lives. Venus and Persephone, as the rulers of Taurus, in the ingoing spiritual conjunction were enabling him to raise and to materialise 'thoughtful' visions in beauty from this deep past.

Another thing I would like to stress is, that without the acceptance of a planet function called Persephone, it is impossible to explain sufficiently how an artist is able to materialise visions of beauty. This can't be done with only Venus, symbol of harmony and beauty. To fully interpret Rodin's chart and to understand his being and life, it was essential to include this possibility.

At the conclusion of our contemplations, what a rich 'goldmine' the chart and life of Rodin has been for us. His Demeter in the 7th degree of Scorpio, diving deep, even supplied diamonds (Sun!) to be picked up from the unconscious sea bed (see the second image of this degree). We learned and understood the lessons of life. Again, we found evidence for what I have said before, namely that the left and right brain were mutually sparking, and heaven supplied us with rich esoteric insights. Enough reasons to take our leave from Rodin by wholeheartedly thanking him for all he has given to the world.

CHAPTER NINE

Wim Koppejan and a Caravan of Camels

Name	Willem Ary Koppejan
Birthdate	19 August 1913
Birthplace	Amsterdam (The Netherlands), 52°N20' and 4°E53'
LMT	4h 00m 00s am (Council Register of Births in Amsterdam)
GT	3h 40m 30s am
RLT	4h 00m 02s am
RST	1h 47m 36s – Ascendant 16°09' Leo (uncorrected), Sun 25°33' Leo, Moon 20°37' Pisces (uncorrected),
Conception	Amsterdam
House system	Placidus.

From the birthchart we take the following basic data, needed in order to calculate the conception correction.

1. With 16°09' Leo rising, the natal Moon is 20°37' Pisces and the natal Sun 25°33' Leo. We draw a line from the Sun to the same degree of the opposite sign and locate the Moon at the left-hand side at the ingoing arch which means the Moon is *waning*. The Moon is positioned above the horizontal axis of Ascendant and Descendant which means the Moon is *above the horizon*. The scheme in Chapter 6 shows this to be the *3rd order* of Bailey which says, 'Moon/Descendant, longer/forwards'.
2. We count the distance between the Moon 20°37' Pisces and the *Descendant* 16°09' Aquarius which is 34°, ignoring the minutes.
3. We divide this distance of 34° by 13° (the average daily motion of the Moon) = 3 days.
4. 3 days longer than 273 days (the average time of pregnancy) = 276 days.
5. 276 days subtracted from the birthdate 19.8.1913 =

WIM KOPPEJAN

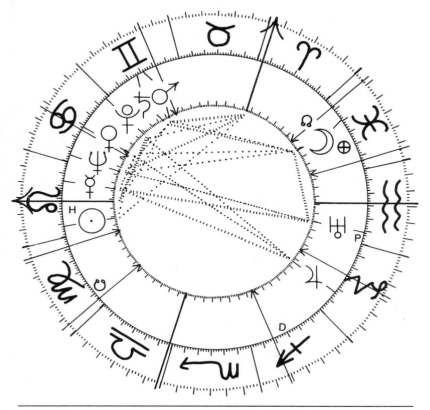

Radix							
		MC	28 22 Ari	Sun	25 33 Leo		1
		ASC	15 52 Leo	Moon	20 36 Pis		8
WIM KOPPEJAN			Plac	Mercury	7 49 Leo		12
		11.	8 28 Gem	Venus	14 46 Can		11
Date:	19 8 1913	12.	16 32 Can	Mars	13 35 Gem		11
Time:	3 38 20 E O	2.	3 28 Vir	Jupiter	8 26 Cap	R	5
Latitude:	52 23 N	3.	26 39 Vir	Saturn	16 34 Gem		11
Longitude:	4 53 E			Uranus	4 46 Aqu	R	6
		Node	25 33 Pis 8	Neptune	26 51 Can		12
		Part ft	10 56 Pis 8	Pluto	0 48 Can		11
				Perseph	3 15 Acq		6
Aspects: Radix/Radix		Orb:	8 0	Hermes	22 03 Leo		1
				Demeter	5 10 Sag		4

MC Tri	Sun 2 49	MC ssq	Mar 0 13	MC Sqr	Nep 1 30	MC Sxt	Plu 2 26
ASC ssx	Ven 1 6	ASC Sxt	Mar 2 17	ASC Sxt	Sat 0 42	ASC ssq	Plu 0 4
Sun ssx	Nep 1 19	Moo Tri	Ven 5 50	Moo Sqr	Mar 7 1	Moo Sqr	Sat 4 2
Moo ssq	Ura 0 50	Moo Tri	Nep 6 15	Mer qcx	Jup 0 37	Mer Opp	Ura 3 4
Ven ssx	Mar 1 11	Ven Opp	Jup 6 20	Ven ssx	Sat 1 48	Mar Cnj	Sat 2 59
Mar ssq	Nep 1 43	Jup Opp	Plu 7 38	Ura Opp	Nep 7 54	Nod qcx	Sun 0 0
Nod Tri	Nep 1 19						

16.11.1912, which is the first possible, regular date of conception. Another way of calculating is by subtracting a full year from the birthdate 19.8.1913, giving 19.8.1912; subtract 276 days (see 4) from 365 days = 89 days to be added to the date of 19.8.1912 to find the date of 16.11.1912.

6. According to Bailey's 3rd order, see the first paragraph, *'Moon Radix is Ascendant Conception'*, we need to know the sidereal time of the natal Moon (20°37′ Pisces), and also (because according to the 3rd order *'or Descendant Conception'*) for the opposite point of 20°37′ Virgo which can be found in the table of houses for 52°N20′. This ST has to be interpolated in order to be accurate:

interpolated ST of the Ascendant of the
position of the natal Moon:
Pisces 20°37′ at ST 17h 44m 56s
and its opposite point
20°37′ Virgo at ST 5h 06m 30s.

Amsterdam = Longitude 4°E53′ multiplied by 4 minutes = 00h 19m 32s, rounded off to 00h 19m 30s, which is the difference between RLT and GMT.

Recapitulating these basic facts in the following scheme:

Scheme for Calculating the 3rd Order

Moon *above* the horizon and *waning*
Moon conception = Descendant or Ascendant radix,
Moon radix = Descendant or Ascendant conception.

Distance between natal Moon (Pisces 20°37′)
and Descendant radix (Aquarius 16°09′)
= 35° : 13° =
3 days longer than 273 days =
276 days before 19.8.1913 =
16.11.1912

Possibility (1)
From the ephemeris we take the ST at noon at 16.11.1912 and the interpolated ST of the Ascendant equal to the position of the natal Moon, the difference between these two items supplies the RLT, as follows:

16.11.1912 (276) noon ST	15h 41m
RLT	+2h 04m
ST Pisces 20°37′	17h 45m

We convert the RLT +2h 04m into GMT by subtracting 19m 30s from it, = +1h 44m (30s) and we calculate the progression of the conception Moon in GMT +1h 44m by using Diurnal Proportional Logarithms, to be found in the ephemeris:

RLT	+2h 04m 00s	
Difference from GMT	−0h 19m 30s	
GMT	+1h 44m (30s)	= Log. 11413
Daily motion of the Moon 11°51'		= Log. 3065 +
Progression of the Moon		Log. 14478 = +0°51'

Checking the ephemeris for 16.11.1912, we take the position of the Moon at noon and adjust this position by adding to it the progression in +1h 44m at a daily motion of 11°51', which is the speed from 16 to 17 November = +0°51' as follows:

16/11 Moon at noon	18°57' Aquarius
Progress +1h 44m	+0°51'
Corrected Descendant	19°48' Aquarius
Corrected Ascendant	19°48' Leo

19°48' Leo is rising at 52°N20' at
approx. ST 2h 09m
approx. 21m later
than the official time
Corrected LMT 4h 21m am
Corrected natal Moon 20°47' Pisces
Corrected natal PF 15°02' Pisces

In this case the true birthtime could have been 4h 21m am, which should have been registered at the Birth Registration Office as 4h 30m rather than 4h 00m am. Therefore this possibility has to be excluded. The second possibility of the same date is calculated as follows:

Possibility (2)
From the ephemeris we take the ST at noon at 16.11.1912 and find in the table of houses for Amsterdam (52°N20') the ST of the Ascendant equal to the *opposite* position of the natal Moon, 20°37' Virgo. The difference between these two items supplies the RLT, as follows:

16/11 (276) noon ST	15h 41m
RLT	−10h 35m
ST 20°37' Virgo	5h 06m

Converting the RLT = −10h 35m into GMT by adding 19m 30s (see 11) to it, which is −10h 54m (30s), and we calculate the progression of the conception Moon in −10h 54m:

RLT   − 10h 35m
Difference from GMT   00h 19m (30s)
GMT   − 10h 54m (30s) = Log.   3428
Daily motion of the Moon 11°51′   = Log. + 3065
Progression of the Moon   Log.   6493 = −5°23′

Checking the ephemeris for 16.11.1912, we take the position of
the Moon at noon and adjust this position by subtracting from it
the progression in − 10h 54m at a daily speed of 11°51′ from 15 to
16 November = − 5°23′, as follows:

16/11 Moon at noon	18°57′	Aquarius
Progression in − 10h 54m	−5°23′	
Corrected Descendant	13°34′	Aquarius
Corrected Ascendant	13°34′	Leo

13°34′ *Leo* is rising at 52°N20′
at approx. ST 1h 32m (03s)
approx. 15m (33s) earlier than the official time
Corrected LMT approx. 3h 44m (27s) am
Corrected natal Moon 20°29′ Pisces
Corrected natal PF 8°30′ Pisces

A birthtime of 15m 33s earlier is not impossible, although it
means just over the allowed limit of 15′ either side of the
birthtime.

Possibility (3)
Leaping a fortnight forwards to 262 days gives us the next
possibility of *29.11.1912*

From the ephemeris we take the ST at noon at 29.11.1912 and find
in the tables of houses for Amsterdam (52°N20′) the ST of the
Ascendant equal to the position of the natal Moon, the difference
between these two items supplies the RLT, as follows:

29.11.1912 (262) noon ST	16h 32m
RLT	+01h 13m
ST 20°37′ Pisces	17h 45m

Converting the RLT = + 1h 13m into GMT by subtracting from it
19m 30s = + 0h 53m 30s and we calculate the progression of the
conception Moon in + 0h 53m:

RLT   +01h 13m
Difference from GMT   − 00h 19m 30s
GMT   + 00h 53m 30s = Log.   14341
Daily motion of the Moon 14°17′   = Log. + 2254
Progression of the Moon   Log.   16595 = +0°32′

Checking the ephemeris for 29.11.1912, we take the position of
the Moon at noon and adjust this position by adding to it the
progression in +0h 53m at a daily motion of 14°17' from 29 to 30
November = +0°32', as follows:

29.11.1912 Moon at noon	11°03' Leo
Progression in +53m	+0°32'
Corrected Ascendant	11°35' Leo

11°35' Leo is rising at 52°N20'
at approx. ST 1h 20m (52s)
which is approx. 26m (44s) earlier than the official time
corrected LMT approx. 3h 33m (16s) am
corrected natal Moon 20°24' Pisces
corrected natal PF 6°28' Pisces

The correction of a birthtime to almost 27m earlier than recorded,
also has to be excluded, as it clearly would have been registered
as 3h 30m am instead of 4h 00m.

Possibility (4)
The second possibility of the *same* conception date is calculated as
follows. From the ephemeris we take the ST at noon at 29.11.1912
and find in the tables of houses for Amsterdam (52°N20') the ST
of the Ascendant equal to the opposite position of the natal
Moon, 20°37' Virgo. The difference between these two items
supplies the RLT, as follows:

ST at noon 29.11.1912 (262)	16h 32m
RLT	+12h 34m
ST of 20°37' Virgo	5h 06ms (adding 24h = 29h 06m)

Converting the RLT = +12h 34m into GMT by subtracting 19m
30s from it = +12h 14m 30s we calculate the progression of the
conception Moon in +12h 14m:

RLT	+12h 34m
Difference from GMT	−00h 19m 30s
GMT	+12h 14m (30s) = Log. 2927
Daily motion of the	
Moon 14°17'	= Log. +2254
Progression of the Moon	Log. 5181 = +7°17'

Checking the ephemeris for 29.11.1912, we take the position of
the Moon at noon and adjust this position by adding to it the
progression in +12h 14m at a daily motion of 14°17' from 29 to 30
November = +7°17', as follows:

29.11.1912 (262) Moon at noon	11°03′ Leo
Progression in +12h 14m	+7°17′
Corrected Ascendant	18°20′ Leo

18°20′ Leo is rising at 52°N20′
at approx. ST 01h 59m (38s)
approx. 12m later than the official time
corrected LMT approx. 4h 12m am
corrected natal Moon 20°43′ Pisces
corrected natal PF 13°30′ Pisces

This corrected birthtime could very well have been the right one.

Possibility (5)

Leaping a fortnight backwards in time from 16.11.1912 presents the next possibility of 290 days = 2.11.1912. From the ephemeris we take the ST at noon at 2.11.1912 and find in the tables of houses for Amsterdam (52°N20′) the ST of the Ascendant equal to the position of the natal Moon. The difference between these two items supplies the RLT, as follows:

2.11.1912 (290) ST at noon	14h 45m (34s)
RLT	+3h 00m (22s)
ST 20°37′ Pisces	17h 45m (56s)

We convert the RLT = +3h 00m 22s into GMT by subtracting 19m 30s from it = +2h 40m 52s and we calculate the progression of the conception Moon in +2h 40m 52s:

RLT	+3h 00m 22s	
Difference from GMT	−0h 19m 30s	
GMT	+2h 41m = Log.	9570
Daily motion of the Moon 14°10′	Log.	+2289
Progression of the Moon	Log. 11859	= +1°34′

Checking the ephemeris for 2.11.1912, we take the position of the Moon at noon and adjust this position by adding to it the progression in +2h 41m at a daily motion of 14°10′ from 2 to 3 November = +1°34′, as follows:

2.11.1912 Moon at noon	14°19′ Leo
Progression in +2h 41m	+1°34′
Corrected Ascendant	15°53′ Leo

15°53′ Leo is rising at 52°N20′
at ST 1h 45m (28s)
2m earlier than the official time
corrected LMT approx. 3h 58m am

corrected natal Moon 20°36′ Pisces
corrected natal PF 10°56′ Pisces

Possibility (6)
For practical reasons the second possibility of the same
conception day turns out to be calculated on the next day,
3.11.1912.
 From the ephemeris we take the ST at noon of 3.11.1912 and we
take the ST of the opposite position of the natal Moon. The
difference between these two items supplies the RLT, as follows:

3.11.1912 ST at noon	14h 49m
RLT	−9h 43m
ST of 20°37′ Virgo .	5h 06m

We convert the RLT = −9h 43m into GMT by adding to it +19m
30s = −10h 02m (30s), and we calculate the progression of the
conception Moon in −10h 02m:

RLT	−9h 43m		
Difference from GMT	+0h 19m 30s		
GMT	−10h 02m 30s	= Log.	3788
Daily motion of the Moon 14°10′		= Log.	+2289
Progression of the Moon		Log.	6077 = −5°55′

Checking the ephemeris for 3.11.1912, we take the position of the
Moon at noon and adjust this position by subtracting from it the
progression in −10h 02m at a speed of 14°10′, which is the speed
from 2 to 3 November = −5°55′, as follows:

3.11.1912 Moon at noon	28°29′ Leo
Progression in −10h 02m	−5°55′
Corrected Ascendant	22°34′ Leo

22°34′ *Leo* is rising at 52°N20′
at approx. ST 2h 24m
approx. 36m later than the official time
approx. corrected LMT 4h 36m am

This time would have been registered as LMT 4h 30m instead of
4h 00m and therefore has to be excluded, unless we assume the
registration was a faulty one and should have been 4h 30m am,
which is hard to believe. To our knowledge the time of pregnancy
was normal, and therefore there is no reason to calculate also the
7 month and 8 month conception possibilities.

Summary of Possibilities

Date	No. days	CC	PF	ST	Time difference	☽
16/11	276	19°48′ ♌	15°02′ ♓	2h 09m	21m later	20°47′ ♓
16/11		13°34′ ♌	8°30′ ♓	1h 32m	16m earlier	20°29′ ♓
29/11	262	11°35′ ♌	6°28′ ♓	1h 21m	27m earlier	20°24′ ♓
29/11		18°20′ ♌	13°30′ ♓	1h 59m	12m later	20°43′ ♓
2/11	290	15°53′ ♌	10°57′ ♓	1h 45m	2m earlier	20°36′ ♓
2/11		22°34′ ♌	17°55′ ♓	2h 24m	36m later	20°55′ ♓

As we have already discussed in connection with Salvador Dali, in cases where we find a corrected Ascendant of *x* degrees and 50 to 59 minutes, at the end of the degree, as in the most probable case here, Leo 15°53′, we have to keep in mind that the images of the next degree are seen to be shining through the personality also, the native being the carrier of a double Ascendant degree symbol. I have calculated examples of a corrected Ascendant of, for example, 29°59′ Pisces, and although this inevitably demonstrated the attributes of an Aries personality, the real Pisces characteristics could also be discerned deep inside. I have found that we have to consider the same thing with natal Moon positions of, for example, 29°59′ Capricorn.

In this case we can be pretty sure that the corrected Ascendant in 15°53′ Leo is the right one, because we were informed 'that the conception took place on Sunday afternoon' which would have been the case on 2 November 1912, by my calculation at precisely GMT 14h 39m 22s Amsterdam. The corrected Ascendant of 16th Leo (the fifth CC of 290 days) was accepted by Koppejan as the right one although he was actually more aware, even physically, of the next degree, 17th Leo:

> *Janduz: 'Near an oasis, a white man in Arab dress*
> *rides a richly caparisoned camel.*
> *He is accompanied by his servant and a caravan of camels.'*
> *Rudhyar: 'A volunteer church choir makes a social event of a*
> *rehearsal.'*

Regarding the Abramitic first image of Janduz, which was recognisable in him, throughout his entire life Koppejan clearly exemplified this image of one who knew the way across the desert, and so was able to go ahead of a caravan of camels, showing them which way to go, and leading them along green oases. To the many people around him, for whom life was indeed a spiritual desert, he became a pioneering example suggesting the direction they might take. It is well known that camels can store

water in their bodies, drawing on this supply for long periods
without replenishment if necessary. In a similar way he carried
the necessary spiritual resources within himself on which to draw
as he crossed such arid territory. However, taking into account
the double Ascendant mentioned previously, we also recognise
'the fields and gardens, basking in the sun, refreshed by a storm',
the inherent second image of 16th Leo.

The contents of the 1st image of 17th Leo are clearly expressed
in the circuit of his natal chart. We find the Sun in 25°33' Leo
(Janduz: 'A man is swimming courageously in a sea with high
waves, trying to reach the beach where an upturned triangle sits
upon the coastal sand,' and Rudhyar: 'As light breaks through
clouds, a perfect rainbow forms') in the 1st house. Mercury is in
7°49' Leo (Janduz: 'A fire from which rise high flames,
illuminating under an arch a radiant triangle formed of short
flames and enclosing in its centre an eye,' and Rudhyar:
'Proletarian, burning with social passion, stirs up crowds').
Hermes is conjunct the Sun, in 22°05' Leo (Janduz: 'A man with
two faces, one looking forward and one looking back is standing
at the edge of a lake lit up by a brilliant star, which is reflected in
the water,' Rudhyar: 'The bareback rider in a circus thrills excited
crowds'). These high-pitched positions and images undoubtedly
are the signs of a highly evolved individual.

Because the Sun in its own sign, Leo, means a stillstand, the
solar energy has to radiate into the opposite sign of Aquarius, his
Descendant, and reach for the positions of Persephone in 3°15'
Aquarius (Janduz: 'A gentleman of noble appearance is
ascending the steps of a palace, with his back to us. In the
courtyard, at the left, facing towards us, a rider of middle age is
about to depart on horseback, carrying in front of him a carefully
locked chest,' and Rudhyar: 'A Hindu pundit reveals himself
suddenly a greater healer'), and Uranus in 4°46' (Janduz: 'A
beautiful young nude woman with a crown of flowers in her hair
is contemplating her image reflected by the mirroring surface of a
pond, beside her an easel, a palette with brushes and the tools of
a sculptor,' and Rudhyar: 'A world leader is guided by the spirits
of his ancestors.') Uranus as the higher ruler of Aquarius in its
own sign is also a stillstand, which enforces powerfully reciprocal
positions both of the Sun in Leo and Uranus in Aquarius, and
with degree symbols which speak for themselves.

Fortunately, this sparking arch between Leo and Aquarius is
beautifully 'bridged over' by the outgoing trines of Saturn and
Mars to Uranus. Saturn, lower ruler of Aquarius, is at 16°34'
Gemini (Janduz: 'A man without hands is seated before a table on
which are placed various beautiful fruits and books. At his feet

water is spilling out of a broken jar,' Rudhyar: 'Head of a youth changes into that of a mature thinker'), in an ingoing conjunction with Mars at 13°34' Gemini (Janduz: 'In the darkness of the night, at the edge of a wood, a masked man is standing in the undergrowth, with a dead horse at his feet. A bit deeper in the wood two foxes are devouring two chickens which they have just killed,' and Rudhyar: 'Two people, living far apart, in telepathic communication.') The solar energy is beamed back in sextiles to the Sun in Leo by Mercury and Hermes, the two rulers of Gemini, and both placed in conjunction with the Sun. The conjunction of this trio with the Ascendant also enabled him to manifest these qualities physically. This burning life energy (Sun) was wholeheartedly and entirely dedicated (Persephone) to the wish (Uranus) to express (Gemini) well-thought-out and structured astro-cosmological concepts. He was fully conscious of the fact that the Moon in 20°36' Pisces (Janduz: 'Tossed around by the sea, a man is seated passively in a little boat without oars, hands around his knees. On the tide-line in the foreground lies a great stranded fish attracting birds of prey,' Rudhyar: 'A child, watched by a Chinese servant, caresses a white lamb') in the 8th house and in conjunction with the Part of Fortune and the north node was not included in the circuit, but on the whole he succeeded throughout his life, in integrating them and living up to their demands nevertheless, a most difficult and heavy task for a double Leo. More so because these positions are shaping ingoing (ripening) squares with the aforementioned Mars and Saturn in Gemini, particularly with regards to the contents of both images involved. He dedicated a lifetime to building up a vast library and extensive astrological archives of a diversity and variety not to be found elsewhere. He took this task very seriously but because he passed away unexpectedly, he was unfortunately not able to synthesise all his knowledge into a publication, though luckily his wife Helene has been able to do this. Koppejan himself left behind a rich spiritual heritage on which people can draw and work fruitfully for years to come. In the end a desert blossomed into flowering fields because of his outpouring of the water of life.

The Moon in Pisces in the 8th house shaped ingoing mundane trines with Pluto in 0°46' Cancer (Janduz: 'An entire family, or several generations, is picking the grapes which are growing on the vines against the wall of their home,' and Rudhyar: 'A sailor is ready to joist a new flag to replace the old one') and Venus in 14°43' Cancer (Janduz: 'Two thrones under two canopies, on the left one lies a mongrel dog asleep, and on the right a big crowned rat lies in wait,' and Rudhyar: 'Merry and sluggish people resting

after a huge feast') in the 11th house, and Neptune 26°52' Cancer
(Janduz: 'A man puts a bridle on his horse. A heifer bends its
head gently towards a woman who leads it,' and Rudhyar: 'A
furious storm rages through a residential canyon') in the 12th
house. The mutual reception between Neptune and the Moon
enhanced this function, and he answered a constant demand for
counselling, and restored the personalities of his clients, by also
cleaning and purifying them spiritually and astrally, and so,
painfully transforming and resolving their chaotic and often
defiled life-circumstances. And this was something for which he
was not always appreciated, or honoured.

Jupiter at 8°26' Capricorn in the 5th house (Janduz: 'A man falls
near a broken key lying on the earth beneath a standing cross on
the right,' and Rudhyar: 'An angel carrying a harp comes
through a heavenly lane') is induced by the Moon in Pisces and
Demeter in Sagittarius and in an outgoing sextile with his Moon
in addition. From here Saturn in Gemini is again activated, and
his ability to see inwardly the cosmic blueprints or structures of
almost any subject on which he concentrated his thoughts was
quite remarkable. He was constantly in contact with the angelic
forces and this demand was often so powerful that it was
impossible for him to continue speaking, as I have often
witnessed. See also Mercury opposite Uranus, as we have
discussed.

His pioneering quality was demonstrated not only by his
testing the Rule of Hermes in so many cases but also, and much
more, by the way he worked through those cases spiritually in
order to radiate Christ-centred light into their Higher Self
bodies, whether they were alive or deceased. This, of course, was
the basis of his therapeutic practice as well, and to my knowledge
it has not yet been achieved in full consciousness by any other
practitioner. We note, too, that the Moon was in an outgoing
square with Demeter in 5°10' Sagittarius, motivating his work on
the astral levels, something which nowadays is a fairly common
practice but which in his day was quite rare. The time and energy
spent on this ministry entirely exhausted his spiritual strength
many times and might have caused his mysterious and
unexpected death. The same pioneering ability was
demonstrated in the interpretation of the 360 degrees of the
zodiac and their introduction, long before those symbols were
commonly accepted. The Part of Fortune is found in 10°57'
Pisces, the second image shows clearly what was at the core of his
loving and caring heart:

'Seekers for illumination are guided into the sanctuary'.

Because of the fact that the Part of Fortune is at the edge of the next degree, we should also look at 12th Pisces:

'Candidates are being examined by the Lodge of Initiates'.

In his circle of friends and clients he was known and very much beloved for his generosity, his profound knowledge and the 'knowing of the Sun' as he called it, as well as for his crystal-clear insights on what he called the 'astro-cosmological' levels, demonstrating always that what 'freely was received, freely should be given'. His astrological concept of the 'Grail principle'; his 'aspects theory' based on psychological values; the sevenfold man; his astrological recognition of healing herbs and food and therefore his dietetic concepts; and finally his knowledge of astrological colour-chromatics, enabled him to counsel so many people appropriately, opening up new horizons for them. The horary chart for 20 August 1953 at Gizeh (the so-called 'Great Pyramid date') was and still is a landmark in his and our lives. His desire to describe astrological and cosmological structures, which would sort out and eliminate once and for all the 'Babylonian' confusion which exists also in this field, was unfortunately not completely fulfilled, and much of that material is part of the rich spiritual capital he left behind.

On 15 May 1942 Koppejan founded his 'Medical Psychological and Paedagogical Institute'. Based upon the corrected Ascendant in 15°53' Leo we find on that date his progressed Mars was in 0°40' Cancer and therefore right on his initiating Pluto. His progressed Part of Fortune was in 20°07' Pisces in an exact conjunction with his natal Moon in 20°37' Pisces in the 8th house. From this time on, the interpretation of the degree symbols, started in 1936, became a fundamental part of the project, and between 1943 and 1956 they were written down and made available. That start meant a profound and thorough conversion of the material, and not surprisingly, a transformation of his own being. In 1979 he was still working on this subject, but hoped during the next few years to be able to publish the results, illustrated by at least three examples for any degree, calculated by his adaptation of Bailey's conception correction method.

His solar return for 18 August 1941 showed remarkable things, in particular the conjunction of Mercury in 25°27' Leo with his natal Sun in 25°33' Leo in the 1st house, pointing towards his intention of writing down all that had been unfolded to him spiritually. The progressed Pluto in 4°33' Leo formed an opposition with his natal Uranus in 4°46' Aquarius, and that planet, which stands for understanding astrological values, was impelled by this initiating force into finding an outlet for spiritual and therefore astrological knowledge. The solar return Uranus was in 0°13′ Gemini, the same degree which was so prominent when he began to interpret the degree symbols. Uranus in an ingoing semi-sextile with Pluto, according to his own aspect theory, facilitates the capacity for inner vision, a faculty of the astral Demeter soul body which functions as a mirror receiving the astrally reflected cosmic images and pictures.

The transits for 15 May 1942 (do realise this was in occupied Holland, in the middle of the war, at a time when the practice of astrology was prohibited by the Germans), hold Mercury in 15°41′ Gemini in an exact ingoing sextile with his corrected natal Ascendant in 16th Leo. Koppejan interpreted this aspect as an introjection of knowledge and wisdom, like respiration, a mobile linking of facts whereby the inner coherence of those facts becomes visible in the wisdom of higher knowledge. Not only Uranus in his solar return, but also the transits of Saturn and Uranus, both rulers of Aquarius, are found in the 1st degree of Gemini, at respectively 0°52′ and 0°02′.

In a letter circulated on 9 June 1956 he acknowledged the foundation of the above-mentioned Institute and stressed the fact that between 1942 and 1956 twice seven years had passed and therefore Uranus by that time was to be found in the 1st degree of Leo. He wrote: ' "Initiates" will be able to understand the meaning of this jump over fourteen years, covering 60 degrees, and what these positions hold. To me, on this day, the "jubilee" of 9.6.1956, it is a great joy to be able to announce and to present the publication of the 360 degrees of the zodiac.'

His progressed Sun on 9 June 1956 was in 7°10′ Libra and in an exact outgoing sextile with his natal Mercury in 8th Leo: what had been given to him cosmically was made ready to be radiated out to people. In the solar return for 19 August 1955 Saturn in 15°16′ Scorpio was in an exact outgoing square with his corrected Ascendant in 16th Leo. The shaping of it in the coming year was physically exhausting, demanding strenuous efforts. On 9 June 1956 transiting Mercury in 0°24′ Gemini showed the link with what he had commenced in 1942. Also, we find the transit of Jupiter in 25°26′ Leo right upon his natal Sun, abundantly crowning the richness of his interpretations of twice 360 degree symbols, presented on 675 loose folio pages. Bearing in mind the shower of 1st degrees we have found, we won't be surprised to find that he also announced in his circular letter that 'by the 360 degrees of the zodiac, starting in this connection with Aries, the basic problems of our existence on earth are expressed. The twelve degrees of the same number in all twelve signs, full circle, and in every aspect, work out such a basic problem ... it is

intended to write down these thirty basic problems and they will
be published in approximately 400 loose folio pages.' To my
knowledge this gigantic plan has not been realised, but we have
elaborate examples of the 22nd, the 27th and the 29th degrees. I
have answered his call for co-operation by working through and
enlarging on the material of his archives, particularly in
connection with musicians.

Wim Koppejan passed away on 20 May 1979. His progressed
Ascendant was found in 0°48' Libra (Rudhyar: 'Pierced by a dart
of light a butterfly is made perfect'), again a 1st degree, in an
outgoing square with his natal Pluto in 1st Cancer. Had he
undertaken a task which was physically too heavy or was this
moment a cosmic recognition of a task well done? His progressed Venus was in 3°17' Libra in an exact ingoing, strengthening,
trine with his natal Persephone in 3°15' Aquarius. With regards
to the considerable amount of astrological material he has
collected and worked on, this significant aspect, shaped between
the two rulers of Taurus, confirms the conclusion that this part of
the job was beautifully completed and that a field sown with
innumerable seeds has been prepared, promising a rich harvest
in the future. Finally, his natal Saturn in the 17th degree of
Gemini, in spite of all the difficulties of the first image of this
degree, has been able to express in an appropriate and
constructive form, and in a revolutionary way, all that which was
planned, because we find on 20.5.1979 the transit of Pluto in
16°47' Libra in an exact trine with it, and both planets in
harmonious aspects with his conception Jupiter in 16°26'
Sagittarius in the 9th house. Jupiter in the conception chart
(2.11.1912 GMT 14h 39m 22s Amsterdam) was in conjunction
with the Part of Fortune in 26°40' Sagittarius, the exact MC in that
chart, indicating a task of teaching and developing knowledge
and wisdom. The stillstand in Sagittarius urged him to reach for
the new impulses of Pluto in 29°47'℞ Gemini in the 4th house.
These positions in my opinion show his motives for incarnation.
His morally justifiable teachings have given to many people who
had lost their bearings the means by which to start a further
development of their entire existence.

In his solar return for 18 August 1978 we find the Ascendant in
0°17' Taurus in a harmonious sextile with natal Pluto. Jupiter in
26°30' Cancer was in exact conjunction with his natal Neptune,
and both planets are the rulers of the 8th house. The solar return,
seen by him as a present from the Higher Self, and in this case
seen with hindsight, seems to imply a rich profit, offered to him
as the reward for all that he suffered with the Moon in Pisces in

the 8th house and for all he was therefore willing to sacrifice, in effect a valuable increase in his etheric and astral abilities. Neptune in 15°34' Sagittarius was trine his corrected Ascendant degree. This could mean that the physical sacrifices he deliberately made, in order to attain the purification of his Moon-etheric soul-body required by the 8th house, by Pisces, and by the therapeutic life task he carried out, meant a bounteous growth for his physical body and spiritual counterpart.

I vividly remember the evening before his birthday in 1979 when we met, and he, with a happy smile, told me how much he, with Mercury in his solar return conjunct his natal Sun, was hoping to be able to write everything down at last. At the same time, having just finished calculating his solar return, I gave him a photograph of a beautiful rainbow, which I had taken (see again the second image of his Sun degree).

We often have the strong impression that the natal chart continues to function even after death, and I have many examples confirming this. It can be seen as the need to help from the unseen levels of light. In this case it is clearly noticeable. Since 1979 much work has been done with regard to his spiritual bequests. His wife Helene managed during the ten years since then, to translate his interpretations of the degree symbols into English, and to an extent expand them in the way he had planned. I was invited to recalculate all the material needed for this publication which has led to the writing of this book. His oldest friend Wil van Panhuys was prepared to retranslate Helene's English manuscript back into Dutch, ready to be published in Holland.

In the light of all this, it seems sensible to have a look at his solar return and progressions for 1989. And remarkably we find in the solar return for 18 August 1989 Venus at 0°32' Libra, again a 1st degree, square his natal Pluto in 1st Cancer. Venus here forms a trine with the transiting 1st degree planets discussed on page 87 in connection with the founding and acknowledging of his Institute in 1942 and 1956. It is all the more remarkable because this year at last, the time seems right to present his life's work and it will finally be published in England and in Holland, ten years after his passing away. We know that Venus in Libra is a stillstand and needs to jump to the opposite sign of Aries, by which co-operation a powerful impulse has pushed its way up to reactivate his Pluto in 1st Cancer in the 11th house of spiritual friends. The Part of Fortune in 7°31' Gemini relates to Saturn in the 8th of Virgo on the day he passed away, in conjunction with the Part of Fortune of that day, and to what had to be left behind as an unfinished inheritance, which needed to be put into a responsible form at the cost of much meticulous and detailed work.

His progressed Ascendant for 1989 is in 7°50′ Libra and the Part of Fortune in 7°26′ Sagittarius. This is not only exactly related to his own Mercury in the 8th of Leo but also to Saturn in the 8th of Virgo in 1979. And that is not all, because we find the Part of Fortune in his solar return for 1989 in an exact conjunction with the natal Moon in the 8th of Gemini of his wife Helenę and the Part of Fortune of his progressed chart for 1989 on my own natal Moon in the 8th of Sagittarius. To this overwhelming number of 8th degrees has to be added the progressed Mars in the 8th of Taurus in 1988 and 1989 in the chart of Wil van Panhuys. And finally we find activating squares and profitable trines with Saturn in the 8th of Virgo in 1979, and sextiles, trines and squares with Mercury in the 8th of Leo in Wim's natal chart. It becomes increasingly clear, that what has been achieved through a fruitful co-operation, is undoubtedly related to his own natal chart, to the transits of Saturn in 1979, and to his solar return and progressions for 1989.

Finally, and quite by 'chance', this essay has been written with transiting Jupiter in the 1st of Gemini, the very degree so strongly connected with the interpretations of the degrees of the zodiac.

I would like to finish this brief review with the words he himself once wrote, words which typify the human I consider to have been one of the finest I have known.

> *I don't want to bruise you (Cancer),*
> *I don't want to cause any pain (Scorpio),*
> *I don't want you to suffer (Pisces),*
> *I want to sow (Taurus), to clean (Virgo), and to lay building-stones*
> *(Capricorn),*
> *I want to give some knowledge (Gemini)*
> *and offer my hand in working together (Libra)*
> *so that you understand (Aquarius),*
> *I want to give impulses (Aries),*
> *to give and to lead (Leo)*
> *and to indicate the directions where to go (Sagittarius),*

> *I'm only a shabby little fellow,*
> *offering jewels in the utter darkness.*

> *20.8.1953*

CHAPTER TEN

Novalis and the Hymns to the Night

Name	'Novalis' (Georg Friedrich Philipp, Baron von Hardenberg)
Birthdate	2.5.1772
Birthplace:	Wiederstedt (Harz, Germany) 51°N41', 11°E34'
LMT	10h 00m am (Thomas Ring)
GMT	9h 13m 44s am
RLT	10h 00m 00s am
RST	00h 43m Ascendant 4°35' Leo (uncorrected), PCA: Sun 12°26' Taurus, (Schoch 12°47'), Moon 6°38' Taurus (uncorrected), (Schoch 6°40')
House system	Placidus.

In order to be able to calculate a conception correction date, it is essential to know the precise sidereal time at noon and the position of the Moon at noon. To calculate these items for dates before 1800, we can use the tables of Schoch or Neugebauer. If these are unavailable, we can use astrological software, such as the PCA Electric Ephemeris, already mentioned, or the Astrolabe software programe by Robert Hand, and trust the result will be accurate.

Unfortunately, the PCA I am using, does not offer the sidereal time. However, at the time I was working on the chart and conception correction of Novalis, I found a simple way to calculate these items accurately, and that technique will be demonstrated in this chapter. I am sure Novalis was kind enough to 'channel' telepathically some astronomical clues on how to use software and possibly even some astrological insights as well, for which I am grateful!

Remembering what was said in Chapter 6, we locate in the chart the following basic facts:

From the birthchart we take the following basic data, needed in order to calculate the CC:

1. With 4°35' Leo rising, the natal Moon is 6°38' Taurus and the natal Sun 12°26'. We draw a line from the Sun to the

NOVALIS

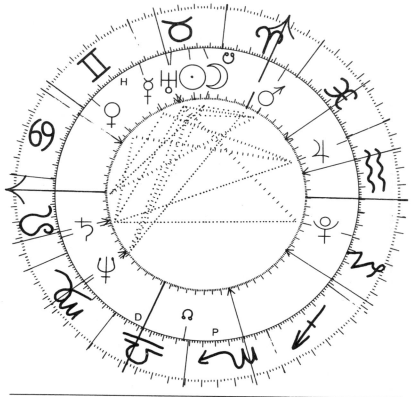

Radix				Sun	12	26	Tau	10
	MC	11 50 Ari		Moon	6	38	Tau	10
	ASC	4 35 Leo		Mercury	2	17	Gem	11
NOVALIS		— Plac —		Venus	25	1	Gem	11
	11.	21 29 Tau		Mars	4	53	Ari	9
Date: 2 5 1772	12.	2 48 Can		Jupiter	28	57	Aqu	8
Time: 10 0 0 E O.8	2.	21 11 Leo		Saturn	22	59	Leo	2
Latitude: 51 41 N	3.	12 26 Vir		Uranus	19	25	Tau	10
Longitude: 11 34 E				Neptune	13	30	Vir R	3
	Node	28 20 Lib	4	Pluto	21	9	Cap R	6
	Part ft	28 46 Can	12	Perseph	8	40	Sco	4
Aspects: Radix/Radix Orb: 8 0				Hermes	11	15	Gem	11
				Demeter	9	00	Lib	3

MC ssx	Sun 0 37	MC qcx	Nep 1 40	ASC Sqr	Moo 2 3	ASC Sxt	Mer 2 18
ASC Tri	Mar 0 18	Sun Cnj	Moo 5 49	Sun Cnj	Ura 6 58	Sun Tri	Nep 1 3
Moo ssx	Mar 1 45	Moo Tri	Nep 6 52	Mer Sxt	Mar 2 36	Mer Sqr	Jup 3 20
Ven Tri	Jup 3 56	Ven Sxt	Sat 2 2	Mar ssq	Ura 0 28	Jup Opp	Sat 5 58
Sat Sqr	Ura 3 35	Sat qcx	Plu 1 51	Ura Tri	Nep 5 55	Ura Tri	Plu 1 44
Nep Tri	Plu 7 39	Nod Tri	Jup 0 37	Nod ssq	Nep 0 10		

same degree of the opposite sign and locate the Moon at the left side at the ingoing arch which means the Moon is *waning*. The Moon is positioned above the horizon axis of the Ascendant and the Descendant, which means the Moon is *above* the horizon. The scheme in Chapter 6 shows this to be the *3rd order* of Bailey which says *Moon/Descendant and longer/forwards*.

2. We find the distance between the Moon 7th Taurus and the *Descendant* 5th Aquarius to be 91°, ignoring the minutes.

3. Divide this distance of 91° by 13° (the average daily motion of the Moon) = 7 degrees or days;

4. 7 days longer than 273 days (the average time of pregnancy) = 280 days;

5. 280 days subtracted from the birthdate 2.5.1772 = 25.7.1771, which is the first possible, regular date of conception. Another way of calculating is by subtracting a full year from the birthdate giving 2.5.1771; subtract 280 days (see 4) from 365 days = 85 days to be added to the date of 2.5.1771 to find the date of 25.7.1771.

6. The date of 25.7.1771 shows the Moon at 19°14′ Capricorn and the next day at 1°20′ Aquarius, which is needed to calculate both possibilities of the same date and also the daily progression of the Moon. On the next day, 27.7.1771, the Moon is at 13°19′ Aquarius.

7. According to the 3rd order of Bailey, see the first paragraph, '*Moon Radix is Asc. or Desc. conception*', we need to know the ST of the natal Moon 6°38′ Taurus, and also (because according to the 3rd order *or Descendant Conception*) for the opposite point of 6°38′ Scorpio which can be found in the table of houses for 51°N41′. This ST has to be interpolated in order to be accurate.

Moon *above* the horizon and *waning*:

Scheme for Calculating the 3rd Order

Moon conception = Descendant or Ascendant radix
Moon radix = Descendant or Ascendant conception

Distance between the Moon (6°38′ Taurus)
and the *Descendant* (5° Aquarius)
= 91° : 13°

= 7 days *longer* than 273 days
= 280 days before the birthdate
= 25.7.1771

In the tables of houses for *51°N41'* *(Wiederstedt)* we locate the

interpolated ST of the Ascendant
equal to the position of the natal Moon
6°38' Taurus at ST 19h 05m
and its opposite point 6°38' Scorpio at ST 9h 29m

First we provide our 'own' ephermeris with the computer, as follows:

1. We calculate the *ST at noon for Greenwich* by entering in our computer: the date, the GMT at noon 12h 00m, and Greenwich (51°N29' and 0°E00'), to locate the Ascendant at noon and checking the tables of houses for Greenwich we find the required ST, as follows:

    26.7.1771
    GMT noon 12h 00m
    Greenwich 51°N29' – 0°E00'

2. From the tables of houses for Greenwich we locate the interpolated ST of the position of the calculated Ascendant, as follows:

    Ascendant 23°53' Libra at
    approx. ST 8h 16m
    Moon Aquarius 1°20'

3. We write down this position of the Moon at noon for Greenwich, and we calculate in the same way the positions of the Moon and the ST for the previous day and for the following day, in order to calculate the daily progression of the Moon.

    27.7.1771
    GMT noon 12h 00m
    Greenwich
    Ascendant 24°35' Libra at
    ST 8h 20m
    Moon 13°19' Aquarius

    25.7.1771
    GMT at noon 12h 00m
    Greenwich
    Ascendant 23°12' Libra
    ST 8h 12m
    Moon 19°14' Caricorn

4. In the tables of houses we look for the *birthplace* *(Wiederstedt)* or, if this is known, the town of conception

(in this case we assume it was indeed the same) 51°N41',
we locate the interpolated ST of the Ascendant equal to
the position of the natal Moon, 6°38' Taurus, and also the
second possibility for the same date, the ST of its opposite
point 6°38' Scorpio. The difference between these two
sidereal times supplies the RLT. By now we are ready to
start our calculations.

Possibility (1)

26.7.1771 Noon ST	8h 16m
RLT	+10h 49m
ST 6°38' Taurus	19h 05m

Next, we convert the RLT (+10h 49m) into GMT by subtracting
46m from it = GMT +10h 03m and we calculate the progression
of the conception Moon in GMT +10h 03m by using diurnal
proportional logarithms, to be found in the ephemeris:

RLT	+10h 49m		
Difference from GMT	−0h 46m		
GMT	+10h 03m	= Log.	3780
Daily motion of the Moon	11°59'	= Log.	+3016
Progression of the Moon		Log.	6796 = +5°01'

Checking the calculated positions for 26.7.1771, we take the
position of the Moon at noon and we adjust this position by
adding to it the progression in +10h 03m at a daily motion of
11°59' which is the motion between 26 and 27 July = +5°01', as
follows:

Moon at 26.7.1771 at noon	1°20' Aquarius
Progression in +10h 03m	+5°01'
Corrected Descendant Radix	6°21' Aquarius
Corrected Ascendant Radix	6°21' Leo

Ascendant 6°21' Leo is rising at 51°N41' at
approx. ST 0h 54m
approx. 11m later
than the official time
corrected LMT 10h 11m am.
corrected natal Moon 6°44' Taurus
corrected PF 0°39' Leo

Possibility (2)
We calculate the second option of the same date as follows:
As before we take the same ST at noon but for this second option
we take the ST of the Ascendant equal to the *opposite* point of the

natal Moon. The difference between the two sidereal times
supplies the RLT, as follows:

ST 26.7.1771 at noon	8h 16m
RLT	+1h 13m
ST 6°38' Scorpio	9h 29m

We convert the RLT (+1h13m) into GMT by subtracting 46m from
it = +0h 27m, and we calculate the progression of the conception
Moon in GMT +0h 27m:

RLT	+1h 13m		
Difference from GMT	−0h 46m		
GMT	+0h 27m	= Log.	17270
Daily motion of the Moon	11°59'	= Log.	+3016
Progression of the Moon		Log.	20286 = +0°14'

Checking the positions for 26.7.1771, we take the position of the
Moon at noon and we adjust this position by adding the
progression in +0h26m at a daily motion of 11°59' which is the
speed between 26 and 27 July = +0°14', as follows:

Moon at noon 26.7.1771	1°20' Aquarius
Progression in 0h 27m	+0°14'
Corrected Descendant Radix	1°34' Aquarius
Corrected Ascendant Radix	1°34' Leo

Ascendant 1°34' Leo is rising at 51°N41' at
approx. ST 0h 28m
approx. 15m earlier
than the official time
corrected LMT 9h 45m am
corrected natal Moon 6°30' Taurus
corrected PF 25°38' Cancer

Possibility (3)
The next conception possibility is a fortnight later than 26 July =
266 days = 9 August, and we calculate in the same way as before:
We calculate the *ST at noon for Greenwich* by entering in our
computer: the date, the GMT at noon 12h00m, and Greenwich
(51°N29' and 0°E00', to locate the Ascendant at noon, and check
in the tables of houses for Greenwich to find the required ST, as
follows:

9.8.1771
GMT noon 12h 00m
Greenwich 51°N29' and 0°E00'

From the tables of houses for *Greenwich* we locate the interpolated ST of the position of the calculated Ascendant, as follows:

Ascendant 3°32' Scorpio at
approx. ST 9h 11m
Moon at noon 0°07' Leo

We write down the position of the Moon at noon in Greenwich and we also calculate in the same way as before the positions of the Moon and the ST for the previous day and for the following day, in order to calculate the daily progression of the Moon.

8.8.1771
GMT noon 12h 00m
Greenwich
Ascendant 2°51' Scorpio at
ST 9h 07m
Moon 15°12' Cancer

10.8.1771
GMT at noon 12h 00m
Greenwich
Ascendant 4°13' Scorpio at
ST 9h 15m
Moon 15°19' Leo

We take the ST at noon as calculated and, as we did in the previous calculation of 26.7.1771, the ST of the Ascendant equal to the position of the natal Moon and also for the second possibility of the same date, the ST of its opposite point. The difference between the two sidereal times supplies the RLT, as follows:

ST at noon 9.8.1771	9h 11m
RLT	+9h 54m
ST Moon 6°38' Taurus	19h 05m

We convert the RLT into GMT by subtracting 46m from it = +9h08m and we calculate the progression of the conception Moon in GMT +9h08m, as follows:

RLT	+9h 54m		
Difference from GMT	−0h 46m		
GMT	+9h 08m	= Log.	4196
Daily motion of the Moon	15°12'	= Log.	+1984
Progression of the Moon		Log.	6180 = +5°47'

We take the position of the Moon at noon and we adjust this position by adding the progression in GMT +9h08m at a daily

motion of 15°12', which is the motion between 9 and 10 August =
+5°47', as follows:

Moon at noon 9.8.1771	0°07' Leo
Progression in +9h 08m	+5°47'
Corrected Ascendant radix	5°54' Leo

Ascendant 5°54' Leo is rising at 51°41' at
approx. ST 0h 51m
approx. 8m later
than the official time
corrected LMT 10h 08m a.m.
corrected natal Moon 6°42' Taurus
corrected PF 0°12' Leo

The second possibility of this date can be ignored.

Possibility (4)
The calculation of the next conception date, a fortnight before the
first date of 26.7.1771, is 13.7.1771 of 294 days, as follows:

Again, first we have to calculate the *ST at noon for Greenwich* by
entering in our computer the date, the GMT at noon 12h00m, and
Greenwich (51°N29' and 0°E00'), to locate the Ascendant at noon
and checking in the tables of houses for Greenwich to find the
required ST, as follows:

13.7.1771
GMT noon 12h 00m
Greenwich 51°N29' – 0°E00'

From the table of houses for Greenwich we locate the
interpolated ST of the position of the calculated Ascendant, as
follows:

Ascendant 14°54' Libra at
approx. ST 7h 24m
Moon at noon 6°44' Leo

We write down the position of the Moon at noon in Greenwich
and we also calculate in the same way the positions of the Moon
and the ST for the previous day and for the following day, in
order to calculate the daily progression of the Moon.

12.7.1771
GMT noon 12h 00m
Greenwich

Ascendant 14°12′ Libra at
noon ST 7h 20m
Moon at noon 21°43′ Cancer

14.7.1771
GMT at noon 12h 00m
Greenwich
Ascendant 15°35′ Libra at
noon ST 7h 28m
Moon at noon 21°48′ Leo

We take the calculated ST at noon 13.7.1771 and we take the interpolated ST of the Ascendant equal to the position of the natal Moon and also for the second possibility of the same date, the ST of its opposite point. The difference between the two sidereal times supplies the RLT, as follows:

ST at noon 13.7.1771	7h 24m
RLT	+2h 05m
ST 6°38′ Scorpio	9h 29m

We convert RLT +2h 05m into GMT by subtracting 46m from it = +1h 19m, and we calculate the progression of the conception Moon in GMT +1h 19m:

RLT	+2h 05m		
Difference from GMT	−0h 46m		
GMT	+1h 19m	= Log.	12607
Daily motion of the Moon	15°04′	= Log.	+2022
Progression of the Moon		Log.	14629 = +0°50′

We take the position of the Moon at noon and we adjust this position by adding the progression in +1h 19m at a daily motion of 15°04′ which is the motion between 13 and 14 July, = +0°50′, as follows:

Moon at noon 13.7.1771	6°44′ Leo
Progression in +1h 19m	+0°50′
Corrected Ascendant radix	7°34′ Leo

Ascendant 7°34′ Leo is rising at 51°N41′ at
approx. ST 1h 02m
approx. 19m later
than the official time
corrected LMT 10h 19m am
corrected natal Moon 6°46′ Taurus
corrected PF 1°54′ Leo

The second possibility of the same day can be ignored.

Summary of Possibilities

Date	No. days	CC	PF	ST	Time difference	☽
26/7	280	6°21' ♌	0°39' ♌	0h 55m	12m later	6°43' ♉
		1°33' ♌	25°38' ♋	0h 28m	15m earlier	6°30' ♉
9/8	266	5°54' ♌	0°12' ♌	0h 51m	8m later	6°42' ♉
13/7	294	7°34' ♌	1°54' ♌	1h 02m	19m later	6°46' ♉

Considering these calculated conception correction possibilities, I would like to suggest the 7th degree of Leo as the right one, which is the first conception correction of *280 days (26.7.1771)*, not only because of one of Novalis' beautiful poems the 'Hymns to the Night' (see in particular the second image of this degree, and the star myths he has woven into his fairy-tales of Sais and Klingsor) but also because of the splendour of his genius, illustrated by the magnificence of both degree symbols:

7th LEO

Janduz: '*A man mounted on the back of a lion*
carries in his right hand a sceptre,
which is topped with a magnificent diamond,
twinkling like a star.'

Rudhyar: '*The constellations of stars*
shine brilliantly in the darkness of desert skies'.

With regard to the stars in both images, it is interesting to see how these are echoed in the words of Ernst Kamnitzer,[23] at the conclusion of his preface to Novalis' *Fragments*:

> ... and so I hope that one day a star will be called Novalis. Not a very big one, but one with a peculiar sweet shine, which recalls his youth, his death and his love. A star which will only be visible for a short time every night. A star one forgets, but which is searched for over and over again when one does remember, the star called Novalis has to be like that.

It might also be of interest to know that I wrote the following on 13.9.1988, inspired by the transit of Venus in the 7th degree of Leo, conjunct his corrected Ascendant.

The degree symbols involved in connection with his chart, progressions and transits are fully quoted to demonstrate the tremendous impact they have had.

The circuit of his chart starts with the Sun at 12°26' Taurus

(Rudhyar: 'A porter is cheerfully balancing a mountain of baggage') ingoing conjunct Uranus 19°25' (Rudhyar: 'Wisps of clouds like wings, are streaming across the sky') and receiving the ingoing reflecting Moon at 6°38' Taurus (Rudhyar: 'Woman of Samaria comes to draw water from the well'). These positions indicate that it is indeed justifiable to speak of a highly developed 'old' and mature (Taurus) soul incarnating, although only for a lifetime of 29 years. A bright shining star soon to be eclipsed, as the natal Sun was on the day of his birth, but only after giving to the world a wonderfully brilliant and intense light of cosmic dimension, encapsulated in his work. He was hardly understood in his own time, and in our time his rich seed-thoughts are still waiting to be germinated. He has given to the world an immense number of extremely valuable thoughts and concepts, touching almost any subject, only just beginning to be unfolded and understood nowadays, and his 'Fragments' are still underestimated. This Moon 'above and waning', and in the 10th house, is a clear example of what is said in Chapter 3.

From Taurus the energy flows straight towards Venus, lower ruler of Taurus, at 25°01' Gemini (Rudhyar: 'Frost-covered trees, lace-like, against winter skies'), together with Mercury at 2°17' ('A troubadour playing a lute, standing beside a waterfall') ingoing conjunct with Hermes at 11°15' (Janduz: 'Two women in deep sorrow are weeping in front of a crooked laurel,' and Rudhyar: 'A black slave-girl demands her rights from her mistress'), all three in the 11th house. The image of Gemini 12th poignantly underlines the feelings at a time of great bereavement, and this will be enlarged upon later. Remarkably, both planets are positioned in their own sign, which is called a double stillstand, a maximally strong piling up of innumerable facts, recognised in their mutual relationships as wisdom, En-Soph, visible in everything he observed.

Mercury ingoing square with Neptune in Virgo 13°30' retrograde (Rudhyar: 'A splendid family tree engraved on a sheet of parchment') inexorably requires him to face a process of new growth into the source of transcendental inspiration and fantasy, which in turn activated his self-knowledge and wisdom in the outgoing square with Hermes. The image of this Neptune degree is significant with regard to his choice of name, also to be discussed later. The stillstand of both Mercury and Hermes in their own sign, forced him to deal with the intricacies of synthesised and philosophical thinking (Sagittarius). As if the functions of the three planets in Gemini were lifted up and transported into the opposite sign of Sagittarius, a continuing urge required to activate Jupiter, ruler of Sagittarius, at 28°57'

Aquarius in the 8th house, strengthened by the outgoing mundane trines (expansive) of Mercury and Venus, and the ingoing trine (strengthening) of Jupiter with Hermes. This enabled him to think in chains of mutually related thoughts, arising directly from cosmic sources and flashing down in condensed revelations of a richness and expansion rarely seen.

Novalis, in his function as actuary, found only three hours a day to 'work' and wrote in no time an extensive study of 500 folio pages about the philosopher Fichte. Identifying with his own positions in Gemini, Novalis wrote about him, 'every stroke of his quill-pen became a link in a teleological chain'. Schulz, one of his biographers, is aware of the danger that the movability of his spirit, dealing with the finest details in his thinking will only lead to nothing, splintering his mind. We refer to his Mercury and Hermes in Gemini in mundane squares to Neptune in Virgo.

Jupiter is at 28°57' Aquarius, but is also operating in the next degree, the 30th degree (Janduz: 'A king treading towards a throne', and Rudhyar: 'Moonlit fields, once Babylon, are blooming white'; compare this with Rudhyar's version in his Mandala, further on) and it is this Jupiter which spun high-powered electric lines, arching to Saturn at 22°59' Leo (Janduz: 'A man with two heads walks along a lake wherein a brilliant shining star is reflected', and Rudhyar: 'A bare-back rider in a circus thrills excited crowds') in the 2nd house. At the University of Jena, Novalis read Philosophy and Law and was in particular interested in human rights. He was on friendly terms with Schlegel, Fichte and Goethe. He was also strongly influenced in his thinking by the pietistic-Lutheran belief of the Hernhutter Brotherhood. Novalis wrote: 'My favourite study is like my bride, Sophia is her name – Philo-sophia is the soul of my life and the key unlocking my inner Self,' and 'I feel in everything the elevated links of a wonderful Unity in which I will grow and which will become the fullness of my Self.' In these words we can easily recognise a young man, in self-knowledge already fully aware of the great purposes in his life.

We find Saturn in the 23rd of Leo in a strong outgoing (activating) square with Uranus in the 20th of Taurus, completing the heavy task of shaping seed-thoughts into new forms; Saturn in Leo creates (Leo) new frames and structures, containers (Saturn), to receive those newly revealed Uranian and cosmic truths in transformed shapes, like seed waiting to germinate and unfold (Taurus, see Persephone at 8°40' Scorpio), as is so often mentioned by his biographers. Persephone in Scorpio means a spiritual growth towards a future by painful and dolorous experiences of death and transformation. From Jupiter a line also moves straight to Uranus conjunct the Sun. From Leo we are focusing in the Sun, where we started, giving a 'closed' circuit.

Bearing in mind the relevant fixed cross positions, it is fascinating to find a man with the Sun and Uranus in Taurus, and whose real name was Friedrich von Hardenberg, had chosen the name Novalis. He derived it from the old name of his thirteenth-century forefathers (remember the second image of his Neptune in Virgo, the 14th degree), which was 'Von Rode' or, in Latin, Novali, after the new red soil, made fertile and ready to receive seeds (Taurus). Significantly, Novalis had in his chart almost all the rulers of the fixed cross, except Mars and Venus, positioned in the signs of that cross, and, in addition, Jupiter at 28°57' Aquarius, a heavily afflicted fixed cross as well. What an appropriate name he gave himself, he who certainly meant to give to the world new spiritual seeds in a new matrix, or even create and prepare new soil for humanity, with his creative work. According to Professor van der Leeuw: 'In this name is expressed the programme of the poet who was aware his task lies in the sowing of seeds in newly prepared soil.' The planets of the fixed cross concerned are: the Sun, ruler of Leo, in Taurus conjunct Uranus, ruler of Aquarius, opposite Persephone, ruler of Taurus, in Scorpio, and Saturn, lower ruler of Aquarius, in Leo. His entire being, nailed on that cross, was focusing on the determination to create, and on the fertile soil as well as the seeds; and with Persephone, higher ruler of Taurus in Scorpio, the will to transform those seeds and their growth into elements of another, higher dimension, prepared for another future. Persephone we find in 8°40' Scorpio (Rudhyar: 'A dentist is repairing teeth ruined by civilised habits'), which clearly refers to what for instance is said about Saturn in Leo.

With the Part of Fortune in the 1st of Leo, one can postulate a Higher Self whose plan is to give humanity the highest spiritual and cosmic value, astonishing in its originality:

> Janduz: 'At the left a lion is standing upright on a rock
> watching the sun rising at the right,
> while a man with a defiant gesture
> is showing him a severed lion's head.'

Rudhyar: 'Under emotional stress blood rushes to a man's head.'

All the planets in difficult squares and tense oppositions in this fixed cross are reinforced by the position of Persephone, the higher ruler of his Sun sign, Taurus, at 8°40' Scorpio in the 4th house. The higher line moving out from the Sun in Taurus, goes directly to this Persephone, the lower lines we have discussed already. Transforming forces from Scorpio, endorsed by Persephone, doyenne of germinating and slowly ripening seeds and germs, are strengthening the positions and movements mentioned above, and finally reaching for Mars, ruler of Scorpio, at 4°53' Aries in the 9th house (Rudhyar: 'A white triangle, with golden wings on its upper sides'). By now we understand how Persephone, out of death ripening leads to the resurrection of transforming Mars in Aries, pushing Pluto at 21°09' Capricorn in an activating outgoing square. Unfortunately we cannot be sure of the right degree of Pluto because, calculated with Schoch, this position is 22°06' Capricorn but with PCA it is 21°09'.

This extremely hard-working salt-mine engineer (Pluto in the 6th house), managed to find time to study mathematics, science, geology and mineralogy, and to write also very fine poetry of outstanding quality, aphorisms and paradoxes. In many of his writings the cosmic meaning is recognisable straight away, and can be translated in an astrological sense. One example: 'Poetry establishes transcendental health, the poet is in fact a transcendental healer' (*Fragments II*, no.326) and here we recognise clearly Neptune and Mercury, the axis of Pisces (poetry) and Virgo (health), and also his Neptune in Virgo.

* * *

When I came across Novalis amidst the astrological material I had to recalculate, I was astonished to find out that for many years I have 'known' him very well. In 1950, the time I had started my career as a musician and was appointed as an organist, one of my favourite hymns, one which became most comforting at a time when I was suffering a sad loss, turned out to be the fifth of his *Spiritual Songs*.[37] I would like to quote the three verses we sang, but in the straightforward English translation by William Lindeman:

> *If I but have Him,*
> *if He is but mine,*
> *if my heart unto the grave*
> *ne'er His faithfulness forgets:*
> *know I naught of sorrow;*
> *only love, devotion, gladness feel.*

> *If I but have Him,*
> *all I gladly leave,*
> *follow on my walking staff*
> *faithfully my Lord alone,*
> *silent let the others*
> *go down busy, wide, and open streets.*

> *Where I have but Him,*
> *is my fatherland;*
> *and each gift falls in my hand*
> *as though an inheritance.*
> *I find long-lost brothers*
> *now again in His disciple band.*

In 1795 when he was 23, Novalis met 12 year old Sophia von Kühn and between them a beautiful love-bond developed which was to transform his life totally. Sadly, Sophie died on 19 March 1797 of lung tuberculosis and a liver disease, at the age of only 15 years, which threw Novalis into total despair and deep sorrow. As it is usual in Hernhutter circles to pay a visit to the beloved ones on Easter morning, the first time Novalis did so was on 16 April. At her graveside, soon afterwards on 13 May, he experienced what has been called a vision, a revelation and a conversion, in my opinion a profound experience of Eternity, an experience which he described two years later in the third of his famous *Hymns to the Night*.

It will be constructive to have a more detailed look at this cosmic event and, looking at the planets and the degree symbols involved, we will be impressed by the way everything seemed to have come together, totally directing us to what was at the base of it all.

It happened on 13.5.1797 about LMT 7h 00m pm, with transiting Jupiter in the 10th of Aries, in exact conjunction with his progressed Moon, and both planets exactly opposite his natal Demeter in the 10th of Libra (Rudhyar: 'A canoe leaving narrow rapids reaches calm waters'). He had a Demetrian 'umbrella' experience of Eternity, whereby, as we know from the third of his *Hymns to the Night*, as he blew away the dust from the grave, he saw ages and ages of past and future time passing by and fading away again, century after century, accompanied by flashing thunderbolts and a deep fear, experienced moments of an indescribable joy, flashing enthusiasm, until the Higher Self of his 'Söphchen' appeared to him, joyfully joining his own reborn spirit, to be merged with the shape of the risen Christ. Because constrained by the planetary positions in Aries, a Plutonic initiation took place which completely changed the course of his life.

This bond with Sophia's Higher Self was a constant inspiration in his life, but the agony of being no longer able to be with her, reinforced at the same time a desire not to live, longing as he was to die and to be reunited with her. In spite of his repeatedly expressed desire for death, he was thought not to be suicidal. His friend Schlegel didn't think he would do such a thing.

Mercury, in an ingoing square with Neptune, must also have caused a life-style in which his health began to suffer more and more and as an inevitable result he died very young of tuberculosis, curiously enough, on the anniversary of the day on which he and Sophie would have been married. Looking at the Janduz image of 14th Gemini ('A masked man standing beside the carcass of a dead horse'), we can see the other side of the coin, also visible in his revelation. Novalis almost certainly had been infected by her disease.

To understand, we must remember that Novalis had his natal Moon in an ingoing conjunction with the Sun and both in an ingoing conjunction with Uranus, which was the ruler of the 8th house of death and transformation. His natal Jupiter in the 8th house was constantly flashing towards this Uranus, and constantly expanding his insights into the world of death, and as he reflected on it, he became more and more at home in this world on the other side. And this could be an important reason why (and how could we expect otherwise?) he was, in an almost extravagant way, in so much sorrow about the death of Sophie and why this wounded him so deeply. To understand how much she meant for him spiritually, we have to know that from the time of their engagement, he wore a golden ring with her image, and on the inside was engraved: 'Sophie is my guardian spirit'. So it is not surprising to find that after her death he continued the bond with her Higher Self and what followed was a matter of course.

Referring to his revelatory experience, Professor G. van der Leeuw[28] puts it in this way:

> Novalis experienced a conversion, the love for Sophie and for the risen Christ merged into each other, religion and sublimated erotic love joined together in the overwhelming conviction, that true life can only be found in death. Here on this grave the foundations are laid for Novalis' finest poetry, the *Hymns to the Night*, and also for his deep philosophical and scientific insights.

To my mind 'conversion' has a missionary ring to it, and I feel 'revelation' is better, a revelation of Christ-centred higher consciousness is still better. Also, the fact the risen Christ is mentioned confirms what I said earlier on about the Plutonic initiation. Gerhard Schulz[28] refers to the words 'Christ and Sophie', which Novalis wrote down in his diary, pointing towards the role of mediator (Hermes, Gemini) between this world and the next which his bride Sophie had taken, comparable with that of Christ. Novalis experienced these mystic truths under the Demeter cover of that very moment at the grave of Sophie.

On the evening of this revelation, transiting Mercury at 13°22' Gemini was in an exact ingoing square with his natal Neptune at 13°30' Virgo. There was also the solar return for 2.5.1797 in which we find Mars in 13°11' Gemini conjunct transiting Mercury, and his progressed Neptune still in 14th Virgo. Because his natal Mercury and the return Mercury were also conjunct his natal Hermes in 12th Gemini, it is clear that during this Neptunian transcendental experience the winged Hermes established an elevated contact between both Higher Selves. See the second image of this Mercurial 14th degree of Gemini:

> Rudhyar: *'Bridging physical space and social distinctions,*
> *two men communicate telepathically.'*

Sophia died on 19.3.1797 at LMT 9h 30m am, with transiting Pluto at 29°23' Aquarius in the 8th house of this chart, which means conjunct Novalis' Jupiter in Aquarius 28°57' in his 8th house. And because of Pluto, I was inclined to speak of an initiation, rather than a vision, and surely it was a revelation too since this occurred in Aquarius. It is very interesting not only to look at the 29th degree but also to look at the next degree, the 30th, as well. Rudhyar in his Mandala version says:

> *'Deeply rooted in the past of a very ancient culture,*
> *a spiritual brotherhood in which many individual minds are*
> *merged into the glowing light of a unanimous consciousness,*
> *is revealed to one who has emerged successfully from this*
> *metamorphosis.'*

By now all that has been said becomes as clear as crystal. The contents of this symbol are answering any questions about what happened that very special night. More is to be said, because if we look at his solar return chart, based on the corrected Ascendant of 7th Leo, we note with amazement that the MC degree in this chart was 5th Taurus, and anyone who is familiar with the degree symbols knows immediately what this means:

> Rudhyar: *'Completely transformed by the deepest sorrow,*
> *a young widow is kneeling at a grave.'*

The solar return Ascendant was at 19°55' Leo, in an activating square with his natal Uranus, ruler of the 8th house (death and transformation), at 19°25' Taurus, connected with the transit of Venus at 19°19' Taurus that evening, right on his natal Uranus, precisely a 'revelation' in love and Love.

As if all this was not enough, Sophie's progressed Uranus on the day she died was in 30th Gemini, as was the Part of Fortune, on that evening about 7h pm, in approximately 29°25' Gemini, both in exact triangle with his natal Jupiter in the 8th, and in addition, as we said, Pluto at the time of her death was in the 30th of Aquarius. This must be enough for the reader to understand what a tremendous impact it had on Novalis.

Finally, on the day he died, 25 March 1801 at GMT 11h 43m 44s, we find the Ascendant at 3°55' Leo and Saturn at 17°38' Leo in the 1st house. Although it is impossible to go deep into these facts, we have to refer to the conception chart (26.7.1771 GMT 22h 01m 30s) with the Sun at 3°34' Leo in a wide conjunction with Saturn at 17°35' Leo. During the burial we find this Saturn still in the same position. We will try to translate this information, compared with the birthchart, although this has never been done before. In my opinion it could mean that because of these positions he freely undertook, in co-operation with Persephone in Scorpio in the 7th house of the conception chart, the manifestation on earth of seed thoughts which would transform humanity's conception of spiritual truths. This he achieved, physically and spiritually, in only one 29-year Saturn cycle.

* * *

The following lines came into my mind during the interpretation of one of the greatest spiritual poets of the Romantic style period.

Transformation

Pain, wiped out and made transcendent,
vaporising burning tears,
has unruffled roaring oceans
into lakes of stilled emotions,
where eternal peace appears.

* * *

It may well be worthwhile to give a list of studies, published in English:

Haussmann, J. F., 'German Estimates of Novalis from 1800 to 1850', in *Modern Philology* 9 The University of Chicago Press, pp. 399–415.

Carlyle, Thomas, 'Novalis', in *Foreign Review* 1829 no.7, and in *Essays on the Greater German Poets and Writers*, London, 1829.

Frye, Lawrence, 'Spatial Imagery in Novalis' *Hymnen an die Nacht'*, in *DVJ* 41 (1967) pp. 568–91.

Haywood, Bruce, *The Veil of Imagery*, Harvard Germanic Studies I, Cambridge Mass., s'Gravenhage, 1959.

Wagner, Lydia Elizabeth, *The Scientific Interest of Friedrich von Hardenberg (Novalis)* Michigan 1937.

Dyck, Martin, *Novalis and Mathematics, a study on Mathematics and its relation to Magic, Music, Religion, Philosophy, Language, and Literature,* Chapel Hill, 1960.

Neubauer, John, 'Stimulation Theory of Medicine in the *Fragments* of Novalis', Diss. NW. University Evanstone 1965.

Rehder, Helmut, 'Novalis and Shakespeare', in *PMLA* 63 (1948) pp. 604–24

Harrold, Charles F., 'Carlyle and Novalis', in *Studies in Philology*, Chapel Hill, USA, 1930, pp. 47–63

Peacock, Ronald, 'Novalis and Schopenhauer, a Critical Transition in Romanticism', in *German Studies presented to L. A. Willoughby,* Oxford 1952, pp. 133–43.

CHAPTER ELEVEN

Francis Bacon and the Noble Chancellor

Birthdate	22 January 1560/1 = Julian 22 January 1561 = Gregorian 1 February 1561
Birthplace	London, 51°N31′, 0°W06′
LMT	7h 28m am (uncorrected)
GMT	7h 28m 24s am
RLT	7h 28m am
RST	16h 12m 15s, Ascendant: PCA 4°53′ Aquarius (uncorrected) (WAK/SCHOCH 4°30′) Sun 12°18′ Aquarius – Moon 29°14′ Aries (PCA) (uncorrected) (SCHOCH 29°18′)
House system	Placidus.

Bacon, according to Baumgartner (in a German astrological magazine), was said to have been born at 7h 28m am and was also supposed to have been born after a seven-month pregnancy. As a result of this information we will have to calculate six possible conception dates, for 8, 7½ and 7 months respectively. We will also have a look at the normal gravidity of 9 months, and another conception correction will be given for exactly LMT 7 hours am instead of 7h 28m.

Bacon's birthdate is often recorded as 1560–1, which causes some confusion. The clue is that in those days it was common to start the new year on 25 March (Jul.) In the case of Bacon's birthdate, 22 January was officially still the year 1560 although astronomically it was the year 1561. This can be illustrated by Bacon's baptismal entry in the records of St Martin in-the-Fields, see plate V, page 49, in Dodd's biography.[24] The date of 22 January was also recorded in Rawley's biography,[36] which was the Julian date, and quoted by Alfred Dodd: 'Francis Bacon, the Glory of his Age and Nation, the Adorner and Ornament of learning, was borne in York House or York Place in the Strand, on the two-and-twentieth day of January in the year of our Lord 1560 [i.e. 1561].'

The birthtime and natal positions are recorded in Jean Overton

SIR FRANCIS BACON

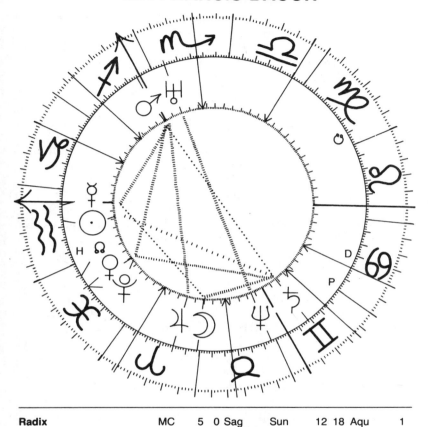

Radix					MC	5	0	Sag		Sun	12	18	Aqu		1
					ASC	4	53	Aqu		Moon	29	14	Ari		2
SIR FRANCIS BACON					— Plac —					Mercury	6	3	Aqu	R	1
					11.	22	46	Sag		Venus	9	13	Pis		1
Date:	22	1	1561		12.	10	31	Cap		Mars	6	30	Sag		10
Time:	7 28	0	E O		2.	5	13	Ari		Jupiter	19	22	Ari		2
Latitude:	51	31	N		3.	12	20	Tau		Saturn	14	10	Gem	R	4
Longitude:	0	6	W							Uranus	25	5	Sco		9
					Node	4	7	Pis	1	Neptune	27	45	Tau	R	3
					Part ft	21	48	Ari	2	Pluto	9	52	Pis		1
										Perseph	1	48	Can		5
Aspects: Radix/Radix		Orb:	8 0							Hermes	25	30	Aqu		1
										Demeter	14	24	Can		6

MC Sxt Mer 1 3	MC Cnj Mar 1 30	MC ses Jup 0 37	MC Sqr Nod 0 52
ASC Cnj Mer 1 11	ASC Sxt Mar 1 37	ASC ssx Nod 0 45	Sun Cnj Mer 6 15
Sun Tri Sat 1 52	Moo Sqr Mer 6 49	Moo ssq Sat 0 4	Moo ssx Nep 1 29
Mer Sxt Mar 0 27	Ven Sqr Mar 2 44	Ven Sqr Sat 4 57	Ven Cnj Plu 0 39
Mar Opp Sat 7 40	Mar Sqr Plu 3 22	Sat Sqr Plu 4 18	Ura Opp Nep 2 40
Nod ssx Mer 1 56	Nod Sqr Mar 2 22	Nod ssq Jup 0 15	

Fuller's biography,[34] page 26, as given by the astrologer William
Lilly[35] for an Ascendant of '5 Aquarius rising at 7 hours in the
morning'. Checking this information, however, we find that 5th
Aquarius is rising at LMT 7h 28m and not at 7 hours, and this is
compatible with the time given by Baumgartner.

Although Francis Bacon was registered as the child of Sir
Nicholas and Lady Bacon, it is openly claimed that he was
actually the son of Queen Elizabeth, and Robert Dudley, later Earl
of Leicester, whom she married secretly on 12 September 1560,
after the sudden and mysterious death of his wife on 8
September. It was also commonly known that at the time of the
alleged marriage, the Queen said 'she was about five months off
her confinement', which implies a conception in late April or
May, and also a normal gravidity of nine months, because Bacon
was born on 22 January 1561. None of the authorities quoted so
far have mentioned a seven-month gravidity, and I have no
knowledge of where this information came from. By mid June
1560 people were openly gossiping that 'a child was in the
making', in the light of which it is hard to believe he was
conceived only a fortnight before, on 29 May. (See CC 1, of 238
days.) On 18 April 1560, the Spanish Ambassador had already
written to his king that 'during *the last few days*, Lord Robert has
come so much into favour ... and it is even said that her Majesty
visits him in his chamber, day and night.' This, in my opinion,
tends to confirm the idea that Bacon could easily have been
conceived on 17 April, which I found by calculating the first
regular date for 280 days of pregnancy.

On checking the transits on 29 May 1560 (which is the
conception day for a gravidity of 238 days, 8 months) on the other
hand, we find transiting Mars in the 5th of Cancer exactly square
the Queen's natal Venus (ruler of the 5th house) in Libra. A
conception chart made up for 29 May 1560 (see CC 238 days of 4th
Aquarius) puts the Part of Fortune at 15°34' Gemini, exactly
conjunct the Queen's Persephone at 15°20' Gemini, the higher
ruler of her 5th house (children) and both these instances could
form a strong argument in favour of that date.

5th LIBRA

Janduz: On a high cliff above a lake, a man is on the edge of falling,
his left hand is stretched out towards a woman,
his right hand drops a couple of rings into the lake.

Rudhyar: Inspired disciples listen to the words of their teacher.

There is more to be checked, because Lilly said '7 hours in the morning with an Ascendant of 5th Aquarius'. Does this mean that Lilly, a reputable astrologer, for some reason gave the right Ascendant degree, and the wrong time, either intentionally, or by mistake? Or is the time of 7 hours correct and do we have to accept an Ascendant of 26th Capricorn? Looking at portraits of Bacon and knowing what kind of man he was, a Capricorn Ascendant is hard to believe. His face and his life-story are much more suggestive of Aquarius. Considering all this, I tend to hold on to an uncorrected Ascendant of 5th Aquarius, assuming Lilly had the timing wrong. In this case the birthtime of 7h 28m with an uncorrected Ascendant of 4°53' will be at the base of our calculations. For the moment I prefer to doubt the seven-month possibility because the biographers didn't mention this, although it has been included in the following calculations. Surprisingly the 4th degree of Aquarius is the result for 280 days as well.

Calculating this CCC, and reminding ourselves of what is said in the 'Trutine of Hermes', we locate in the natal chart the following basic facts:

1. 4°53' Aquarius rising, the natal Moon at 29°14' Aries and the natal Sun at 12°18' Aquarius. We draw a line from the Sun at 12°18' Aquarius to the same degree of the opposite sign of 12°18' Leo and locate the Moon at 29°14' Aries at the right-hand side at the outgoing arch which means the Moon is *waxing*. The Moon is positioned below the horizontal axis of Ascendant and Descendant which means the Moon is *below* the horizon. The scheme in Chapter 6 shows this to be the *1st order* of Bailey which says '*Moon/Ascendant and longer/forwards*'.
2. We count the distance between the Moon at 29°14' Aries and the *Ascendant* at 4°53' Aquarius which is 84°, ignoring the minutes.
3. Divide this distance of 84° by 13° (the average daily motion of the Moon) = 6 or 7 degrees or days.
4. 6/7 days longer than 273 days (the average time of pregnancy) = 279/280 days.
5. 279/280 days subtracted from the birthdate (Julian) 22.1.1561 = *(Julian) 17.4.1560*, which is the first possible, regular date of conception. Another way of calculating is by subtracting a full year from the birthdate Julian 22.1.1561 giving Julian 22.1.1560; subtract 280 days (see 4) from 365 days = 85 days to be added to the date of Julian 22.1.1560 to find the date of Julian 17.4.1560, which is the normal pregnancy time of 279 days.

6. According to the 1st order of Bailey, see the first
    paragraph, '*Moon Radix is Asc. or Descendant Conception*',
    we need to know the Sidereal Time of the natal Moon
    (Aries 29°14'), and also (because according to the 1st
    order '*or Descendant Conception*') for the opposite point of
    Libra 29°14' which can be found in the Table of Houses
    for London (51°29' North 0°06' West). This ST has to be
    interpolated in order to be accurate.
7. Because for London the RLT is almost equal to the GMT,
    we don't need to convert the RLT. Summarised in the
    following scheme:

Moon radix is *under* the horizon and *waxing*

Scheme for Calculating the 1st Order

Moon conception = Ascendant or Descendant radix
Moon radix = Descendant or Ascendant conception
Distance between the Moon 29°14' Aries
and the *Ascendant* 4°53' Aquarius
= 84° : 13° =
7 days *longer* than 273 days =
280 days before the birthday =
regular Jul 17.4.1560

By counting forwards in time we find approx.

Jul. 1 May   = approx. 266 days
Jul. 15 May   = approx. 252 days
Jul. 29 May   = approx. 238 days = 8 months
Jul. 12 June = approx. 225 days = 7½ months
Jul. 26 June = approx. 210 days = 7 months

With the help of the PCA computer program Electric Ephemeris,
we provide our own ephemeris, as exemplified on Novalis in
Chapter 10, as follows:

1. We calculate the *ST at noon Greenwich* by entering in our
    computer: the date, the GMT at noon 12h 00m, and
    Greenwich (51°N29', 0°E00'), to locate the Ascendant at
    noon and checking in the tables of houses for Greenwich
    to find the required ST, as follows:

29.5.1560 (JULIAN)
GMT noon 12h 00m
Greenwich 51°N29', 0°E00'

2. From the tables of houses for Greenwich we locate the

interpolated ST of the position of the calculated Ascendant, as follows:

Ascendant 20°39' *Virgo* at
approx. ST 5h 07m
Moon 9°00' Leo

3. We write down the position of the Moon at noon in Greenwich as calculated and we also calculate the positions of the Moon and the ST for the previous day and for the following day, in order to discover the daily progression of the Moon.

28.5.1560 *(JULIAN)*
GMT noon 12h 00m
Greenwich
Ascendant 19°58' Virgo at
ST 5h 03m
Moon 25°42' Cancer

30.5.1560 *(JULIAN)*
GMT noon 12h 00m
Greenwich
Ascendant 21°21' Virgo
ST 5h 11m
Moon 22°30' Leo

4. We look in the tables of houses for the birthplace or, if this is known, the town of conception, and in this case we assume it was indeed the birth town 51°N31', and find the ST of the Ascendant equal to the position of the natal Moon 29°14' Aries and also for the second possibility of the same date, the ST of its opposite point 29°14' Libra, as follows:

interpolated ST of the Ascendant
equal to the position of the natal Moon
29°14' Aries = ST approx. 18h 51m
29°14' Libra = ST approx. 8h 47m

Possibility (1)
The calculation of this first conception date of *Julian 29.5.1560 (238 days = 8 months)* as follows:

We take the ST at noon on 29.5.1560 (Julian date) and the interpolated ST of the Ascendant equal to the position of the natal Moon (29°14' Aries). The difference between the two sidereal times supplies the RLT. We will notice that for this date we don't need the ST of its opposite point for the second option of the same date. In order to be able to subtract −10h 16m from ST 5h 07m we have to add 24 hours to the ST, as follows:

ST at noon 29.5.1560 (Julian)	5h 07m (+24 hours = 29h 07m)
RLT	−10h 16m
ST Moon 29°14' Aries	18h 51m

Because for London the RLT is almost equal to the GMT, we don't need to convert the RLT (which in fact is 1h 44m am) into GMT, ignoring the small difference. We take the position of the Moon at noon and we adjust this position by subtracting the progression of the conception Moon in GMT −10h 16m at a daily motion of 13°18', which is the progression between 28 and 29 May, by using diurnal proportional logarithms, to be found in the ephemeris:

RLT	−10h 16m (= 1h 44m am)	
Difference from GMT	0h 00m	
GMT	−10h 16m	= Log. 3688
Daily motion of the Moon	13°18'	= Log. +2564
Progression of the Moon		Log. 6252 = −5°41'

Moon at noon 29.5.1560 (Julian)	9°00' Leo
Progression in −10h 16m	−5°41'
Corrected Descendant Radix	3°19' Leo
Corrected Ascendant Radix	3°19' Aquarius

which means a birth approx. *4m earlier* than was recorded.

Ascendant 3°19' Aquarius is rising at 51°N31' at
approx. ST 16h 08m
approx. 4m earlier
than the official time
corrected LMT 7h 24m am
corrected natal Moon 29°12' Aries
corrected PF 20°13' Aries

We ignore the second option of adding 3h 40m to the Moon position of 9°00' Leo, by taking the difference between noon ST 5h 07m and ST 8h 47m of the opposite of the natal Moon, 29°14' Libra, which will result in an Ascendant of 11°00' Aquarius, ST 16h 26m, *14m later* than recorded.

There is also a third possibility by taking the ST of the previous day, 28 May, and adding roughly 2° to the Moon position of 25°42 Cancer, which leads us to the result of approx. 28° Capricorn which is approx. ST 15h 55m and *17m earlier*. See the results for a CC of LMT 7h 00m.

Be aware of the fact this CC is for an 8 month birth and not, as was assumed, a 7 month. Therefore, although it seemed satisfactory, we will also calculate the 227 and 212 days, respectively (Jul.) 10 June and 25 June.

Possibility (2)
As we did before, we calculate the *ST at noon on 10 June (Julian) for Greenwich* by entering in our computer the date, the GMT at noon 12h 00m, and Greenwich (51°N29' and 0°E00'), to locate the Ascendant at noon and checking in the tables of houses for Greenwich to find the required ST, as follows:

10.6.1560 (JULIAN)
GMT noon 12h 00m
Greenwich 51°N29' – 0°E00'

2. From the tables of houses for *Greenwich* we locate the interpolated ST of the position of the calculated Ascendant, as follows:

Ascendant 29°00' Virgo at
approx. noon ST 5h 55m
Moon 28°13' Capricorn

3. Writing down the position of the Moon at noon in Greenwich, we calculate in the same way the positions of the Moon and the ST on the previous day and on the following day, in order to calculate the daily progression of the Moon.

9.6.1560 (JULIAN)
GMT noon 12h 00m
Greenwich
Ascendant 28°18' Virgo at
ST 5h 50m
Moon 14°40' Capricorn

11.6.1560 (JULIAN)
GMT at noon 12h 00m
Greenwich
Ascendant 29°41' Virgo
ST 5h 58m
Moon 11°22' Aquarius

4. We take the same ST of the Ascendant equal to the position of the natal Moon and for the second possibility of the same date, the ST of its opposite point. The

difference between the two sidereal times supplies the RLT, as follows:

Calculating this second conception date, *10 June 1560 (Julian)*, we take the ST at noon as follows:

ST noon 10.6.1560 (Julian)	5h 55m
RLT	+ 12h 56m
ST Moon 29°14' Aries	18h 51m

We don't need to convert the RLT into GMT; we calculate the progression of the conception Moon in GMT + 12h 56m, as follows:

RLT	+ 12h 56m	
Difference from GMT	0h 00m	
GMT	+ 12h 56m	= Log. 2685
Daily motion of the Moon	13°09'	= Log. + 2613
Progression of the Moon		Log. 5298 = + 7°05'

We take the position of the Moon at noon and we adjust this position by adding the progression in + 12h 56m at a daily motion of 13°09', which is the motion between 10 and 11 June, as follows:

Moon at noon 10.6.1560	28°13' Capricorn
Progression in + 12h 56m	+ 7°05'
Corrected Ascendant Radix	5°18' Aquarius

Ascendant 5°18' Aquarius is rising at 51°N31' at
approx. ST 16h 13m
approx. 1m later
than the official time
corrected LMT 7h 29m am
corrected natal Moon 29°14' Aries
corrected PF 22°14' Aries

Although almost the same birthtime as the official time, we don't think this degree symbol fits the natal chart. The second option of this date results in 29°47' Capricorn which means a birth approx. 15m earlier, see the additional calculations for LMT 7h 00m.

Possibility (3)

1. For the last conception possibility of 210 days, 7 months, 25 June (Julian date), we calculate as before the ST at noon at 25 June for Greenwich by entering in our computer the date, the GMT at noon 12h 00m, and Greenwich (51°N29' and 0°E00'), to locate the Ascendant at noon and by

checking the tables of houses for Greenwich to find the required ST, as follows:

25.6.1560 (JULIAN)
GMT noon 12h 00m
Greenwich 51°N29' – 0°E00'

2. From the tables of houses for Greenwich we locate the interpolated ST of the position of the calculated Ascendant, as follows:

Ascendant 9°25' Libra at
approx. ST 6h 53m
Moon at noon 5°30' Leo

3. Writing down the position of the Moon at noon in Greenwich, we also calculate in the same way the positions of the Moon and the ST for the previous day and for the following day, in order to calculate the daily progression of the Moon.

24.6.1560 (JULIAN)
GMT noon 12h 00m
Greenwich
Ascendant 8°43' Libra at
ST 6h 50m
Moon 22°01' Cancer

26.6.1560 (JULIAN)
GMT at noon 12h 00m
Greenwich
Ascendant 10°06' Libra
ST 6h 57m
Moon 19°11' Leo

We take the ST at noon but in this case we take the ST equal to the opposite point of the natal Moon, 29°14' Libra and we calculate as before:

ST noon 25.6.1560 (Julian)	6h 53m
RLT	+ 1h 54m
ST 29°14' Libra	8h 47m

As before, we don't need to convert the RLT, and calculate the progression of the conception Moon in GMT + 1h 54m, as follows:

RLT = GMT   +1h 54m = Log.   11015
Daily motion of the Moon   13°41'   = Log.   +2440
Progression of the Moon   Log.   13455 = +1°05'

We take the position of the Moon at noon and we adjust this position by adding the progression in +1h 54m at a daily motion of 13°41', which is the motion between 25 and 26 June = +1°05', as follows:

Moon at noon 25.6.1560   5°30' Leo
Progression in +1h 54m   +1°05'
Corrected Descendant radix   6°35' Leo – Ascendant 6°35' Aquarius

Ascendant 6°35' Aquarius is rising at 51°N31' at
approx. ST 16h 16m
approx. 4m later
than the official time
corrected LMT 7h 32m am
corrected natal Moon 29°16' Aries
corrected PF 23°33' Aries

The second option for this date results in 28°38' Capricorn = ST approx. 15h 55m, which means a birth 17m earlier than the official time. The Ascendant sign, the degree and also 17m earlier, seem very unlikely.

Summary of Possibilities

Date	No. days	CC	PF	ST	Time Difference	☽
29/5	238	3°19' ♒	20°13' ♈	16h 08m	4m earlier	29°12'♈
		11°00' ♒		16h 26m	14m later	
		28° ♑		15h 55m	17m earlier	
10/6	226	5°18' ♒	22°14' ♈	16h 13m	47s later	29°14'♈
		29°47' ♑		15h 57m	15m earlier	
25/6	212	6°35' ♒	23°33' ♈	16h 16m	4m later	29°16'♈
		28°38' ♑		15h 55m	17m earlier	

The results of CC calculations for a *normal* gravidity, which will be further discussed later on, are as follows:

Date	No. days	CC	PF	ST	Time difference	☽
17/4	280	3°47' ♒	20°41' ♈	16h 09m	3m earlier	29°12'♈
1/5	266	7°18' ♒	24°14' ♈	16h 18m	4m later	29°14'♈
14/5	252	5°51' ♒	22°46' ♈	16h 14m	1m later	29°12'♈

The results of CC calculations for a birthtime of *LMT 7 hours in the morning*:

Date	No. days	CC	PF	ST	Time difference	☽
16/4	280	28°29' ♑	15°18' ♈	15h 55m	11m later	29°06' ♈
1/5	266	1°45' ♒	18°39' ♈	16h 04m	20m later	29°11' ♈
4/4	294	6°06' ♑	23°05' ♈	16h 15m	31m later	29°16' ♈
		28°23' ♑	15°12' ♈	15h 55m	11m later	29°06' ♈
14/5	252	29°29' ♑	16°19' ♈	15h 57m	13m later	29°07' ♈

These results are partly the same as we calculated before, and again, in my opinion the Capricorn degrees are total unsuitable and can be ignored. The CC for the short gravidities, based upon 7h am, will be the same as calculated before. The CC calculation for LMT 7h am of the regular date meets difficulties in the sense that we find the conception Moon at the last degrees of Aquarius which shows the time is wrong, and finally, none of the calculations have as a result a birthtime at 7 hours am.

* * *

A corrected birthtime only 4m later than the official time, which we found with CC 212 days, is quite possible, because Bacon was said to be a 7 month child, although the degree symbols of 7th Aquarius do not seem to fit very well: Janduz: 'A man pierces a doll with his sword,' and Rudhyar: 'Out of the cosmic egg, life is born fresh and virginal.' However, these images were actually operating in another area of his life, because he had Mercury in this degree (at 6°03').

The second image of the 6th degree of Aquarius, which is of CC 226 days of approx. 7½ months:

Rudhyar: 'In an allegorical mystery-ritual a man officiates alone.'

at first sight seems to fit much better, firstly because of the theory that Bacon in fact wrote Shakespeare's plays, and also because I found some astrological evidence for this degree which will be discussed later. In spite of this, I prefer 4th Aquarius, which is the CC for 29.5.1560, or 238 days, although this postulates an 8 month pregnancy, and not 7 months as recorded.

4th AQUARIUS

Janduz: 'A gentleman of noble appearance is ascending
the steps of a palace, with his back to us.
In the courtyard at the left, facing towards us,
a rider of middle age is about to depart on horseback,
carrying in front of him a carefully locked chest.'

Rudhyar: 'A Hindu pundit reveals himself suddenly a great healer.'

During the reign of King James I, Bacon was the Lord Chancellor from 1617 until 1621, when he was dismissed from this office, because of alleged bribery (see the first image of Janduz for 4th Aquarius). On a low level this degree could indeed indicate such a thing, but on an elevated level it is always seen as one of the purest Aquarius degrees, and this is clearly apparent in the case of Bacon, a man who showed great nobility throughout his life, and functioned on a highly spiritual level. According to Dodd, no charge against Bacon was proved, and there was not even a trial. Dodd found strong evidence that Bacon had been the victim of a conspiracy in the palace.

A look at his chart certainly indicates a man of extraordinary stature: Bacon was a 'double' Aquarius, with not only the Sun (12°18') and the Ascendant (3°19'), but with, in addition, Mercury (6°03') ingoing conjunct Hermes (25°30') in this altruistic sign. In addition, both Mercury and the Sun are connected in strong ingoing trines with the lower ruler of Aquarius, Saturn, at 14°10'℞ Gemini in the 4th house. This would make him determined, and well able, to comprehend and to re-state cosmic truths retrieved from the deep past, structuring, renewing, and teaching them Hermetically in an innovative form of speech and writing. Actually, at this point it should be noted that according to the Schoch tables, Saturn is at 13°45'℞, and Uranus at 24°18' Scorpio, instead of 25°05'. The outgoing, activating squares with Uranus in Scorpio (which, although in wide squares, still have to be regarded as such because of the ingoing conjunctions with Hermes) required him to stretch his spiritual consciousness beyond limits in order to uncover the cosmic secrets hidden in Scorpio, and to process them into reformulated philosophical teachings (in the 9th house). At the same time he founded fraternities designed to initiate poets and scholars into an ever-greater knowledge of the ancient wisdoms, and became a true sage himself in the process. We find the positions in Aquarius also in squares with Neptune in 27°45' Taurus in the 3rd house, and remember that an elevated Higher Self knows it has to be prepared to make sacrifices in order to bring about the fruitful growth of all that is given.

Coming 'down' from heavenly Uranus, the solar energy moves on to Mars, ruler of Scorpio but also of Aries, which sign is on the cusp of the 2nd house of financial matters, which is found at 6°30 Saggitarius, in the 10th house of official State functions. Mars is in an ingoing, maturing square with Pluto, ruler of the 2nd house, which, being in Pisces could well have led to the alleged but unproven accusations of bribery, which we will discuss later. In the meantime, because Mars is also in opposition to Saturn in Gemini, he is using his energy to better effect, along with initiating Pluto, by starting the poets and scholars of Pisces along the path to the acquisition of knowledge and wisdom, (Gemini), shaped into re-formed educative and constructive organisations and schemes (opposite Saturn). It is widely believed that, under the pen-name of William Shakespeare, he wrote a considerable number of plays which were themselves the vehicles for metaphysical and esoteric teachings. The circuit moves back from Saturn in Gemini to Mercury, Sun and Hermes in Aquarius and moves again into Scorpio, hiding and coding in symbols and ciphers.

Mars in Sagittarius induces Jupiter at 19°15′ Aries, conjunct the Moon at 29°12′, both in the 2nd house, and again the matter of finances, but spiritually this house has also to be recognised as the storehouse for spiritual capital, which the Higher Self has garnered in previous harvests. The Part of Fortune at 20°13′ Aries in the 2nd, and in conjunction with both planets, has the task of bringing this to fruitful life. In my opinion the course of this part of the circuit points clearly towards both images of 4th Aquarius.

Some interesting esoteric commentaries, which have an immediate bearing on the interpretation of the circuit given above, can be found in the publications of the Francis Bacon Research Trust. I quote below from the *Virgin Ideal*.[49]

> Francis Bacon *secretly* prepared a scheme for the complete instauration or *renovation* of all arts and sciences, bringing the Renaissance to a fruition in Elizabethan England and *'laying bases* for posterity'. Both privately and publicly he launched his divinely inspired *new method and plan* for the *reformation* and *enlightenment* of the whole world, amidst unique phenomena in the heavens. Referred to by his contemporaries as the *'Chancellor* of Parnassus', Bacon headed a *fraternity* of *poet-scholars*. They created for mankind some of the world's finest literature and art, embodying the sciences and precepts of the Ancient *Wisdom* traditions as an 'Open University' of Light, plus an English language capable of becoming the vehicle of the *deepest wisdom teachings* and accurate scientific thought [my italics].

From the words given in italics we can easily recognise what I have said. It is equally clear that the noble man ascending the palace steps, in the first image of 4th Aquarius, also symbolically carries rich spiritual treasures, which are healing for humanity, as illustrated by the second image of Jones. 'The palace' does not only refer to, for instance, Royal palaces, but also to the Heavenly palaces of spiritual light and knowledge and wisdom.

Dodd, on page 23 of his biography, gives Bacon's birthdate as 22 January 1561. Since we know this to be the Julian date, we can assume that all other dates mentioned in his biography and quoted in this chapter are also Julian and have to be converted into the Gregorian calendar by adding ten days. This I found confirmed by the information given by Jean Overton Fuller.

On 14 March 1621 (Jul.) Bacon was suddenly accused in the House of Commons of 'bribery and corruption', on 3 May (Jul.) sentenced by the House of Lords and on 31 May (Jul.) imprisoned in the Tower. I quote Alfred Dodd:

> ... because all England knew he was as honest as the day ... there was not a whisper against his name in the Commons ... up to 14th March he stood before England and the world as a man of irreproachable character and justly so – as we have seen.

> In less than two months – 14th March to 3rd May – the wisest intellectual in the world was ground into the dust in obloquy and shame. His enemies had triumphed. Francis Bacon's conspicious fall diverted men's thoughts from the more scandalous wickedness of the Great Favourite [i.e. Buckingham]. The result of Bacon's ruin was that Buckingham was saved. Bacon was cast down from the height of fortune to become a byword of shame. What a tremendous and mysterious catastrophe! What a fall indeed! So Francis Bacon was sent to the Tower [31 May] a ruined man. Bacon was a victim of a diabolical plot, there was no trial and nothing has been proved against him.

Elsewhere Dodd comments that in fact King James and the Crown were also saved when the King commanded Bacon to be the scapegoat, thus saving himself, Buckingham, and their wicked and crooked friends like Coke, Cranfield, Mompesson and Mitchell from impeachment. It is interesting to know that Bacon was the Keeper of the Seal and had been forced to seal all the monopoly patents and licences, remnants of the feudal rights of the Crown, which ensured a flow of illegal money into the King's purse, to be openly squandered. To avoid a scandal, the crooks cooked up a plot against Bacon so that he was not able to accuse them in court, in his own defence, as he had planned. It was later said that during an audience on 12 April 1621 (Jul; Greg. 22 April) the King forced Bacon to plead guilty to crimes he had never committed, and that from loyalty to the Crown he agreed to do this. It is fascinating to see how obviously and clearly the degree symbols were indicating this course of events in the spring of 1621. We only have to examine the transits and progressions to verify the claim that Bacon was innocent. Without going too deeply into detail, there are some interesting facts I would like to mention.

First of all, however, this seems the right time to have a look at the chart of King James I. We immediately notice he had the natal Moon at 3°55' Leo exactly conjunct the Descendant of Bacon, quite a confirmation for the rightness of the 4th degree of Aquarius as the Ascendant of Bacon. On 12 April 1621 King James had his progressed Moon conjunct his natal Moon in 3°26' Leo and, on top of all, in December 1620 and in January 1621 his progressed Venus, ruler of the 2nd house (and the 9th), at 14°50' Cancer, stressing his desperate financial state. He succeeded in regaining his stability at the expense of Bacon, and he thus illustrated the content of the images involved (see further on) in an embarrassingly exact fashion. Knowing this we are not at all surprised to find transiting Venus at 14°41' Aries square Bacon's natal Demeter in the 15th of Cancer and opposite Bacon's progressed Mars in the 15th of Capricorn. Transiting Mars was in the 18th of Scorpio, which depicts a man with a dagger, on the point of stabbing another man in the back. The King's progressed Neptune was in the 14th of Gemini conjunct Bacon's Saturn, and his progressed Uranus was opposition both in the 14th of Sagittarius. With one mighty blow this royal tidal wave caused a reversal in Bacon's life, completely wiping out his status, and impugning his honour.

In connection with this we will have a look at both images involved, telling quite revealing things, justifying the idea that Bacon's fall was indeed a sacrifice:

15th CANCER JANDUZ IMAGE

Two thrones under two canopies side by side,
a mongrel dog sleeping on the left throne and
on the right one a big crowned rat lies in wait.

15th CAPRICORN JANDUZ IMAGE

At the left a tripod and brazier from which flames are leaping high.
On the right a man is standing with a dead sheep on his shoulders,
he is half sacrificial priest and half butcher.

Not surprisingly we find the fall of Bacon called 'the sacrifice' to save Buckingham and, if I understand well, the King.

Bacon's solar return for 31 January (Greg.) 1621 GMT 20h 44m 30s (based on the Ascendant of 3°19' Aquarius CC I), shows the Ascendant at 24°30' Virgo (Jones image: 'a flag is flying halfmast in front of an official building'!) and the Part of Fortune at 6°52' Capricorn (see the wicked contents of both degree images) certainly indicate a 'diabolical plot'. This was doubly reinforced by the south node at 13°39' Gemini conjunct his natal Saturn (fall!), and augmented by the King's progressed Neptune in the same degree, surely causing bad karma for both. This position confirms the 14th degree of Saturn instead of the 15th degree calculated with the PCA software program. We find Jupiter at 12°04' Taurus, square his natal Sun.

When looking at Bacon's progressions for 1621, we notice first of all the progressed Ascendant is in the 2nd degree of Gemini (a degree of 'imprisonment', see the Janduz image), and the Sun is in the 13th of Aries sextile the natal Sun. In December 1620, when it all began to boil, the progressed Moon was in Cancer and exactly conjunct his natal Persephone, also in Cancer, at approximately 1°48', in the 5th house, and progressing closer and closer to the ingoing conjunction with his natal Demeter in Cancer at approximately 14°24 (see the degree symbols; there can't be any doubt about the reference!) in the 6th house and becoming square with Jupiter in the 20th of Aries in 1622, by which time it was all over. Bacon seems to have been released in June 1621 and pardoned on 12 October. Without the acceptance of the postulated Persephone and Demeter it is impossible to find satisfying answers, but by including them we can. Demeter in Cancer is in its own sign and so is the progressed Moon, and because both were at a stillstand in Cancer, they were forced to reach for, or rather to be thrown into, the opposite sign of Capricorn, which we find on the cusp of the 12th house. In the light of this one can account for the etheric and astral 'ins and outs' of all that happened. All the smeary and dirty tricks of his enemies, which the 12th house stands for, caused those false accusations of bribery, and the imprisonment. Also, do notice that Persephone is the second ruler of the 2nd house. Due to the importance of his State function as Lord Chancellor, but also because of his spiritual stature, of course there were more than only earthly enemies to contend with. It is clear that Bacon with the progressed Mars in the 15th of Capricorn in the 12th house and exactly opposite Demeter in Cancer in the 6th, had to become the scapegoat for the sins of those on the thrones, making a willing sacrifice, to 'digest' all the corruption coming towards him from the King, Buckingham and all the others involved in this scandal. It was the same progressed Mars in Capricorn, which by inducing the natal Saturn in Gemini (see the 14th degree of Gemini: 'a masked man standing beside the carcass of a horse'), caused Bacon to be forced by the King into this role of scapegoat, and at the same time to undertake the Hermetic role of mediator for the sins of others in spite of the fact that he was completely innocent (Hermes, induced by natal Saturn). It must have been intolerable for this noble man to have his official position abused by corrupt people in the name, and sometimes in the person, of the man he believed was King by Divine Right, and to whom he had sworn fealty. He must have come to think that the best way he could serve (Demeter in the 6th house) his King and country was to obey in whatever circumstances. This position of Mars opposite Demeter in Cancer strongly enforced the progressed Moon and natal Demeter. Finally, his progressed MC was in the 30th of Capricorn in the 12th house when his official status faded away and, square his natal Moon in the 30th of Aries, provoked the conflict which abruptly changed his personal life.

On 14 March (Jul. = Greg. 24th) (accused in the House of Commons) we find transiting Uranus at 29°25' Cancer (see his progressed MC as well) in an exact square with his natal Moon, which accounts for the sudden shock these accusations must have caused. His natal Sun was exactly squared by transiting Pluto at 12°08' Taurus but exactly trined by transiting Neptune at 12°17' Libra.

On 3 May (Jul.; Greg. 13 May), when Bacon was sentenced in the House of Lords, we find transiting Venus at 5°27' Taurus and on 31 May (Jul.; Greg. 10 June) transiting Mars at 5°36' Scorpio. Both transits indicate the probability of the *6th* degree of Aquarius which we have calculated in CC II, but are in any case square his Ascendant and Mercury. His progressions, although based on the 4th of Aquarius would be the same for 6th Aquarius, holding Mercury at 5°02' Aries in sextile with a possible Ascendant of 6th Aquarius. The progressed Moon on 3 May was at exactly 5°55' Cancer, which is interesting but does not really account for this drama.

Finally, Bacon was pardoned on 12 (Jul.) 22 (Greg.) October 1621 with transiting Venus at 25°06' Scorpio exactly conjunct his Uranus, Jupiter at 25°55' ℞ Gemini conjunct his natal Hermes, and Neptune at 13°46' Libra in trine to his natal Saturn.

* * *

According to Dodd, 'Bacon died to the world' on 9 April (Jul.; Greg. 19 April) 1626, but it is said he died a 'philosophical death', and there is evidence that he fled to the Continent and lived to a very old age. Among others, Manly Palmer Hall said 'that he feigned death and passed over into Germany, there to guide the destinies of his Fraternities for nearly twenty-five years after his alleged death.' Dodd's opinion was that in 1626 'Bacon made a carefully planned getaway, 'dying' on Resurrection Sunday, which seems indeed to be a mute signal that though he had died to the world he had risen again.'

On the day Bacon 'died', his progressed Mars was at 17°24' Capricorn, and looking at the second image of this degree, we can imagine that he may well have sailed away to Holland and later to America, as is suggested. Was it perhaps on one of His Majesty's galleons, which was flying the Union Jack?! Progressed Venus was at 27°37' Taurus exactly conjunct his natal Neptune! His progressed MC had reached the exact Ascendant degree of 4th Aquarius, which is perhaps another indication of the rightness of CCI. The transiting Sun was at 29°17' Aries, right on his natal Moon, combined with the progressed Moon at 9°54' Virgo and transiting Saturn in the 10th of Virgo, opposite both his natal Venus (9°13' Pisces) and his natal Pluto (9°52' Pisces). Certainly a new start, but was it on earth or was it in heaven? That is the question!

* * *

Life

The World's a bubble, and the Life of Man
Less than a span:
In his conception wretched, from the womb
So is the tomb;
Curst from his cradle, and brought up to years
with cares and fears.
Who then to frail mortality shall trust,
But limns on water, or but writes in dust.

What then remains, but that we still should cry
for being born, or, being born, to die?

Lord Bacon

CHAPTER TWELVE

HRH Princess Beatrice and the Knights

Name	HRH Princess Beatrice of York
Birthdate	8.8.1988
Birthplace	London, 51°N32', 0°E06'
LMT	8h 18m pm (BST)
GMT	7h 18m pm
RLT	7h 18m pm
RST	16h 26m 50s: Ascendant approx. 11°13' Aquarius (uncorrected), Sun 16°26' Leo, Moon 4°54' Cancer (uncorrected)
Houses	Placidus.

From the birthchart we take the following basic data, needed in order to calculate the CC:

1. With 11°13' Aquarius rising, the natal Moon is in 4°54' Cancer and the natal Sun 16°26' Leo. We draw a line from the Sun to the same degree of the opposite sign and locate the Moon at the left-hand side at the ingoing arch which means it is *waning*. The Moon is positioned below the horizontal Ascendant–Descendant axis, which means it is *below* the horizon. The scheme in Chapter 6 shows this to be the *4th order* of Bailey which says 'Moon/Descendant, shorter and backwards'.
2. We find the distance between the Moon at 4°54' Cancer and the *Descendant* at 11°13' Leo to be 36°, ignoring the minutes.
3. We divide this distance of 36° by 13° (the average daily motion of the Moon) = 3 degrees/days;
4. 3 days shorter than 273 days (the average time of pregnancy) = 270 days;
5. 270 days subtracted from the birthdate 8.8.1988 = 12.11.1987 which is the first possible, regular date of conception. Another way of calculating is by subtracting a full year from the birthdate giving 8.8.1987; subtract 270 days (see 4) from 365 days = 95 days to be added to the date of 8.8.1987 to find the date of 12.11.1987.

HRH PRINCESS BEATRICE OF YORK

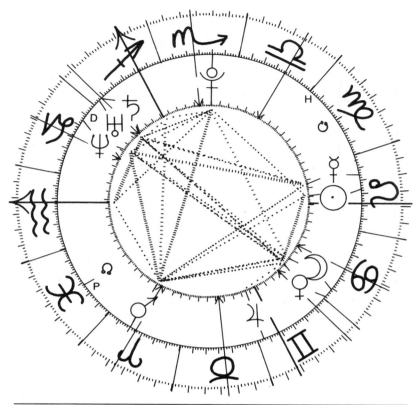

Radix					Sun	16	26	Leo		7
		MC	8 38	Sag	Moon	4	54	Can		5
		ASC	11 13	Aqu	Mercury	22	29	Leo		7
HRH BEATRICE OF YORK		— Plac —			Venus	1	30	Can		5
		11.	26 15	Sag	Mars	9	20	Ari		1
Date:	8 8 1988	12.	14 33	Cap	Jupiter	2	45	Gem		3
Time:	20 18 0 E 1	2.	11 46	Ari	Saturn	26	18	Sag	R	11
Latitude:	51 31 N	3.	16 51	Tau	Uranus	27	21	Sag	R	11
Longitude:	0 6 W				Neptune	7	51	Cap	R	11
		Node	15 28	Pis 1	Pluto	9	53	Sco		8
		Part ft	29 41	Sag 11	Perseph	18	12	Prs		1
Aspects: Radix/Radix Orb: 8 0					Hermes	29	20	Vir		7
					Demeter	5	29	Cap		11

MC	Tri	Mar 0 42	MC	ssx	Nep 0 47	MC	ssx	Plu 1 15	ASC	Sxt	Mar 1 53
ASC	ssq	Sat 0 5	ASC	ssq	Ura 1 8	ASC	Sqr	Plu 1 20	Sun	Cnj	Mer 6 3
Sun	ssq	Ven 0 4	Sun	Tri	Mar 7 6	Sun	Sqr	Plu 6 34	Moo	Cnj	Ven 3 24
Moo	Sqr	Mar 4 26	Moo	Opp	Ura 7 33	Moo	Opp	Nep 2 57	Moo	Tri	Plu 4 59
Mer	ses	Mar 1 51	Mer	Tri	Sat 3 49	Mer	Tri	Ura 4 52	Mer	ses	Nep 0 21
Ven	Sqr	Mar 7 50	Ven	ssx	Jup 1 15	Ven	Opp	Sat 5 12	Ven	Opp	Ura 4 9
Sat	ssq	Plu 1 25	Nep	Sxt	Plu 2 2	Nod	qcx	Sun 0 58			

Ven Opp Nep 6 21 Mar Sqr Nep 1 29 Mar qcx Plu 0 33 Sat Cnj Ura 1 3

6. According to the 4th order of Bailey, see the first paragraph, *'Moon Radix is Ascendant or Descendant Conception'*, we need to know the ST of the Ascendant equal to the position of the natal Moon (4°54' Cancer), and also (because according to the 4th order *'or Descendant Conception'*) for the opposite point of 4°54' Capricorn which can be found in the tables of houses for London 51°N32'). Both sidereal times have to be interpolated in order to be accurate. These basic facts are summarised in the following scheme:

The natal Moon is *below* the horizon and *waning*

Scheme for Calculating the 4th Order

Moon conception = Descendant or Ascendant radix
Moon radix = Descendant or Ascendant conception
Distance between the Moon 4°54' Cancer
and the *Descendant* 11°13' Leo
= 36° : 13°
= 3 days shorter than 273 days
= 270 days before the birthday 8.8.1988
= *'regular'* 12.11.1987

In the tables of houses for London 51°N32', we locate

the interpolated ST of the
Ascendant equal to the position of the natal Moon
4°54' Cancer is rising at ST 22h 10m
and its opposite point 4°54' Capricorn at ST 14h 33m

Possibility (1)
The calculation of the first, regular conception date (270 days), is as follows:
From the ephemeris we take the ST at noon at 12.11.1987 and find in the tables of houses for 51°N32' the interpolated ST of the Ascendant equal to the position of the natal Moon and also for the second possibility of the same date, the ST of its opposite point. In both cases the difference between the two sidereal times supplies the RLT, as follows:

ST 12.11.1987 at noon	15h 24m
RLT	+6h 46m
ST 4°54' Cancer	22h 10m

Converting the RLT +6h 46m into GMT by adding 24s to it (which can be ignored), we calculate the progression of the conception Moon in GMT +6h 46m by using diurnal proportional logarithms, to be found in the ephemeris:

RLT	+6h 46m		
Difference from GMT	0h 00m		
GMT	+6h 46m	= Log.	5498
Daily motion of the Moon	11°51'	= Log.	+3065
Progression of the Moon		Log.	8563 = +3°20'

Checking the ephemeris for 12.11.1987, we take the position of the Moon at noon and we adjust this position by adding the progression in +6h 46m at a daily motion of 11°51', which is the motion between 12 and 13 January = +3°20', as follows:

Moon 12.11.1987 at noon	7°31' Leo
Progression in +6h 46m	+3°20'
Corrected Descendant radix	10°51' Leo = Ascendant 10°51' Aquarius

Ascendant *Aquarius 10°51'* is rising at 51N°32'
at approx. ST 16h 26m
approx. 50s earlier
than the official time,
corrected LMT 20h 17m 10s
corrected natal Moon 4°53' Cancer
corrected PF 29°18' Sagittarius

A correction of approx. 50s earlier, 'regular', and a normal pregnancy of 270 days, is very likely to be the right one.

Examining the natal chart we notice an Aquarius Ascendant with the lower ruler Saturn at 26°18'℞ Sagittarius and Uranus, the higher ruler, at 27°21'℞, both in the 11th house and conjunct the Part of Fortune, in outgoing squares shaped with Hermes, the higher ruler of Gemini, in 29°20' Virgo in the 7th house.

The circuit in this chart starts with the Sun at 16°26' Leo in the 7th house in an outgoing conjunction with Mercury at 22°29' Leo, both opposite the Ascendant. For a Sun in Leo it is vital to open up the spiritual centre (Sun) and to radiate towards Aquarius, to embrace humanity, and to share both leadership and equality.

From there we go to Saturn and Uranus (rulers of Aquarius opposite Leo) in Sagittarius, in the 11th house, emphasising the need for Leo to radiate solar energy and to be in the company of people, to teach and to be taught development and growth (Sagittarius), based on a totally new way of life, reforming and renewing what is already established.

The planets in Sagittarius are reaching for its ruler, Jupiter, at 2°45' Gemini in the 3rd house of learning and teaching, and in the beautiful 3rd degree, like a modern troubadour, perhaps singing and playing the harp or a lute.

From here the flow goes on in two directions, first towards Hermes, the higher ruler of Gemini, at 29°20′ Virgo, and thence towards Mercury in the 23rd of Leo, and from there on but also straight from Jupiter beaming back towards Mercury, ruler of both Gemini and Virgo, discovering self-knowedge (Hermes) but also finding how things are related in a higher sense and facilitating the integration of this sense of unity with her own spiritual attributes (Mercury conjunct the Sun in Leo).

From Mercury in Leo we finish up with the Sun, where we started, a 'closed' circuit, so to speak, which is not very common, and which will ensure the spiritual support for both aims and difficulties. What was intended to be reached for could easily support her whole being.

But there is more to say because the circuit has not touched another and vital part, which is separated from and not so easily included in her being, namely the positions of the Moon in 4°54′ Cancer (conjunct Venus at 1°30′), Mars at 9°20′ Aries, Pluto at 9°53′ Scorpio and Persephone at 18°12′ Pisces. And notably Neptune at 7°51′ Capricorn conjunct Demeter at 5°28′, both in the 11th house.

I think in particular a 'loose' (unintegrated in the circuit) and afflicted Moon, locked up in her own sign of Cancer is, especially for a female, rather difficult. The Moon is in an almost 'sharp' though still outgoing opposition with the higher ruler of Cancer, Demeter, and Neptune, and is the ruler of the 6th house of health, so obviously there are some tense problems here with the homeland of the soul, the astral realms. In fact we have here a second 'stillstand' as with the Sun in Leo. A Moon locked up in her own sign *has* to search for the substantiating forces of Capricorn in experiences, but also in the realm of feelings and reactions, not only because of this, but also because Demeter and Neptune in Capricorn, aiming towards Saturn (ruler of Capricorn) in conjunction with Uranus, are begging for what is so rightly expressed in 11th Aquarius:

Janduz: 'Armoured knights on horseback approach two by two, and ride to the right.
In the background at the left, two of them attack each other as though in a medieval tournament.'

Rudyhar: 'An artist, away from the world, receives a new inspiration.'

I think we should also look at Rudyhar's 'Mandala' version, which in my opinion is more to the point:

'During a silent hour [Capricorn], a man receives a new inspiration
[Neptune]
which may change his life [in sextile with Pluto in 10th Scorpio].'

We notice the importance of Saturn and Uranus in Sagittarius in
outgoing squares with Hermes in 29°20' Virgo because of the Part
of Fortune in 29°18' Sagittarius.

We do hope this native of royal birth, born on the 8th day of the
8th month in the 88th year of this century and at the 8th hour and
18 minutes, who has such an impressive natal chart with
enormous potential, particularly as the planets involved are
positioned in elevated degree symbols, will find her way in life. It
is to be hoped that she will be wisely guided by her parents and
that the way she is brought up and educated will really allow her
to learn properly and responsibly the alternative way of life for
the coming New Age, to remain open to anything regarded as
unusual, allowing her indeed to make that change of life her
personality symbol indicates, and which is so strongly expressed
in her chart. This is emphasised by the number 8, as found in her
birth data, which number certainly directs our attention not only
towards the transforming contents of the 8th sign, Scorpio, but
also to the renewing Christ forces, poured out by Aquarius and
symbolised by this number.

* * *

The calculation of the second option of the same date will give an
Ascendant of approx. 7°00' Aquarius which means a birth of
approx. ST 16h 17m, and 10m earlier than the time given
officially, which can safely be ignored.

The 4th order claims the next possibility 14 days longer (284
days) and we calculate 29 October, taking the same ST as in the
previous calculation, as follows:

ST at noon of 29.10.1987	14h 29m	
RLT	+7h 41m	
ST 4°54' Cancer	22h 10m	

We don't need to convert the RLT to GMT and so we move on to
calculating the progression of the conception Moon in GMT +7h
41m:

RLT = GMT	+7h 41m	= Log.	4947
Daily motion of the Moon	14°10'	= Log.	+2289
Progression of the Moon		Log.	7236 = 4°32'

Checking the ephemeris for 29.10.1987, we take the position of
the Moon at noon and we adjust this position by adding the

progression in +7h 41m at a daily motion of 14°10', which is the motion between 29 and 30 October, as follows:

Moon 29.10.1987 at noon	2°40' Aquarius
Progression in +7h 41m	+4°32'
Corrected Ascendant radix	7°12' Aquarius

Ascendant Aquarius 7°12' is rising at 51°32'
at approx. ST 16h 17m
approx. 10m earlier
than the official time
corrected LMT 20h 08m
corrected natal Moon 4°49' Cancer
corrected PF 25°35' Sagittarius

The calculation of the second option of the same date can be ignored because the result will be approx. ST 16h 07m, which is 20m earlier.

Calculating the last conception date of 26 November (256 days), as follows:

From the ephemeris we take the ST at noon and the ST of the Ascendant equal to the *opposite* position of the natal Moon, because the first option can be ignored. The difference between the two sidereal times supplies the RLT, as follows:

ST at noon of 26.11.1987	16h 19m
RLT	−1h 46m
ST 4°54' Capricorn	14h 33m

We don't need to convert the RLT to GMT and so we move on to calculating the progression of the conception Moon in GMT −1h 46m:

RLT = GMT	−1h 46m	= Log.	11331
Daily motion of the Moon	14°22'	= Log.	+2229
Progression of the Moon		Log.	13560 = −1°04'

Checking the ephemeris for 26.11.1987 we take the position of the Moon at noon and we adjust this position by subtracting from it the progression in −1h 46m at a daily motion of 14°22' which is the speed between 25 and 26 November, = −1°04', as follows:

Moon 26.11.1987 at noon	13°37' Aquarius
Progression in −1h 46m	−1°04'
Corrected Ascendant radix	12°33' Aquarius

Ascendant 12°33' Aquarius is rising at 51°N32'
at approx. ST 16h 30m
approx. 3m earlier
than the official time
corrected LMT 20h 15m
corrected natal Moon 4°56' Cancer
corrected PF 1°03' Capricorn

As we have said before, the corrected Ascendant degree of 11th
Aquarius which is the 'regular' conception date of 12 November
1987, for 270 days, becomes clearly visible in the chart, which
cannot be said of the other two corrected degree symbols. Also, in
view of the accuracy with which royal births are normally
recorded, a corrected birthtime only 50 seconds earlier than the
official time is more likely than a birth with either a 3 minute or a
10 minute difference.

CHAPTER THIRTEEN

Paul Kruger and the Open House

Birthdate	10 October 1825
Birthplace	Bulhoek, Colesberg, South Africa, 30°S45', 25°E05' times 4m = 1h 40m 20s difference with GMT
LMT	'After sunrise'; we take sunrise = LMT 5h 31m 35s am
GMT	LMT minus 1h 40m 20s = GMT 3h 51m (15s)
RLT	5h 31m 35s am
RST	18h 46m 35s: Ascendant *Aries* inverted: *Libra* 16°32' (uncorrected), Sun 16°34' Libra, Moon 20°44' Virgo (uncorrected)
House system	Placidus.

The difference between a calculation for a southern and a northern latitude is that because we are using the tables of houses for northern latitudes, we have to invert the given positions when we are dealing with the southern side of the Equator. And therefore we have to *add or to subtract* (it makes no difference which) *12 hours* in the calculation of the ST and as a result we have to *invert the rising sign*. Also, we have to take the *opposite sign to the position of the natal Moon* when locating the ST of the Ascendant corresponding to this position.

The actual calculation for southern latitudes is a little more time-consuming than it is for northern latitudes, because it is not so easy to figure out quickly which ST and Moon position to take, since we are 'adding or subtracting 1h 40m', which is the difference in time between RLT and GMT.

As an example we turn to the birthchart of Paul Kruger:

The positions originally calculated with the White's ephemeris have been checked and corrected with the PCA Electric Ephemeris. From the birthchart we take the following basic data, needed in order to calculate the CC:

1. With 16°32' Libra rising, the natal Moon is 20°44' Virgo and the natal Sun 16°34' Libra. We draw a line from the Sun to the same degree of the opposite sign and locate the Moon at the left-hand side at the ingoing arch which

PAUL KRUGER

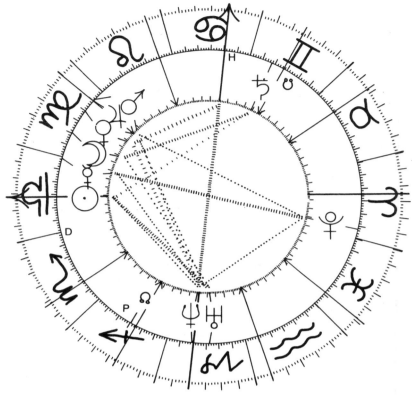

Radix				MC	10 27 Can	Sun	16 34 Lib		12
				ASC	16 34 Lib	Moon	20 44 Vir		12
PAUL KRUGER				—— Plac ——		Mercury	1 35 Lib		12
				11.	5 4 Leo	Venus	10 59 Vir		12
Date:	10 10 1825			12.	5 48 Vir	Mars	4 19 Vir		11
Time:	3 51 15	E O		2.	21 16 Sco	Jupiter	5 35 Vir		11
Latitude:	30 45 S			3.	17 18 Sag	Saturn	21 55 Gem	R	9
Longitude:	25 6 E					Uranus	16 5 Cap		4
				Node	14 47 Sag 2	Neptune	9 8 Cap		3
				Part ft	20 44 Vir 12	Pluto	2 54 Ari	R	6
						Perseph	10 27 Sag		2
Aspects: Radix/Radix		Orb:	8 0			Hermes	7 52 Can		9
						Demeter	0 18 Sco		1

MC Sxt Ven 0 32		MC Opp Nep 1 18		ASC Cnj Sun 0 0		ASC Sqr Ura 0 29
ASC Sxt Nod 1 47		Sun Tri Sat 5 22		Sun Sqr Ura 0 29		Sun Sqr Nep 7 25
Moo Sqr Sat 1 12		Moo Tri Ura 4 39		Mer Sqr Nep 7 33		Mer Opp Plu 1 18
Ven Cnj Mar 6 40		Ven Cnj Jup 5 24		Ven Tri Ura 5 5		Ven Tri Nep 1 51
Mar Cnj Jup 1 16		Mar Tri Nep 4 49		Mar qcx Plu 1 25		Jup Tri Nep 3 33
Ura Cnj Nep 6 56		Nep Sqr Plu 6 15		Nod Sxt Sun 1 47		Nod ssx Ura 1 18

means it is *waning*. The Moon is positioned above the horizontal Ascendant–Descendant axis, which means it is *above* the horizon. The scheme in Chapter 6 shows this to be the 3rd order of Bailey which says *'Moon/Descendant, longer/forwards'*.

2. We find the distance between the Moon at 20°44′ Virgo and the *Descendant* at 16°34′ Aries to be 153°, ignoring the minutes.
3. We divide this distance of 153° by 13° (the average daily motion of the Moon) = 12 degrees or days.
4. 12 days longer than 273 days (the average time of pregnancy) = 285 days.
5. 285 days subtracted from the birthdate is 29.12.1824, which is the first possible, regular date of conception. Another way of calculating is by subtracting a full year from the birthdate giving 10.10.1824; subtract 285 days (see 4) from 365 days = 80 days to be added to the date of 10.10.1824 to find the date of 29.12.1824.

Moon *above* the horizon and *waning*.

Scheme for Calculating the 3rd Order

Moon conception = Descendant or Ascendant radix
Moon radix = Descendant or Ascendant conception

Distance between the Moon 20°44′ Virgo
and the *Descendant* 17° Aries
= 153° : 13°
= 12 days *longer* than 273 days
= 285 days before the birthday
= 29.12.1824

Because of the difference with a calculation for northern latitude, the calculation scheme has to be set up in the order given here, following the numbers:

(1) CC date = ST at noon	xh xxm
(5) RLT − or +	xh xxm
(4) ST	xh xxm
(3) added to or subtracted from (2)	+ 12h 00m
(2) Ascendant natal Moon ST	xh xxm

In cases where the result of (4) is *more* than 24 hours, we subtract from it 24 hours.

According to the 3rd order of Bailey, see the first paragraph, *'Moon radix is Ascendant or Descendant conception'*, we need to know the ST of the natal Moon 20°44′ Virgo, and also (because according to the 3rd order *'or Descendant conception'*) for the opposite point of 20°44′ Pisces which can be found in the tables of houses for 30°N45′). This ST has to be interpolated in order to be accurate.

Please note that for southern latitudes we have to take the *opposite sign to the position of the natal Moon* but don't worry if you make a mistake at this point, because it only really matters if you want to calculate the conception *chart*. In the tables of houses for 30°N45′, we locate the interpolated ST of the Ascendant equal to the natal Moon, as follows:

interpolated ST of the Ascendant equal to the
opposite position of the natal Moon
= 20°44′ *Pisces* at approx. ST 17h 34m
and the opposite point, 20°44′ Virgo at approx. ST 5h 16m

Possibility (1)

1. We calculate the *ST at noon in Greenwich* by entering in our computer:

the date *29.12.1824*
GMT at noon 12h 00m
Greenwich (51°N29′ and 0°E00′)
using Placidus, gives:
Ascendant Aries 18°33′

2. From the tables of houses for *Greenwich* we locate the interpolated ST of the position of this Ascendant, as follows:

Ascendant 18°33′ Aries
rising at ST approx. 18h 31m
Moon at noon 18°42′ Aries

3. In the same way we calculate the positions of the ST at noon and the Moon at noon of the previous and the following day, in order to calculate the daily progression of the Moon:

28.12.1824
GMT noon 12h 00m
Greenwich 51°N29′ – 0°E00′
Ascendant 16°18′ Aries at
approx. ST 18h 27m
Moon at noon 6°39′ Aries

30.12.1824
GMT at noon 12h 00m
Greenwich
Ascendant 20°47′ Aries at
approx. ST 18h 35m
Moon at noon 0°58′ Taurus

4. We note down the ST at noon and the ST of the rising sign equal to the *opposite* of the position of the natal Moon and also for the second possibility of the same date, the ST of the *true* position of the natal Moon. The difference between the two sidereal times supplies the RLT, as follows:

(1) 29.12.1824 ST at noon	18h 31m	
(5) RLT	+11h 03m	
(4) ST	5h 34m	= 29h 34m minus 24h
(3) subtracted from (2)	+12h 00m	
(2) ST Ascendant *opposite* natal Moon	17h 34m (20°44′ Pisces)	

Converting the RLT into GMT we do remember that by *eastern* longitude the difference of 1h 40m between the RLT (5) and the GMT has to be *subtracted* from the RLT in case we have to *add* the RLT to the ST.

RLT (see 5)	+11h 03m	
Difference from GMT	−1h 40m	
GMT	+9h 23m	= Log. 4079
Daily motion of the Moon	12°16′	= Log. +2915
Progression of the Moon		Log. 6994 = +4°48′

Checking our computerised positions for 29.12.1824, we take the position of the Moon at noon and adjust this position by adding +4°48′ to it, which is the progression in GMT +9h 23m at the daily motion of 12°16′, which is the motion between 29 and 30 December 1824, as follows:

Moon at noon 29.12.1824	18°42′ Aries
Progression in +9h 23m	+4°48′
Corrected Descendant radix	23°30′ Aries – Ascendant 23°30′ Libra

In the tables of houses for the birthplace, latitude 30°N45′, we look up the Ascendant of the sign *opposite* the one we have calculated; 23°30′ *Aries* is rising at ST 19h 04m, which means, compared with the uncorrected ST 18h 46m 35s, a birth 19m later than the official birthtime.

> 23°30' *Aries* is rising at 30°N45' at
> approx. ST 19h 04m =
> approx. 19m later than the official time
>
> corrected LMT approx. 5h 48m 35s
> corrected natal Moon 20°54' Virgo
> corrected PF 27°50' Virgo
> *inverting the rising sign:*
> *corrected Ascendant 23°30' Libra*

Having arrived at this point, I can imagine you will feel relieved you made it so far, although perhaps with some cold perspiration on your forehead! Well, I won't blame you, it is quite a thing to do! Although I dare say, it will be possible to carry out this calculation plus the other four, still to come, in roughly speaking 30 minutes by the time you are an experienced 'conceptionist'. Now, bravely carrying on with the next calculation, which is the second option of the same date:

Possibility (2)
As before, we note down the ST at noon, but for this second option we take the ST of the position equal to the *true* position of the natal Moon, 20°44' Virgo. The difference between the two sidereal times supplies the RLT, as follows:

(1) 29.12.1824 ST at noon	18h 31m
(5) RLT	− 1h 15m
(4) ST	17h 16m
(3) added to (2)	+ 12h 00m
(2) ST Ascendant natal Moon 20°44' Virgo	5h 16m

Converting the RLT into GMT as before, we remember the difference between RLT (5) and GMT has to be *added* to the RLT because we have to *subtract* the RLT from the ST, as follows:

RLT	− 1h 15m		
Difference from GMT	+ 1h 40m		
GMT	− 2h 55m	= Log.	9153
Daily motion of the Moon	12°03	= Log.	+ 2992
Progression of the Moon		Log.	12145 = − 1°28'

We note down the position of the Moon at noon on 29.12.1824, and adjust this position by subtracting − 1°28', which is the progression in GMT − 2h 55m at the daily motion of 12°03', which is the motion between 28 and 29 December 1824, as follows:

Moon at noon 29.12.1824	18°42′ Aries
Progression in −2h 55m	−1°28′
Corrected Descendant radix	17°14′ Aries
Corrected Ascendant radix	17°14′ Libra

In the tables of houses for 30°N45′, we look up *Ascendant 17°14′* Aries, which is rising at approx. ST 18h 48m, which means a birth approx. 2m later than the official birthtime.

17°14′ *Aries* is rising at 30°N45′ at
approx. ST 18h 48m =
approx. 2m later than the official time
corrected LMT 5h 33m
corrected natal Moon 20°45′ Virgo
corrected PF 21°25′ Virgo
inverting the rising sign:
corrected Ascendant 17°14′ Libra

Possibility (3)
The calculation of the next possibility is that of 271 days, a fortnight later, 11.1.1825, and the first option of this date is calculated as follows:

1. As before, we calculate the *ST at noon for Greenwich* in order to locate the Ascendant at noon and to find in the tables of houses for Greenwich the required ST, as follows:

    11.1.1825
    GMT noon 12h 00m
    Greenwich 51°N29′, 0°E00′
    Ascendant 14°38′ Taurus
    Moon at noon 18°53′ Libra

2. From the tables of houses for Greenwich we locate the interpolated ST of the position of this Ascendant, as follows:

    Ascendant 14°38′ Taurus
    rising at approx. ST 19h 22m
    Moon at noon 18°53′ Libra

3. We note down the position of the Moon at noon at Greenwich and we also calculate in the same way the positions of the Ascendant in order to find the ST at noon, and the position of the Moon, for the previous day and for the following day, in order to calculate the daily progression of the Moon.

10.1.1825
GMT noon 12h 00m
Greenwich
Ascendant 12°51' Taurus rising at
approx. ST 19h 18m
Moon at noon 4°45' Libra

12.1.1825
GMT at noon 12h 00m
Greenwich
Ascendant 16°22' Taurus rising at
approx. ST 19h 26m
Moon 2°45' Scorpio

We note down the ST at noon and the ST of the rising sign and position equal to the opposite of the position of the natal Moon and also for the second possibility of the same date, the ST of the true position of the natal Moon. The difference between the two sidereal times supplies the RLT, as follows:

(1) 11.1.1825 ST at noon	19h 22m	
(5) RLT	+10h 12m	
(4) ST	5h 34m	(= 29h 34m − 24h)
(3) added to (2)	+12h 00m	
(2) ST Ascendant opposite natal Moon	17h 34m	(20°44' Pisces)

To convert the RLT into GMT, the difference between the RLT (5) and the GMT has to be *subtracted* from the RLT because we have to *add* the RLT to the ST, as follows:

RLT	+10h 12m	
Difference from GMT	−1h 40m	
GMT	+8h 32m	= Log. 4491
Daily motion of the Moon	13°52'	= Log. +2382
Progression of the Moon		Log. 6873 = +4°56'

We take the position of the Moon at noon on 11.1.1825 and adjust this position by adding +4°56', which is the progression in GMT +8h 32m at the daily motion of 13°52', which is the motion between 11 and 12 January 1825, as follows:

Moon at noon 11.1.1825	18°53' Libra
Progression in +8h 32m	+4°56'
Corrected Ascendant radix	23°49' Libra

In the tables of houses for 30°N45', we look up the Ascendant of the opposite sign to the one we have calculated, 23°49' *Aries*, which is rising at ST 19h 05m, which means compared with the uncorrected ST 18h 46m 35s, a birth approx. 18m later than the estimated birthtime 'after sunrise':

23°49' *Aries* is rising at 30°N45' at
approx. ST 19h 05m =
approx. 18m later than the official time,
corrected LMT approx. 5h 49m 35s
corrected natal Moon 20°54'. Virgo
corrected PF 28°09' Virgo
inverting the rising sign:
corrected Ascendant 23°49' Libra

This result is almost exactly similar to the first possibility of 285 days, 29.12.1824!

Possibility (4)

For calculating the second possibility of this date, we note down the ST of the Ascendant equal to the *true* position of the natal Moon 20°44' Virgo. The difference between the two sidereal times supplies the RLT, as follows:

(1) 11.1.1825 ST at noon		19h 22m
(5) RLT		−2h 06m
(4) ST		17h 16m
(3) added to (2)		+12h 00m
(2) ST Ascendant natal Moon Virgo 20°44'		5h 16m

Converting the RLT into GMT, we noted that by *subtracting* the RLT from the ST, we have to *add* 1h 40m to it.

RLT	−2h 06m		
Difference from GMT	+1h 40m		
GMT	−3h 46m	= Log.	8043
Daily motion of the Moon	14°08'	= Log.	+2300
Progression of the Moon		Log.	10343 = −2°13'

We take the position of the Moon at noon and adjust this position by subtracting −2°13' which is the progression in GMT −3h 46m at the daily motion of 14°08', which is the speed between 10 and 11 January 1825, as follows:

Moon at noon 11.1.1825	18°53' Libra
Progression in −3h 46m	−2°13'
Corrected Ascendant radix	16°40' Libra

In the tables of houses for 30°N45', we look up Ascendant 16°40' *Aries*, which is rising at ST approx. 18h 45m, compared with the uncorrected ST 18h 46m 35s, a birth 1m later than the official birthtime.

16°40' *Aries* is rising at 30°N45' at
approx. ST 18h 45m =
approx. 1m later than the official time
corrected LMT 5h 32m a.m.
corrected natal Moon 20°44' Virgo
corrected PF 20°50' Virgo
inverting the rising sign:
corrected Ascendant 16°40' Libra

Possibility (5)
The calculation of the last possibility of 256 days, again a fortnight later, 25.1.1825, as follows:

1. As before we calculate the *ST and the Moon position at noon* for *Greenwich* by entering in our computer the date, the GMT at noon 12h 00m, and Greenwich (51°N29' and 0°E00'), to locate the Ascendant at noon and to find the required ST in the tables of houses for Greenwich, as follows:

25.1.1825
GMT noon 12h 00m
Greenwich 51°N29' – 0°E00'
Ascendant Gemini 5°41'
Moon at noon 14°44' Aries

2. In the tables of houses for Greenwich we locate the interpolated ST of this Ascendant, as follows:

Ascendant 5°41' Gemini rising at
approx. ST 20h 18m

3. We write down the ST and the position of the Moon and we calculate in the same way also the positions of the Moon and the ST of the previous day and the following day, in order to calculate the daily progression of the Moon.

24.1.1825
GMT noon 12h 00m
Greenwich
Ascendant 4°23' Gemini rising at
approx. ST 20h 14m
Moon 2°50' Aries

26.1.1825
GMT at noon 12h 00m
Greenwich
Ascendant 6°58' Gemini rising at
approx. ST 20h 22m
Moon 26°44' Aries

4. We note down the ST of the Ascendant equal to the *opposite* position of the natal Moon 20°44' Pisces and also for the second possibility of the same date, the ST of the *true* position of the natal Moon 20°44' Virgo. The difference between the two sidereal times supplies the RLT, as follows:

(1) 25.1.1825 ST at noon	20h 17m	
(5) RLT	+9h 17m	
(4) ST (= 29h 34m minus 24h)	5h 34m	
(3) added to or substracted from (2)	+12h 00m	
(2) ST Ascendant opposite natal Moon	17h 34m (20°44' Pisces)	

Converting the RLT into GMT, remember that by *adding* the RLT to the ST, we have to *subtract* 1h 40m from the RLT:

RLT	+9h 17m	
Difference from GMT	−1h 40m	
GMT	+7h 37m = Log. 4984	
Daily motion of the Moon	12°00' = Log. +3010	
Progression of the Moon	Log. 7994 = +3°48'	

We take the position of the Moon at noon on 25.1.1825 and adjust this position by adding +3°48', which is the progression in GMT +7h 37m at the daily motion of 12°00', which is the motion between 25 and 26 January 1825, as follows:

Moon at noon 25.1.1825	14°44' Aries
Progression in +7h 37m	+3°48'
Corrected Descendant radix	18°32' Aries – Ascendant 18°32' Libra

In the tables of houses for 30°N45', we look up the Ascendant of the opposite sign, 18°32' *Aries*, which is rising at ST approx. 18h 50m, which means compared with the uncorrected ST 18h 46m 35s, a birth approx. 3½m later than the official birthtime.

18°32' *Aries* is rising at 30°N45' at
approx. ST 18h 50m =
approx. 3½m later than the official time
corrected LMT 5h 35m

corrected natal Moon 20°46' Virgo
corrected PF 22°44' Virgo
inverting the rising sign:
corrected Ascendant 18°32' Libra

The second option of this date can be ignored because the result is approx. 13th Libra which means a birth approx. ST 18h 35m = 11m before sunrise and not likely.

* * *

Because Kruger's official birthtime was vaguely given as 'after sunrise', it has been necessary to calculate all the possibilities. All of them are within a likely time margin which makes it all the more difficult to sort out which is the correct one.

Looking at the degree symbols involved, it doesn't take much imagination to decide that 18th Libra, found in the second conception possibility of 29.12.1824 (285 days), seems to have a priority, not only because it is fairly rare to find a natal Sun in exactly the same position as the Ascendant degree, which is why we have to exclude 17th Libra (CC IV, 11.1.1825, 271 days), but much more because we find the Sun in an exact ingoing square with Uranus at 16°04' Capricorn in the 4th house. This would make him determined to develop freedom in his own 'house' or in his country, into the openness and the 'hospitality', portrayed in the Janduz image of 18th Libra, and which this freedom fighter demonstrated throughout his entire life:

Janduz: 'A comfortable house, bordered with flowers, doors and windows wide open, showing a cosy and comfortable interior.'

Rudhyar: 'Two men placed under arrest are being brought to court.'

Looking at the symbol of a 'comfortable home', one thinks about Cancer and its rulers the Moon and Demeter. Cancer is on the MC, at the top of the chart, with Hermes, ruler of Gemini, at approximately 7°52', just into the 9th house. Looking at his natal Moon at 20°44' Virgo in the 12th house, the area of sacrifice, decay, abandonment and surrender, we find it shares the sign with Mars (4°19'), Jupiter (5°36') and Venus (10°59'), all of them very near the cusp of the 12th house. However, this configuration in Virgo shapes ingoing trines with Neptune (9°08') and Uranus (16°04') in Capricorn, which two planets are operating in the 4th house of the home. Because of this, a doubled degree symbol of a ruined cottage, as pictured in 17th Libra, is hard to accept. Kruger's life taken as a whole was far too distinguished to carry such a ruinous hallmark.

In another context, however, it can be seen that this quartet in

Virgo, shaping four outgoing squares with Saturn at 21°55′ Gemini, in conjunction with the south node at 14°46′, was probably responsible for the failures in his battle to stabilise a religious ideology of permanent freedom for the people of his land. In addition, the ingoing squares between the Virgo planets and Persephone, the higher ruler of Taurus, at 10°27′ Sagittarius, reiterate in a double sense the need for future growth in this area.

Neptune in the outgoing conjunction with Uranus was at the same time demanding that sacrifices be made in order that he might achieve freedom in his own house, as well as in his homeland. In fact, at the end of his life, this conjunction, with the added weight of the planets in Virgo square Saturn in Gemini, may have been the cause of his eventual exile, when, finding no international support, he had to leave home and country, to live out the remainder of his life in Switzerland.

The circuit in his chart starts with the Sun at 16°34′ Libra in conjunction with the Ascendant. In Libra one encounters unequal environmental conditions and situations, which require constant balancing, and equalising into harmonious circumstances. Particularly with the ingoing square of Uranus in Capricorn in the 4th house, one would have to encounter the opposite of freedom and openness – constraint – and in Capricorn, cramping restriction and limitation (not to say slavery), to be converted into freedom. It is an interesting fact that the first signs of the system which since 1948 has been called 'apartheid', became visible (when it was made extremely difficult for natives to be naturalised and to vote), during the sixteen years he was the President of the Republic of Transvaal, and this is something the whole world still finds difficult to accept, placing this country, rightly or wrongly, into a distinct, separated position, set apart. It is also fascinating to discover that the whole subject is encapsulated in Paul Kruger's chart. In this connection it has to be said that although his Sun has a strong trine with Saturn, ruler of Capricorn, in Gemini, Saturn conjunct the leaking South node shows a moral approach split into good and evil, black and white, causing an almost schizophrenic duality. Tragically and ironically there was no freedom at the end of his personal life, and observing the events since 1900, there has been little freedom in his country either. The second image of 18th Libra shows why.

The Sun in Libra induces the ruler of Libra, Venus, which we find at 10°59′ Virgo and shares the presence and influences of Mars, Jupiter and the Moon, as we mentioned earlier on, in heavy squares with Saturn in Gemini, the task being to achieve balance in a morally responsible sense, while encountering heavy political resistance from foreign governments. Saturn in Gemini in the 9th house conjunct the south node at 14°46' implies a dirty karmic mark to be wiped out. The second image of 15th Gemini:

'Two Dutch children are studying their lessons together.'

Clearly we have spotted an interesting facet of the South African case, a heavy karmic weight (Saturn) carried not only by Kruger personally but also by the collective souls of both the South African and the Dutch nations, for whom he was the intermediary (see Hermes in the 8th of Cancer, the sign which rules Holland), something which unfortunately is not yet recognised and accepted by those involved.

The line from Libra leads straight away to the difficult position of Venus in the 12th house, stressing the impulse to sacrifice and to suffer, and then moves back to Mercury, ruler of Virgo, conjunct the Sun. In fact this is all the circuit has to offer, and it will not have been easy to reach and integrate the other planets. The course of his life shows clearly in how much he has managed to reach out for those qualities, his solar centre being at stake in a tremendous, tense trial in the battle for independence. His Pluto at 2°54' Aries in opposition with the Sun, signifies part of the solar task to grow into the requisite freedom (Sun ingoing square Uranus) and how his failure came to be seen as momentous writing on the walls of the as yet unformed United Nations, an unanswered cry for recognition and the right to exist, to be recognised as a nation.

All the energy derived from the oppositions between the Sun in conjunction with the Ascendant and Pluto, drove him towards the harmonising of chaotic and obstructive situations. Although he did indeed make whatever sacrifices were necessary, he had to endure the painful experience of seeing his solar energy burn away like the smoke from burning sacrifices, into 'nothing'. But was it nothing, or is it true that all his and other people's suffering, including that of the coloured people, will be transformed into Glory at some future time? Venus particularly, and the other planets in Virgo, shape outgoing squares with Saturn in Gemini in the 9th house, and an ingoing trine with Neptune in Capricorn in addition. It must have been enormously disappointing to see how, in spite of all the efforts made, freedom was constantly eroded and the soil washed away from under his feet, and how the sacrifices on behalf of freedom and openness had to overcome obstacles, hard as a rock. Is it not true that only a morality and a conscience which is as clear as crystal, can successfully resist the black forces which want to take away freedom? In this context I don't mean black people, but rather the forces of darkness which always appear where gold and diamonds, outcrystallised light, are found in abundance. In cases where moral sense is insufficient, or lacking altogether, Hermes in Cancer (induced by Saturn in Gemini), can only cause bitter life circumstances, providing a difficult road to self-knowledge. It is doubtful how far Kruger learned his personal lessons.

It may have been the grand dream of a great leader, expressing the quality of his own personality, to turn a ruined cottage (his Sun degree,) into a beautiful open and hospitable home (his personality symbol of 18th Libra) projected to and reflected by a paradisial country. When van Riebeeck, on behalf of the Dutch East Indian Company, officially started a Dutch settlement, they arrived in a country where no living soul was to be found, not even a black-skinned Adam. From 1795, oppressed by English invaders, the Boers were gradually forced to move to the North. In 1835 the Great Trek began and Kruger as a little boy, was part of it. Crossing hitherto empty country, they encountered hostile Bantu tribes, Zulus, Xhosas and others, originating from central Africa, by ill chance moving south at the same time as the Trekkers moved north and also searching for fresh fields for their cattle – a basic conflict began which is still unresolved nowadays. As we know the British also claimed those new areas and in the end the Boers were forced to bow the knee again, and the way this was achieved was abominable and disgusting. We find Kruger constantly trying to harmonise these conflicting parties. His Sun in conjunction with the Ascendant in Libra, opposition his Pluto in Aries, endowed him with heroic power. During one of those bloody confrontations with the Zulus, Kruger alone, and with great risk to his own life, retrieved the body of General-Commander Potgieter, who had been killed in the battle, right out of the Zulu fortresses.

Checking the authenticity of the corrected birthtime, I looked at the events in October 1900, when Paul Kruger was forced to leave his country in order to find help in a hopeless and tragic situation, caused by the overwhelming pressure of Imperial Britain, and I found the following substantial evidence for the 18th degree.

His progressions for 1.10.1900 show quite extraordinary things, such as his progressed Ascendant at 9°35' Capricorn, in an exact conjunction with his natal Neptune, which is positioned sharply at the edge of the 4th house, symbolising his home and his country, so that we are not surprised to find that he actually had to leave, both in a political, and in a physical sense.

Most extraordinary of all, his progressed Mercury, ruler of his 9th and 12th houses, had reached the position of 17°27' Capricorn, square his Ascendant. One who is familiar with the Sabian symbols, immediately knows the reason why he literally sailed away aboard the warship *Gelderland*, graciously sent by Her Majesty Queen Wilhelmina of the Netherlands (CC Ascendant 16th Aquarius) who was the only one in the whole world willing to help this extremely brave fighter for freedom and independence. The only difference from this image was that, ironically, it was not the Union Jack, flying from a British warship as is pictured by Rudhyar, but the proud flag of another free country whose people are of the same breed as the Afrikaner Boers.

18th CAPRICORN

'The Union Jack flag flies from a new British destroyer.'

Looking at his progressed chart for 1.10.1900 we find an 18th degree four times. I consider this to be a strong confirmation of the validity of his corrected Ascendant degree. We find the Moon at 17°29' Gemini, and Saturn at 17°22' Gemini, trine the Ascendant, Mercury at 17°27'℞Capricorn square to it, and Mars at 17°56' Libra in conjunction with it.

Before we can begin to understand what is really going on in South Africa, we should investigate much more, and we will find 18th degrees everywhere. If we look at the date of the Dutch settlement in the Cape for instance, by pioneering Jan van Riebeeck, on 6.4.1652, we find the Sun in 18th Aries and Venus in 18th Taurus. Surprisingly we will also find 18th degrees in the charts of several prominent people involved in contemporary South African politics. The chart of the founding of the Union of South Africa on 31 May 1910, in Cape Town, at 12h 00m noon, shows Neptune at 17°36' Cancer. There are more examples, like the great defender of the case of the Boers, General Jan Smuts with Mars and Pluto in the 18th of Taurus, the Most Reverend Desmond Tutu, Archbishop of South Africa with Uranus in the 18th of Aries, Mr Matthijs Botha with Saturn in the 18th of Gemini and Mr Pieter Botha with his progressed Uranus in the 18th of Aquarius from 1961 till 1985 which, while extremely interesting, and well worth working out in more detail, is of course a subject in itself, and not possible to pursue in this book. However, it forms a clear example of the theory which we touched on in Chapter 1, the cosmic tasks undertaken by a number of people who share a particular degree number, in this case the 18th degrees, albeit in different signs. We came across a series of 15th degrees in the circumstances surrounding Bacon's life, which serves to draw our attention to a completely different, but equally compelling problem. We also came across the 18th degree of Capricorn in Chapter 8, dealing with Rodin, and I think we have found one of the answers. The split, as we extensively examined in that chapter, occurs also in the case of South Africa with the appearance of apartheid. Perhaps the world's commentators have something further to look at, something which could at least further an understanding of what is happening over there.

Paul Kruger died in Switzerland on 14 July 1904. We find an 18th degree twice, Venus in 17°48' Sagittarius and Saturn in 17°06' Gemini, exactly on the cusps of the 3rd and 9th houses. Intuitively working through the basic problem of the 18th degrees, Paul Kruger with his corrected Ascendant 18th Libra certainly contributed physically not only to defining the tensely contrasting opposites which are inherent in Gemini, but also to constructing the idealistic pathways by which they can be reconciled.

CHAPTER FOURTEEN

Daniel Barenboim and the Lit-Up Forge

Name	Daniel Barenboim
Birthdate	15.11.1942 (AST but Daily Saving Time),
Birthplace	Buenos Aires (Argentina) 34°S36′, 58°W27′
LMT	11h 35m am (source: *Astrological Journal*, July 1989.)
GMT	14h 35m pm (Shanks: +3 hours)
RLT	10h 41m 12s am
RST	2h 15m 19s = uncorrected Ascendant 13°48′ Leo; inverted Aquarius; uncorrected Moon 26°39′ Aquarius, Sun 22°37′ Scorpio.

The calculation of a birth for a southern latitude but *western* longitude, as would be the case in South American countries such as Argentina, Peru, Brazil and Chile or, for instance, in the Falkland Islands, will be exemplified with the conception correction of the birthchart of the well-known conductor Daniel Barenboim, born in Buenos Aires in Argentina.

In comparison with Paul Kruger's conception correction, the difference in calculation occurs in the conversion of the RLT into GMT (GMT is *later* than RLT) which has to be carried out by the same method which we use for any birth for a western longitude, as for instance in the cases of Bacon, Baden Powell and HRH the Princess of York.

Checking the difference in time between the given birthtime and the time of the corrected Ascendant, we have to be aware that for southern latitudes, it is not Aquarius, Pisces and Aries which are the fast-rising signs but conversely the signs of Leo, Virgo and Libra. This is of importance when considering the margin of 15 minutes before or after the given birthtime. For northern latitudes these signs are rising approximately one degree per four minutes in time, while for southern latitudes this can be 2½ degrees in the same length of time, which is the case in northern latitudes with the signs of Aquarius to Aries. We wonder if this concept of conversion could be applied to the interpretation of the birthchart as well.

Reminding ourselves what is said in the Trutine of Hermes, we locate the following basic facts:

From the birthchart we take the following basic data, needed in order to calculate the CC:

1. With 13°48' Aquarius rising, the natal Moon is 26°39' Aquarius and the natal Sun 22°37' Scorpio. We draw a line from the Sun to the same degree of the opposite sign, Taurus, and locate the Moon at the right-hand side of the outgoing arch, which means it is *waxing*. The Moon is positioned below the horizontal axis of Ascendant and Descendant, which means it is below the horizon. The scheme in Chapter 6 shows this to be the 1st order of Bailey, which says 'Moon/Ascendant, longer/forwards'.

2. We find the distance between the Moon in 27th Aquarius and the *Ascendant* in the 14th Aquarius to be 13°, ignoring the minutes.

3. We divide this distance of 13° by 13° (the average daily motion of the Moon) = 1 (day).

4. 1 day longer than 273 days (the average time of pregnancy) = 274 days.

5. 274 days subtracted from the birthdate, 15.11.1942 = 14.2.1942, which is the first possible regular date of conception. Another way of calculating is by subtracting a full year from the birthdate giving 15.11.1941; subtract 274 days (see 4) from 365 days = 91 days to be added to the date of 15.11.1941 to find the date of 14.2.1942.

6. According to the 1st order of Bailey, see the first paragraph, *'Moon Radix is Ascendant or Descendant Conception'*, we normally need to know the interpolated ST of the natal Moon 26°39' Aquarius, and also the ST of the opposite point of 26°39' Leo, which can be found in the tables of houses for 34° *North* 36', but note that for *southern* latitude we have to take the *opposite sign of the position of the natal Moon*, i.e. Leo, and for the 2nd option the *true position*, i.e. Aquarius. Don't worry if we make a mistake at this point, because it only really matters if one wants to calculate the conception chart. In the tables of houses for 34°*North*36', we locate the interpolated ST of the Ascendant equal to the natal Moon, as follows:

interpolated ST of the Ascendant equal to the
opposite position of the natal Moon
= 26°39' *Leo* at approx. ST 3h 20m
and the true position of 26°39' *Aquarius* at approx. ST 16h 30m

Moon *below* the horizon and *waxing*

Scheme for Calculating the First Order

Moon conception = Descendant or Ascendant radix
Moon Radix = Descendant or Ascendant conception

Distance between the Moon (26°39′ Aquarius)
and the *Ascendant* (13°48′ Aquarius)
= 13° : 13°
= 1 day *longer* than 273 days
= 274 days before the birthday
= *14.2.1942 regular*

Because of the difference with a calculation for northern latitude, the calculation scheme has to be set up in the order given here, following the numbers, in the same way that we did in the case of Paul Kruger's CC:

(1) CC date = ST at noon		xh xxm
(5) RLT − or +		xh xxm
(4) ST		xh xxm
(3) added to or subtracted from (2)		+12h 00m
(2) Ascendant natal Moon ST		xh xxm

In this case we notice that the difference between RLT and GMT is 3h 53m 48s (3h 54m), which is the result of 58°*West*27′ multiplied by 4′. This result is *later than RLT* (see 5). For *western* longitudes we have to *add* this result to the RLT in cases where the difference between RLT and GMT is a *plus*, and to *subtract* from the RLT in cases where this is a *minus*.

As an exercise I would like to leave the reader to calculate the actual CC, but I will give the results of this conception correction which are as follows:

Summary of Possibilities

Date	No. days	CC	ST	Time difference	PF	☽
14/2	274	11°54′ ♒	2h 08m	7m earlier	15°52′ ♉	26°35′ ♒
1/2	288	12°37′ ♒	2h 12m	2½′ earlier	16°38′ ♉	26°38′ ♒
1/3	260	14°09′ ♒	2h 18m	2½′ later	18°12′ ♉	26°40′ ♒

Because the birthtime is pretty accurate at 25 minutes before noon, I think we can dismiss the first possibility of 7 minutes earlier, but only 2½ minutes earlier or later is very well possible. Examining the birthchart I am inclined to accept the third option of the 15th degree of Aquarius and in particular if we look at the strong positions and aspects of for instance the Sun and Venus in Scorpio and Jupiter in Cancer.

In this case we assumed that the conception indeed took place in Buenos Aires but of course, it could have been in England. Although it is hard to believe that in the middle of World War II people were sailing to Argentina.

* * *

15th AQUARIUS

Janduz: 'A lit-up forge. A man comes out of the opening, built of stone, with a torch in his hand giving a beautiful flame.'

Rudhyar: 'Two love-birds on a fence sing out their pure happiness.'

CHAPTER FIFTEEN

Baden Powell and the Archer of the Sun

Name	Lord Robert Stephenson Smyth Baden-Powell
Birthdate	22.2.1857
Birthplace	London (England) 51°N31', 0°W06'
LMT = GT = RLT	Approx. 6h 21m 30s am (time calculated from No. 837 in Leo's *1001 Nativities* which gives 'Ascendant Aquarius 12°') although there is another birthtime of 6h 00m am (Archives Koppejan).
RST	16h 30m (Ascendant 11°58' Aquarius, uncorrected), natal Sun 3°38' Pisces, natal Moon 4°21' Aquarius.

The conception correction of a fast rising sign such as Aquarius presents many more possibilities than a slow rising sign such as Leo, which makes it much harder to determine the right degree. In this case we find at least nine possibilities.

From the birthchart we take the following basic data, needed in order to calculate the CC:

1. With 12th Aquarius rising, the natal Moon is at 4°21' Aquarius and the natal Sun at 3°38' Pisces. We draw a line from the Sun to the same degree of the opposite sign and locate the Moon at the left-hand side at the ingoing arch which means the Moon is *waning*. The Moon is positioned above the horizontal axis of Ascendant and Descendant, which means the Moon is *above* the horizon. The scheme in Chapter 6 shows this to be the *3rd Order* of Bailey which says '*Moon/Descendant, longer/forwards*'.

2. We find the distance between the Moon in 5th Aquarius and the *Descendant* in 12th Leo to be 172°, ignoring the minutes.

3. We divide this distance of 172° by 13° (the average daily motion of the Moon) = 13° or days.

LORD BADEN-POWELL

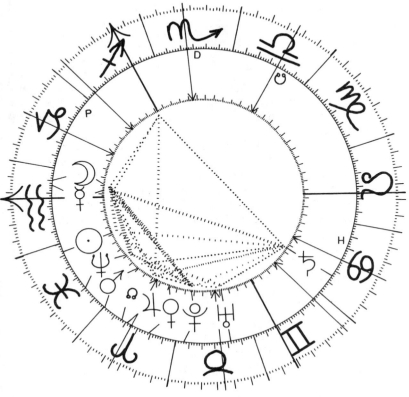

Radix		MC	9	5	Sag		Sun	3	38	Pis		1
		ASC	11	58	Aqu		Moon	4	21	Aqu		12
LORD BADEN-POWELL		──	Plac	──			Mercury	6	58	Aqu		12
		11.	26	40	Sag		Venus	19	57	Ari		2
Date:	22 2 1857	12.	15	2	Cap		Mars	29	57	Pis		1
Time:	6 21 30 E O	2.	12	35	Ari		Jupiter	10	48	Ari		1
Latitude:	51 31 N	3.	17	24	Tau		Saturn	7	29	Can	R	5
Longitude:	0 6 W						Uranus	21	17	Tau		3
		Node	8	2	Ari 1		Neptune	19	30	Pis		1
		Part ft	12	41	Cap 11		Pluto	3	54	Tau		2
							Perseph	29	22	Sag		11
Aspects: Radix/Radix	Orb:	8 0					Hermes	23	35	Can		6
							Demeter	12	52	Sco		8

MC	Sxt	Mer	2 6	MC	Tri	Jup	1 43	MC	qcx	Sat	1 35	MC	Tri	Nod	1 3
ASC	Sxt	Jup	1 10	Sun	ssx	Moo	0 43	Sun	ssq	Ven	1 19	Sun	Tri	Sat	3 51
Sun	Sxt	Plu	0 16	Moo	Cnj	Mer	2 38	Moo	Sxt	Mar	4 23	Moo	ssq	Nep	0 10
Moo	Sqr	Plu	0 27	Mer	Sxt	Jup	3 50	Mer	qcx	Sat	0 31	Mer	Sqr	Plu	3 5
Ven	ssx	Ura	1 20	Ven	ssx	Nep	0 26	Mar	Sqr	Sat	7 32	Jup	Sqr	Sat	3 19
Sat	ssq	Ura	1 13	Sat	Sxt	Plu	3 36	Ura	Sxt	Nep	1 46	Nep	ssq	Plu	0 37
Nod	Sxt	Mer	1 4	Nod	Cnj	Jup	2 46	Nod	Sqr	Sat	0 33	Nod	ssq	Ura	1 45

4. 13 days longer than 273 days (the average time of pregnancy) = 286 days.
5. 286 days subtracted from the birthdate 22 February 1857 = 10 May 1856, which is the first possible, regular date of conception. Another way of calculating is by subtracting a full year from the birthdate giving 22 February 1856; subtract 286 days (see 4) from 365 days = 79 days to be added to the date of 22 February 1856 to find the date of 10 May 1856.
6. According to the 3rd order of Bailey, see the first paragraph, *'Moon radix is Ascendant or Descendant conception'*, we need to know the ST of the natal Moon (4°21′ Aquarius), and also of the opposite point of 4°21′ Leo which can be found in the tables of houses for London. This ST has to be interpolated in order to be accurate.

Scheme to Calculate the 3rd Order

Moon conception = Descendant or Ascendant radix
Moon radix = Ascendant or Descendant conception

Distance between the Moon and the Descendant = 172°:13 = 13 days longer than 273 days
= 286 days before the birthdate = 10.5.1856
(conception presumably London)

We have to calculate also the next possibilities:

14 days forwards = 272 days = 24.5.1856
14 days forwards = 258 days = 6.6.1856

In the tables of houses for London 51°N31′ we locate the

interpolated ST of the Ascendant equal to the
position of the natal Moon Aquarius 4°21′ at ST approx. 16h 11m
and its opposite point 4°21′ Leo at approx. ST 0h 43m

The calculation of this first conception possibility, which is 10 May 1856, of 286 days, is as follows:

Possibility (1)
From the ephemeris we take the ST at noon and find in the tables of houses the interpolated ST of the Ascendant equal to the position of the natal Moon and also for the second possibility of the same date, the ST of its opposite point. The difference between the two sidereal times supplies the RLT, as follows:

ST 10 May at noon	3h 14m
RLT	+12h 57m
ST Moon 4°21' Aquarius	16h 11m

Because the difference in time between RLT and GMT is only 24 seconds, there is no need to convert the RLT into GMT and we calculate the progression of the conception Moon in GMT +12h 57m by using diurnal proportional logarithms, to be found in the ephemeris, as follows:

RLT = GMT	+12h 57m	= Log.	2679
Daily motion of the Moon	12°21'	= Log.	+2885
Progression of the Moon		Log.	5564 = +6°40'

Checking the ephemeris for 10 May 1856, we take the position of the Moon at noon and we adjust this position by adding to it the progression in +12h 57m at a daily motion of 12°21', which is the motion between 10 and 11 May = +6°40', as follows:

Moon 10 May at noon	4°30' Leo
Progression in +12h 57m	+6°40'
Corrected Descendant radix	11°10' Leo
Corrected Ascendant radix	11°10' Aquarius

Ascendant Aquarius 11°10' is rising at 51°N31' at
approx. ST 16h 28m
approx. 2m earlier
than the official time
corrected LMT 6h 19m am
corrected natal Moon 4°20' Aquarius
corrected PF 11°52' Capricorn

The calculation of the second option of this conception date is as follows:

Possibility (2)
From the ephemeris we take the same ST at noon at 10 May, but now we take the interpolated ST of the Ascendant equal to the *opposite* position of the natal Moon, 4°21' Leo. The difference between the two sidereal times supplies the RLT, as follows:

ST 10 May at noon	3h 14m
RLT	−2h 31m
ST opposite Moon 4°21' Leo	0h 43m

Because the difference in time between RLT and GMT is 24 seconds, there is no need to convert the RLT into GMT, and we calculate the progression of the conception Moon in GMT

– 2h 31m by using diurnal proportional logarithms, to be found in the ephemeris, as follows:

RLT = GMT   – 2h 31m = Log.   9794
Daily motion of the Moon   12°40′   = Log. + 2775
Progression of the Moon   Log.   12569   =   – 1°20′

Checking the ephemeris for 10 May, we take the position of the Moon at noon and we adjust this position by subtracting from it the progression in – 2h 31m at a daily motion of 12°40′, which is the motion between 9 and 10 May = – 1°20′, as follows:

Moon 10 May 1856 at noon   4°30′ Leo
Progression in – 2h 31m   – 1°20′
Corrected Descendant radix   3°10′ Leo
Corrected Ascendant radix   3°10′ Aquarius

Ascendant 3°10′ Aquarius is rising at 51°N31′ at
approx. ST 16h 08m
approx. 22m earlier
than the official time
corrected LMT 5h 59m am
corrected natal Moon 4°09′ Aquarius
corrected PF 3°41′ Capricorn

For the calculation of the next option of the same conception date, we had better take the next day, 11 May, as follows:

Possibility (3)
From the ephemeris we take the ST at noon at 11 May, and take the ST of the Ascendant equal to the *opposite* position of the natal Moon, 4°21′ Leo, as follows:

ST 11 May 1856 at noon   3h 18m
RLT   – 2h 35m
ST opposite Moon 4°21′ Leo   0h 43m

Because the difference in time between RLT and GMT is 24 seconds, there is no need to convert the RLT into GMT, and we calculate the progression of the conception Moon in GMT – 2h 35m by using diurnal proportional logarithms, to be found in the ephemeris, as follows:

RLT   – 2h 35m = Log.   9680
Daily motion of the Moon   12°21′   = Log. + 2885
Progression of the Moon   Log.   12565   = – 1°20′

Checking the ephemeris for 11 May, we take the position of the Moon at noon and we adjust this position by subtracting from it the progression in −2h 35m at a daily motion of 12°21', which is the motion between 10 and 11 May, = −1°20', as follows:

Moon 11 May at noon	16°51' Leo
Progression in −2h 35m	−1°20'
Corrected Descendant radix	15°31' Leo
Corrected Ascendant radix	15°31' Aqu · us

Ascendant 15°31' Aquarius is rising at 51°N31' at
approx. ST 16h 38m
approx. 8m later
than the official time
corrected LMT 6h 29m am
corrected natal Moon 4°25' Aquarius
corrected PF 16°18' Capricorn

The next conception date is 14 days forwards to 24 May = 272 days, as follows:

Possibility (4)
From the ephemeris we take the ST at noon and note down the interpolated ST of the Ascendant equal to the position of the natal Moon and also for the second possibility of the same date, the ST of its opposite point. The difference between the two sidereal times supplies the RLT. As we will see, this date will supply us with three options to be calculated, as follows:

ST 24.5.1856 at noon	4h 09m
RLT	+12h 02m
ST Moon 4°21' Aquarius	16h 11m

Because the difference in time between RLT and GMT is 24 seconds, there is no need to convert the RLT into GMT, and we calculate the progression of the conception Moon in GMT +12h 02m by using diurnal proportional logarithms, to be found in the ephemeris, as follows:

RLT = GMT	+12h 02m	= Log.	2998
Daily motion of the Moon	13°42'	= Log.	+2435
Progression of the Moon		Log.	5433 = +6°52'

Checking the ephemeris for 24 May 1856, we take the position of the Moon at noon and we adjust this position by adding to it the progression in +12h 02m at a daily motion of 13°42', which is the motion between 24 and 25 May = +6°52', as follows:

Moon at noon 24.5.1856	28°13' Capricorn
Progression in +12h 02m	+6°52'
Corrected Ascendant radix	5°05' Aquarius

Ascendant Aquarius 5°05' is rising at 51°N31' at
approx. ST 16h 12m
approx. 18m earlier
than the official time
= LMT 6h 03m am
corrected natal Moon 4°11' Aquarius
corrected PF 5°38' Capricorn

For the calculation of the second option we had better take the next day 25 May, in order to be able to subtract from the Moon position of the same date, as follows:

Possibility (5)
From the ephemeris we take the ST at noon of 25 May and the interpolated ST of the Ascendant equal to the *opposite* position of the natal Moon, 4°21' Leo, the difference between the two sidereal times supplies the RLT, as follows:

ST 25 May at noon	4h 13m
RLT = GMT	−3h 30m
ST 4°21' Leo	0h 43m

Because the difference in time between RLT and GMT is 24 seconds, there is no need to convert the RLT into GMT, and we calculate the progression of the conception Moon in GMT −3h 30m by using diurnal proportional logarithms, to be found in the ephemeris, as follows:

RLT = GMT	−3h 30m = Log.	8361	
Daily motion of the Moon	13°42' = Log.	+2435	
Progression of the Moon	Log.	10796 =	−2°00'

Checking the ephemeris for 25 May 1856, we take the position of the Moon at noon and we adjust this position by subtracting from it the progression in −3h 30m at a daily speed of 13°42', which is the speed between 24 and 25 May = −2°00', as follows:

Moon at noon 25 May	11°55' Aquarius
Progression in −3h 30m	−2°00'
Corrected Ascendant radix	9°55' Aquarius

Ascendant 9°55' Aquarius is rising at 51°N31' at
approx. ST 16h 25m
approx. 5m earlier
than the official time
corrected LMT 6h 16m am
corrected natal Moon 4°18' Aquarius
corrected PF 10°35' Capricorn

There is also a third possibility of the same date, 25 May, as follows:

Possibility (6)
From the ephemeris we take the ST at noon at 25 May, and we take the same ST of the Ascendant equal to the position of the natal Moon, as follows:

ST 25 May at noon	4h 13m
RLT	+11h 58m
ST Moon 4°21' Aquarius	16h 11m

Because the difference in time between RLT and GMT is 24 seconds, there is no need to convert the RLT into GMT, and we calculate the progression of the conception Moon in GMT +11h 58m by using diurnal proportional logarithms, to be found in the ephemeris, as follows:

RLT = GMT	+11h 58m	= Log. 3022
Daily motion of the Moon	13°53'	= Log. +2377
Progression of the Moon		Log. 5399 = +6°55'

Checking the ephemeris for 25 May, we take the position of the Moon at noon and we adjust this position by adding to it the progression in +11h 58m at a daily motion of 13°53', which is the motion between 25 and 26 May = +6°55', as follows:

Moon 25 May at noon	11°55' Aquarius
Progression in +11h 58m	+6°55'
Corrected Ascendant radix	18°50' Aquarius

Ascendant 18°50' Aquarius is rising at 51°N31' at
approx. ST 16h 45m
approx. 15m later
than the official time
corrected LMT 6h 36m am
corrected natal Moon 4°29' Aquarius
corrected PF 19°41' Capricorn

The calculation of the next conception date, *6 June 1856 (258 days)*, also gives us three options to work out, as follows:

Possibility (7)
From the ephemeris we take the ST at noon and find in the tables of houses the interpolated ST of the Ascendant equal to the position of the natal Moon and also for the second possibility of the same date, the ST of its opposite point. The difference between the two sidereal times supplies the RLT, as follows:

ST 6 June 1856 at noon	5h 00m
RLT	+11h 11m
ST Moon 4°21' Aquarius	16h 11m

Because the difference in time between RLT and GMT is 24 seconds, there is no need to convert the RLT into GMT, and we calculate the progression of the conception Moon in GMT +11h 11m by using diurnal proportional logarithms, to be found in the ephemeris, as follows:

RLT = GMT	+11h 11m	= Log.	3316
Daily motion of the Moon	12°40'	= Log.	+2775
Progression of the Moon		Log.	6091 = +5°54'

Checking the ephemeris for 6 June, we take the position of the Moon at noon and we adjust this position by adding to it the progression in +11h 11m at a daily motion of 12°40', which is the speed between 6 and 7 June, = +5°54', as follows:

Moon 6 June at noon	29°50' Cancer
Progression in +11h 11m	+5°54'
Corrected Descendant radix	5°44' Leo
Corrected Ascendant radix	5°44' Aquarius

Ascendant 5°44' Aquarius is rising at 51°N31' at
approx. ST 16h 14m
approx. 16m earlier
than the official time
corrected LMT 6h 05m am
corrected natal Moon 4°13' Aquarius
corrected PF 6°19' Capricorn

For the calculation of the second option of the same conception date, we take the next day, 7 June, as follows:

Possibility (8)
From the ephemeris we take the ST at noon and the interpolated ST of the Ascendant equal to the *opposite* position of the natal Moon:

ST 7 June at noon	5h 04m
RLT	−4h 21m
ST opposite Moon 4°21' Leo	0h 43m

Because the difference in time between RLT and GMT is 24 seconds, there is no need to convert the RLT into GMT, and we calculate the progression of the conception Moon in GMT

−4h 21m by using diurnal proportional logarithms, to be found in the ephemeris, as follows:

RLT = GMT	−4h 21m	= Log.	7417
Daily motion of the Moon	12°40′	= Log.	2775
Progression of the Moon		Log. 10192	= −2°18′

Checking the ephemeris for 7 June, we take the position of the Moon at noon and we adjust this position by subtracting the progression in −4h 21m at a daily motion of 12°40′, which is the speed between 6 and 7 June = −2°18′, as follows:

Moon 7 June at noon	12°30′ Leo
Progression in −4h 21m	−2°18′
Corrected Descendant Radix	10°12′ Leo
Corrected Ascendant Radix	10°12′ Aquarius

Ascendant 10°12′ Aquarius is rising at 51°N31′ at
approx. ST 16h 25m
approx. 5m earlier
than the official time
corrected LMT 6h 16m am
corrected natal Moon 4°18′ Aquarius
corrected PF 10°52′ Capricorn

The calculation of the third and last option of this conception date is as follows:

Possibility (9)
From the ephemeris we take the ST at noon at 7 June, and the interpolated ST of the Ascendant equal to the true position of the natal Moon, 4°21′ Aquarius, the difference between the two sidereal times supplies the RLT, as follows:

ST 7 June at noon	5h 04m
RLT	+11h 07m
ST Moon 4°21′ Aquarius	16h 11m

Because the difference in time between RLT and GMT is 24 seconds, there is no need to convert the RLT into GMT, and we calculate the progression of the conception Moon in GMT +11h 07m by using diurnal proportional logarithms, to be found in the ephemeris, as follows:

RLT	+11h 07m	= Log.	3342
Daily motion of the Moon	12°22′	= Log.	+2880
Progression of the Moon		Log. 6222	= +5°44′

Checking the ephemeris for 7 June, we take the position of the Moon at noon and we adjust this position by adding to it the progression in +11h 07m at a daily motion of 12°22', which is the speed between 7 and 8 June = +5°44', as follows:

Moon 7 June at noon	12°30' Leo
Progression in +11h 07m	+5°44'
Corrected Descendant radix	18°14' Leo
Corrected Ascendant radix	18°14' Aquarius

Ascendant 18°14' Aquarius is rising at 51°N31' at
approx. ST 16h 44m
approx. 14m later
than the official time
corrected LMT 6h 35m am
corrected natal Moon 4°28' Aquarius
corrected PF 19°04' Capricorn

Summary of Possibilities

Date	No. days	CC	PF	ST	Time difference	☽
10/5	286	11°10' ♒	11°52' ♑	16h 28m	2m earlier	4°20' ♒
		3°10' ♒	3°41' ♑	16h 08m	22m earlier	4°09' ♒
11/5	285	15°31' ♒	16°18' ♑	16h 38m	8m later	4°25' ♒
24/5	272	5°05' ♒	5°38' ♑	16h 12m	18m earlier	4°11' ♒
25/5	271	9°55' ♒	10°35' ♑	16h 25m	5m earlier	4°18' ♒
		18°50' ♒	19°41' ♑	16h 45m	15m later	4°29' ♒
6/6	258	5°44' ♒	6°19' ♑	16h 14m	16m earlier	4°13' ♒
7/6	257	10°12' ♒	10°52' ♑	16h 25m	5m earlier	4°18' ♒
		18°14' ♒	19°04' ♑	16h 44m	14m later	4°28' ♒

These calculations make it clear, that sometimes it is easier to take the conception day before or after the calculated date, in order to be able to subtract from or to add to the difference between RLT and GMT from the Moon position.

In this case the official birthtime was approx. 6h 21m (based upon an 'Ascendant of 12th Aquarius') but another birthtime of 6h 00m (see CC IV of 18m earlier, 6th Aquarius) has also been given and therefore it is advisable to calculate all the conception possibilities, since even the 18m and 22m later have to be considered as possible.

Working out which corrected Ascendant degree is the true one in such a case is not easy, and we must consider the degree symbols for verification. Let us therefore consider the main features of his life, and see whether the postulated images confirm the personality of this famous man.

Colonel Lord Baden-Powell was known as the hero of Mafeking, a small town in the Cape province of Southern Africa, which, under his command, survived a seven-month siege by the Boers led by General Cronjé, in the winter of 1899/1900. Also called 'The Wolf who Never Sleeps', he was an active army officer whose assignment was the training of police officers in South Africa.

Having learned field-craft from the Zulus, he wrote a manual for army reconnaissance patrols, called *Aids for Scouting*. News of his methods filtered back to England, where they were adopted by English youngsters, who formed themselves into groups to practise scouting, and this came as a big surprise to Baden-Powell. Noticing the effect it had, however, he organised a trial camp on Brownsea Island in 1908, and wrote his book *Scouting for Boys*. This was very much along the lines of Seton's manual for the North American youth movement called the 'Woodcraft Indians', which in turn was based on the methods of the Canadian fur-trappers, and the North American Indians. It romanticised the idea of the lonely tracker in the woods of Canada and North America, copying the primitive and hard life of the trappers and Indians, constantly alert for bears, wolves and other dangers, and having to find the way through the wilderness, alone and self-sufficient by day, dreaming by a campfire at night. We can imagine Old Shatterhand with his Winchester outmanoeuvring the grizzly bears. Good stuff for young boys! Baden-Powell's idea originally was to strengthen the inexperienced young men who arrived to serve in the army straight from English public schools, to teach them the first lessons in survival and to harden them up. He successfully adapted this idea to the needs of their younger brethren at home. In addition, he intended to shape a movement of peace and brotherhood, and this impulse was taken up worldwide.

Who does not remember his first smoky and half-burned 'loaf' of bread, cooked on his own hand-cut stick! And how proud we were of the first badges we successfully achieved! And the huge bonfires in the night, surrounded by hundreds of youngsters, singing their well-known songs accompanied by guitars. Scouts and pioneers dedicated to the ideals of brotherhood and service. Happy memories of times spent in nature and solving the typical problems involved in doing so.

Baden-Powell's chart shows a Sun at 3°38' Pisces ingoing conjunct with the higher ruler of Pisces, Neptune at 10°30', and

Mars at 29°56' in a wide outgoing conjunction, all three in the 1st house: clear signs of the man who feels his being completely immersed in nature (Pisces and Neptune), sensing the mystical presence of God in the whole of creation around him.

The idealistic and enthusiastically aiming Jupiter, lower ruler of Pisces, is in pioneering Aries at 10°49', with a measure of peace and harmony from Venus at 19°56', outgoing conjunct, finding his trails and tracks, purposes and aims, strongly surviving in a totally independent way, as Aries wants to live. This solar energy, basically determined to live in unity with nature and wildlife, flows to martial, active Aries and straight back to Pisces with Mars, ruler of Aries. Pisces' Neptune is 'locked' in its own sign, and needs the sense and order of Virgo to discover how to deal practically with life in nature, how to find the tools to survive in the wilderness with its wild beasts, but much more how to serve nature. This leads us to sensible and practical Mercury, ruler of serving Virgo, positioned in the sign behind his Sun sign, in altruistic and brotherly 6°57' Aquarius and the Moon at 4°21' ingoing conjunct, in the 12th house, but virtually conjunct the Ascendant, so physically living all this. We find the Moon in 5th Aquarius (Rudhyar: 'A world-leader is seen guided by his ancestor's spirits') of this world-famous 'Chief Scout' a strong example of this second image. See also his Jupiter at 10°49' Aries, second image: 'The ruler of a country is being officially introduced.'

From Aquarius we find a difficult ingoing quincunx from Saturn, lower ruler of Aquarius, at 7°28' Cancer in the 5th house, to the Moon, which is conjunct Mercury. Saturn and the Moon are, of course, in mutual reception.

The higher way from Aquarius leads to its ruler Uranus at 21°20' Taurus in the 3rd, with Pluto at 3°50' far behind it, but important because induced by the planets in Aries. Here we find the basis for the peace and brotherhood movement. Jupiter in Aries, ruler of the 10th and the 11th houses, aiming with strong impulses, intends to initiate the growth of high, idealistic oneness with natural conditions. Jupiter in Aries is inducing Pluto in Taurus conjunct Uranus, and Mars in the 30th of Pisces, in an exact outgoing activating square with Persephone, higher ruler of Taurus, in Sagittarius, leading back to Jupiter in Aries.

In this circuit we find all the planets included and, because of Mars in Pisces, the energy flows back to the Sun in Pisces. Although his Part of Fortune in Capricorn in the 11th house is not included, I find this task, trine Pluto and Uranus in Taurus, fulfilled anyway. Overviewing all the possibilities, I am inclined to accept the 6th degree of Aquarius (CC IV of 272 days), as the true one:

6th AQUARIUS

*Janduz: 'On the edge of a prairie, at the left, an archer draws his bow
to send his arrow into the sun, so to speak.
The prairie is dried out and little flames of fire traverse it
in all directions up to the feet of the archer,
who does not seem to see the flames.'*

*Rudhyar: 'In an allegorical mystery-ritual
a man officiates alone.'*

Baden Powell died on 8 January 1941 with transiting Jupiter at 5°47' Taurus and the progressed Pluto at 5°35' Taurus, both not only square his corrected Ascendant but also in exact trines with his Part of Fortune at 5°38' Capricorn in the 11th house. This confirms the rightness of the Ascendant degree and the Part of Fortune we accepted. But in addition, and more importantly, what he has set into development with the scout movement, was an idealistic impulse which, in a personal sense, meant an abundance of growth for the future of his entire being. The Part of Fortune is the result of what the physical, the spiritual and the soul bodies have set out to achieve in a particular life. What is so extraordinary is that at the same time both planets are square with his Ascendant, his physical being. What on one hand meant a huge profit for his Part of Fortune meant on the other hand a polemic physical change, as if his physical body was harshly activated to develop into a totally new type of existence in matter, directed towards a new and unexplored area of life, waiting to be reconnoitred by this Chief Scout who aims his arrows towards the spiritual contents of the Sun, and 'officiates alone'.

CHAPTER SIXTEEN

Pearl Buck and the Good Earth

Name	Pearl Sydenstricker Buck
Birthdate	26 June 1892
Birthplace	Hillsboro, West Virginia, (USA) 39°N54', approx. 80°W00'
Zone	EST (LMT +5 hours = GMT)
LMT	12h 30m
GMT	17h 30m
RLT	12h 10m
RST	6h 30m = Ascendant 6°14' Libra (uncorrected), Sun 5°30' Cancer, Moon 3°08' Leo (uncorrected).
House system	Placidus.

Pearl Buck, the well-known author of *The Good Earth* and other novels, set in China, is an example of a birth in the USA, although the conception took place elsewhere, in this case in China. Our calculation of the conception therefore will be quite different from any other CC calculation.

Before Pearl was conceived, her mother had already lost three babies due to poor food and hygienic circumstances. For the birth of the new baby the doctor, for reasons of health and hygiene, advised her to return temporarily to the USA. Mother and healthy daughter happily returned to China 5 months after the birth to rejoin her husband, who was a Presbyterian evangelist in Tsjiankiang near the River Yantze, near Nanking. Therefore it is clear that baby Pearl was conceived here or in nearby Nanking. The location of Tsjiankiang is 32°N10' 118°E50'.

The difference between this and an ordinary CC is that in this case we have to take the

Interpolated ST of the Ascendant equal to
the position of the natal Moon 3°08' Leo
from the *China location*
instead of the birthplace
i.e. 32°N10' = ST 1h 31m
opposition point 3°08' Aquarius ST 15h 12m

PEARL S. BUCK

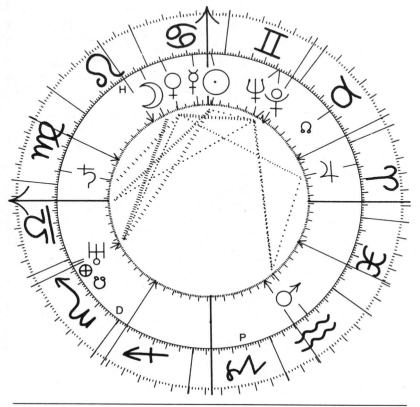

Radix							
	MC	7	9 Can	Sun	5 30	Can	9
	ASC	6	14 Lib	Moon	3 8	Leo	10
PEARL S. BUCK		— Plac —		Mercury	12 44	Can	10
	11.	10 29 Leo		Venus	24 43	Can R	10
Date: 26 6 1892	12.	10 34 Vir		Mars	16 48	Aqu R	5
Time: 17 30 0 E O	2.	2 54 Sco		Jupiter	21 23	Ari	7
Latitude: 39 54 N	3.	3 37 Sag		Saturn	24 11	Vir	12
Longitude: 80 0 W				Uranus	2 3	Sco R	1
	Node	14 29 Tau 8		Neptune	9 47	Gem	9
	Part ft	3 53 Sco 2		Pluto	8 58	Gem	9
				Perseph	20 30	Cap	4
				Hermes	11 15	Leo	11
				Demeter	27 00	Sco	2

Aspects: Radix/Radix   Orb: 8 0

MC Cnj Sun 1 40	MC ssx Plu 1 49	ASC Sqr Sun 0 44	ASC Tri Plu 2 44
Sun Cnj Mer 7 15	Sun Tri Ura 3 27	Moo Sqr Ura 1 6	Ven Sqr Jup 3 20
Ven Sxt Sat 0 32	Ven Sqr Ura 7 20	Ven ssq Nep 0 4	Ven ssq Plu 0 45
Mar Sxt Jup 4 34	Mar Tri Nep 7 1	Mar Tri Plu 7 50	Nep Cnj Plu 0 49
Nod Sxt Mer 1 44	Nod Sqr Mar 2 19		

In the second place, noticing the difference of *East for China* and *West for the USA*, we calculate in the conception correction the

difference between the RLT and the GMT:
118°E50' multiplied by 4m = RLT − or + 7h 55m (20s)
instead of the western longitude
of the birth town (USA 80° West = 5h 20m).

We also have to take into consideration, as usual for *western* longitudes as in this case, that we calculated in the *natal chart* the difference in time for the GMT as 5h 20m *later* than the RLT. Notice, in the CCC we have to calculate this difference for the *eastern* longitude of Tsjiankiang 118°50' east and not west. Therefore the GMT is 7h 55m *earlier* than RLT.

From the birthchart we take the following basic data, needed in order to calculate the CC:

1. With 6°14' Libra rising, the natal Moon is 3°08' Leo and the natal Sun 5°30' Cancer. We draw a line from the Sun to the same degree of the opposite sign and locate the Moon at the right-hand side at the outgoing arch, which means it is *waxing*. The Moon is positioned *above* the horizontal axis of Ascendant and Descendant, which means it is above the horizon. The scheme in Chapter 6 shows this to be the *2nd order* of Bailey which says '*Moon Ascendant, shorter/backwards*'.

2. We find the distance between the Moon at 3°08' Leo and the *Ascendant at 6°14' Libra* to be 64°, ignoring the minutes.

3. We divide this distance of 64° by 13° (the average daily motion of the Moon) = 5 degrees or days shorter.

4. 5 days shorter than 273 days (the average time of pregnancy) = 268 days.

5. 268 days subtracted from the birthdate 26.6.1892 = 2.10.1891, which is the first possible regular date of conception. Another way of calculating is by subtracting a full year from the birthdate giving 26.6.1891; subtract 268 days (see 4) from 365 days = 97 days to be added to the date of 26.6.1891 to find the regular date of 2.10.1891.

6. According to the 2nd order of Bailey, see the first paragraph, '*Moon radix is Ascendant or Descendant conception*', we need to know the ST of the natal Moon 3°08' Leo, and also (because according to the 2nd order '*or Descendant Conception*') for the opposite point of 3°08' Aquarius which can be found in the tables of houses for

Tsjiankiang (32°N10'). Both sidereal times have to be interpolated in order to be accurate.

Scheme for Calculating the 2nd Order
Moon *above* the horizon and *waxing*
Moon conception = Descendant or Ascendant radix
Moon radix = Descendant or Ascendant conception

Distance between the Moon (3°08' Leo)
and the *Ascendant* 6°14' Libra)
= 64° : 13°
= 5 days *shorter* than 273 days
= 268 days before the birthday
= 2.10.1891

The calculation of the first regular conception date is as follows:
From the ephemeris we take the ST at noon and find in the tables of houses for 32°N10' (Tsjiankiang, China) the interpolated ST approx. 1h 31m of the Ascendant equal to the position of the natal Moon (Leo 3°08') and also for the 2nd possibility of the same date, the ST approx. 15h 12m of its opposite point (Aquarius 3°08'), the difference between the respective sidereal times supplies the RLT, as follows:

ST 2.10.1891 at noon	12h 43m	
RLT	+12h 48m	
ST Moon 3°08' Leo	1h 31m (+24hrs = 25h 31m)	

We have to convert the RLT into GMT by subtracting 7h 55m from it = +4h 53m and to calculate the progression of the conception Moon in GMT +4h 53m by using diurnal proportional logarithms, to be found in the ephemeris:

RLT	+12h 48m	
Difference from GMT	−7h 55m	
GMT	+4h 53m	= Log. 6915
Daily motion of the Moon	11°51'	= Log. +3065
Progression of the Moon		Log. 9980 = +2°25'

Checking the ephemeris for 2.10.1891, we take the position of the Moon at noon and we adjust this position by adding to it the progression in +4h 53m at a daily motion of 11°51', which is the speed between 2 and 3 October, = +2°25', as follows:

Moon at noon 2.10.1891	3°08' Libra
Progression in +4h 53m	+2°25'
Corrected Ascendant	5°33' Libra

Ascendant 5°33' Libra is rising at 39°N54' (Hillsboro)
at approx. ST 6h 28m
approx. 2m earlier
than the official time
corrected LMT 0h 28m pm
corrected natal Moon 3°07' Leo
corrected PF 3°11' Scorpio

For the author of this particular famous set of novels, the trilogy
The Good Earth, which illustrates her powerful vision of a Chinese
farmer entirely bound to the soil of his countryland, the 6th of
Libra seems to be very appropriate. See the Janduz picture of this
degree:

6th LIBRA
'A farmer is ploughing his field.
At the end of the field one can see beautiful haystacks,
which encourage him in his work.'

Rudhyar: 'In a trance a pilgrim beholds his ideals made concrete'.

The second possibility of 282 days of pregnancy is 14 days earlier
than the previous date, 18.9.1891, and is calculated as follows:

From the ephemeris we take the ST at noon and the same ST as
in the previous calculation, the difference between the respective
sidereal times supplies the RLT, as follows:

ST 18.9.1891 at noon	11h 48m
RLT	+ 13h 43m
ST Moon 3°08' Leo	1h 31m (+ 24hrs = ST 25h 31m)

We have to convert the RLT into GMT by subtracting 7h 55m
from it and to calculate the progression of the conception Moon in
GMT + 5h 48m:

RLT	+ 13h 43m	
Difference from GMT	− 7h 55m	
GMT	+ 5h 48m	= Log. 6168
Daily motion of the Moon	15°16'	= Log. + 1965
Progression of the Moon		Log. 8133 = + 3°41'

Checking the ephemeris for 18.9.1891, we take the position of the
Moon at noon and we adjust this position by adding to it the
progression in + 5h 48m at a daily motion of 15°16', which is the
motion between 18 and 19 September, + 3°41', as follows:

Moon at noon 18.9.1891   29°25' Pisces
Progression in +5h 48m   +3°41'
Corrected Descendant radix   3°06' Aries = Ascendant 3°06' Libra

Ascendant 3°06' Libra is rising at *39°N54 (Hillsboro USA)*
approx. ST 6h 15m
approx. 15m earlier
than the official time
corrected LMT 0h 15h pm
corrected natal Moon 3°00' Leo
corrected PF 0°36' Scorpio

A birthtime 15m earlier can be ignored. And so can the second
option for the same date. The last possibility to be calculated is
that of 296 days which is 14 days before the previous date,
i.e. 5.9.1891:

From the ephemeris we take the ST at noon, but this time it
turns out to be more convenient to take the ST of the position
opposite to the natal Moon, the difference between the respective
sidereal times supplies the RLT, as follows:

ST 5.9.1891 at noon		10h 57m
RLT		+4h 15m
ST Moon 3°08' Aquarius		15h 12m

Converting the RLT +4h 15m into GMT, we subtract 7h 55m from
the RLT and we calculate the progression of the conception Moon
in GMT, −3h 40m. Notice that, in order to be able to subtract 7h
55m from the RLT +4h 15m, we have to add 12 hours to the RLT
+4h 15 = 16h 15m, and by doing so we have to *subtract* the result
from the Moon at noon, although it seemed to be in *addition*! As
follows:

RLT +4h 15m +12h	+16h 15m (we added 12 hours!)			
Difference from GMT	−7h 55m			
GMT	8h 20m a.m. = −3h 40m =	Log.	8159	
Daily motion of the Moon	11°50'	=	Log.	+3065
Progression of the Moon		Log.	11224 =	−1°49'

Checking the ephemeris for 5.9.1891, we take the position of the
Moon at noon and we adjust this position by subtracting from it
the progression in −3h 40m at a daily speed of 11°50', which is
the speed between 4 and 5 September, = −1°49', as follows:

Moon at noon 5.9.1891	6°05' Libra
Progression in −3h 40m	−1°49'
Corrected Ascendant radix	4°16' Libra

Ascendant 4°16' Libra is rising at 39°N54'
approx. ST 6h 21m
approx. 9m earlier
than the official time
corrected LMT 0h 21m p.m.
corrected natal Moon 3°03' Leo
corrected PF 1°50' Scorpio

CCI (6th Libra) presents a birth only 2 minutes earlier than
recorded and is therefore much more acceptable than CCII (4th
Libra) which is 16 minutes earlier and CCIII (5th Libra), which is 9
minutes earlier.

Assuming we didn't know about a conception in China, we
should have calculated the CCC for the birth place in Hillsboro
(West Virginia) USA. Interestingly, lat. 39°N54' runs straight
over Peking! Let us see what difference this will present.

Remember that in this case we have to deal with a *western*
latitude, and as is said before, the time difference between RLT
and GMT in this case is 80° multiplied by 4 minutes, giving us 5h
20m. In our calculations we have to be aware the GMT will be 5h
20m *later* than RLT.

Also we remember in this case we have to take the ST 1h 13m of
the rising natal Moon at 39° *north* 54', the results of calculating
the consecutive possibilities are:

268 = 2.10.1891
Ascendant 7°08' Libra
ST 6h 36m
6m later
a difference of +1°35' with CCI for China

282 = 18.9.1891
Ascendant 5°10' Libra
ST 6h 26m
4m earlier
a difference of only −0°25' with CC II for China

296 = 5.9.1891
Ascendant 3°55' Libra
ST 6h 18m 30s
12m earlier
a difference of only 0° − 21' with CC III for China

Although, and unusually, we also came to 6th Libra (CC II) in this
calculation, the difference is that we still have to sort out which
date the conception took place in order to calculate the conception

chart, if we want to do so. In our first calculation we found 6th Libra at the regular conception date of 2.10.1891 of 268 days, but in the second calculation it is 18.9.1891 of 282 days. Also, 4m earlier in the second calculation is more than the 2m we found in the first one.

If we ignore the difference of the true conception place, 268 days of pregnancy is more likely than 282, which is rather long. The second calculation therefore would have scored a minus compared with the first one but nevertheless we would have decided the 6th degree of Libra was the one we were looking for, rather than the other degrees we have calculated.

* * *

China is said to be ruled by Cancer and therefore it is perhaps not so surprising to discover that Pearl Buck, whose natal Sun in 6th Cancer was in conjunction with Mercury at 12°44' Cancer in the 10th house, not only chose the subject of Chinese life for her novels, but also decided to be conceived in China and actually lived there for many years. Mercury, in conjunction with Venus at 24°43' Cancer, was very well-placed to describe the rich variety of the old Chinese customs and habits in a harmonious way. These, in her time were still rooted in an ancient, almost medieval culture, expressing a typically Cancerian attachment to tradition and unwillingness to change and to modernise. With the ingoing sextile of Saturn at 24°11' Virgo, in the 12th house, she managed to find a beautiful form for her novels, and to express the structural decay of the old-fashioned Chinese empire which she witnessed. The positions in Cancer are shaping ingoing trines with reforming Uranus at 2°03' Scorpio and in particular with Demeter, the higher ruler of Cancer, at 27°00' Scorpio, with both planets conjuncting the Part of Fortune in 4th Scorpio and the south node in 15th Scorpio. Oppositions are to be found with Persephone in 21st Capricorn in the 4th house, and outgoing squares with Jupiter in 22nd Aries, through which she developed the ideal (Jupiter) of recording (Capricorn) the evolution (Persephone) of an entire race (China, Cancer, 4th house) in a series of novels. This paralleled her own development as she grew up in the midst of those people, learning and maturing under the influence of their racial characteristics. It is interesting to find that she, with Jupiter in Aries in the 7th house in her birthchart, chose a husband who was a Presbyterian evangelist, and who, as an agricultural expert, failed to realise his ideal of improving the obsolete agricultural methods (Jupiter in the outgoing square with Persephone, ruler of Taurus, in Capricorn in the 4th house) of the Chinese peasants (see also her corrected Ascendant degree of 6th Libra).

Persephone is in 20°30' Capricorn, and in an outgoing trine with Saturn, ruler of Capricorn, in the 12th house. Saturn, ruler of the 4th house (the deep past) and the 5th house (children), was undoubtedly behind the karmic principle responsible for much agony and suffering when in 1921 a mentally retarded child was born. Remarkably, as so often happens, this agony precipitated the expression of her literary talents, Mercury, ruler of Virgo, in 13th Cancer, induced by Saturn. Jupiter in 22nd Aries in the 7th house, as we have seen, induced her Pluto in the 9th of Gemini in conjunction with Neptune in the 10th of Gemini, both in the 9th house, and both also inducing Mercury. Interestingly, Saturn in the 25th degree of Virgo in the second image is also expressing bereavement ('a flag at half-mast').

From the Sun in Cancer the circuit flows to the Moon in the 4th of Leo, in conjunction with Hermes in 11°15', shaping ingoing (growing) squares with renewing and reforming Uranus in the 3rd of Scorpio (modernisation was begun by Emperor Kwang-Siu in 1895/8 but torpedoed by Empress Ts'e-si), and Uranus in turn has an outgoing square with Hermes. What was established knowledge for Pearl Buck's spirit (Sun), was for her soul a lack which made it necessary for her to face painful experiences (Moon) in this life, such as the birth of her handicapped child, followed by the death of her beloved mother (both in 1921), and last but not least by witnessing the violent events of the Boxer Rebellion in 1900 and of the *coup d'état* of the Republican General Chiang K'ai-shek in April 1927, who established his own government in nearby Nanking. She and her family were forced to hide in the house of Chinese friends, and were rescued by an American gunboat to be returned to the States, although temporarily. It seems she had to experience all this in order to become aware (Leo, Moon) in the hard way that her soul desired, and to develop a deeply transforming understanding (Uranus in Scorpio) and recognition (Hermes) of all that was stirred up and overturned in the Chinese group soul by the waves of blood and terror of a new rule, designed to modernise and reform Chinese life by the agricultural revolution of Mao Tse-tung. At the same time the transits of Uranus in the 1st degree of Cancer, in conjunction with transiting Pluto in 14th Cancer, were operating classically in regard to this Chinese reformation and revolution. We also recognise that Demeter, the higher ruler of Cancer and significant for the collective group soul of the Chinese race in particular, but also the symbol of her own astral soul-body, is to be found in Scorpio in the horrible 28th degree of Scorpio (Janduz: 'In a farmyard frightened poultry flap their wings in panic as they flee from a wolf which is escaping with a goose in its jaws. At the left, in the background, another wolf is standing on the carcass of a horse, howling at the sky'). The experience of this reforming change was consciously sought by her Higher Self in order to develop the unselfish altruism which it lacked. The Part of Fortune, particularly in conjunction with Uranus, expresses the wish to renew and reform the astral part of her eternal soul (Demeter), and the need to experience this (Moon) through actual external and explosive circumstances in her daily life. We wonder how much the soul bodies of both Pearl Buck and the Chinese nation were disturbed by the damage to their electromagnetic force fields. The revolution went entirely counter to the Cancerian instincts of the Chinese people, and most important even led to brainwashing and the indoctrinating practices of Mao, in which astral sources seem to be completely cut off. It is ironic that in order to overcome the very qualities which pertain to Cancer, the chosen method involved doing violence to the brain and the astral mirroring, both of which are ruled by Cancer, and therefore by the Moon and Demeter.

As we mentioned earlier on, it was the birth of a 'child not wanting to grow' as Pearl called it, and the death of her mother, both related to and concerning motherhood, so vital for a Sun in Cancer, which nevertheless gave her, with Pluto in conjunction with Neptune in Gemini, the inspiring impulse to start writing novels. We recall the outgoing squares between Saturn in Virgo, ruler of the 4th and the 5th houses, in the 12th house, with Pluto and Neptune in Gemini in the 9th house, by which Mercury, the ruler of Gemini, was also activated. By writing novels she was hoping to be able to earn the money needed to give her child the necessary nursing care. Soon afterwards she published with great success *East-Westwind* (1930), *The Good Earth* (1931), and *Oil for China's lamps* (1933), followed in 1946 by *Pavilion of Woman* each of which became a bestseller, one after the other. In all her novels, more than eighty altogether, she managed to project all she had understood and integrated of the internal and external qualities of the Chinese soul, most particularly in *The Good Earth*. This tells the life-stories of three generations of Chinese farmers and peasants, experiencing the big changes of life, caused by the agricultural revolution, peasants dedicated to the soil which they loved, and on which they lived. Here is her corrected Ascendant degree of 6th Libra and in particular the first image:

> *'A farmer is ploughing his field.*
> *At the end of the field one can see beautiful haystacks,*
> *which encourage him in his work.'*

In 1931 she was awarded the American Pulitzer prize and in 1938 the Nobel prize for literature. Through her work she contributed much towards improving the relations between America and China (see the positions in the 10th house). She was rewarded by witnessing the first visit of an American President to China. After 1945 she became active in seeking political equality for people of all races. In her own way she has indeed ploughed and sown the land given to her, and brought it to a rich fertility.

With the Sun in Cancer, and the Moon in Leo in conjunction with intermediating Hermes, and also the ingoing squares involved, Pearl Buck has been a loving mother promoting her dearest wish to dissolve the problems of racial discrimination in an advanced modern (Uranus) way, by an Aquarian style of upbringing and education for her adopted half-blood orphans. She started a private 'Welcome House Adoption Agency' to place more than 150 of the abandoned children of American fathers and Asiatic mothers, aiming to change (Scorpio) their abominable life-circumstances (Moon in Leo) into something which was more human (Uranus) than was encountered in her time by these racially disqualified children. Employing these positions of Uranus and Demeter in Scorpio in the 2nd house of finances, Pearl Buck spent all her money establishing institutes everywhere in which this Aquarian treatment was to be given. With this she must surely have filled the gaps in her etheric body, expressed by the Moon in the ingoing square with Uranus.

Because the Moon is in Leo, the circuit immediately leads back to the Sun in Cancer, and from here Demeter in 28th Scorpio is more and more deeply felt and urged to achieve not only renewing changes, stirred up for her own internal (astral) emotional feelings of concern and care, but also for the renewing change of racial and social life for these ignored and despised coloured children. This deep-rooted desire for renewal was strongly augmented by the ruler of Scorpio (and also by Jupiter in Aries), Mars in 17th Aquarius in the outgoing, activating, square with Uranus in Scorpio, which is influenced straight away because it is the ruler of Aquarius. From here Saturn is induced, leading to Mercury, as we have seen before. The remarkable thing is how strongly Pearl Buck felt the welling up of what has commonly been recognised as unprejudiced humanity and care, demanding democratic equality of rights and duties.

Pearl Buck died on 6 March 1973 in Danby (Vermont, USA).

Her progressed Uranus had moved on to 3°50' Scorpio, exactly on the natal Part of Fortune. The natal Moon at 3°08' Leo was square with this Part of Fortune again pointing to the urge expressed in the radix to achieve an inner change in the etheric side of the soul in particular. Although a stage was reached whereby Uranus had indeed enlightened, enriched and widened her Part of Fortune, the same task remained in the sense of a more comprehensive transformation of that which had been undertaken during her life. In conjunction with the south node in 14°29' Scorpio it will be clear that, although in this life the Part of Fortune has been worked out positively, there is still more to be done in the same area, to be undertaken in future times. For this pilgrim (see the second image of her corrected Ascendant degree) there is much more to dream:

Rudhyar: *'In a trance a pilgrim beholds his ideals made concrete.'*

CHAPTER SEVENTEEN

HRH Willem-Alexander, Prince of Orange

Name	HRH Willem-Alexander Claus Ferdinand, Prince of Orange-Nassau.
Birthdate	27 April 1967
Birthplace	Utrecht, The Netherlands, 52°N05', 5°E08'
LMT	19h 57m
GMT	18h 57m
RLT	19h 17m 32s
RST	9h 38m 35s:Ascendant (uncorrected) 7°55' Scorpio, Sun 6°49' Taurus, Moon 21°53' Sagittarius (uncorrected).
House system	Placidus.

The conception correction of this royal birth is most exceptional and instructive, not only because the length of pregnancy is known to have been far beyond normal – approximately 300 days – but also because the conception presumably took place somewhere in the Greater Antilles. Because the time of birth is exactly known, it should be possible to present a satisfactory CC calculation. Unfortunately this is not the case, unless we accept a time of pregnancy of 317 days, an extraordinarily long period which seems to be out of the question. What remains is the acceptance of a birth 4 minutes later than the official time, which is unusually inexact for a royal birth. In any case, this serves as an example of the difficult detective work which sometimes has to be undertaken in the course of this type of calculation. As in this case, the knowledge of the parents' whereabouts when the conception took place is not always available, and the question mark with which we are left at the end of our labours only means that there are some imponderables remaining, and not that the method is faulty.

For the birthchart we take the following basic data, needed in order to calculate the CC:

1. With 7°55' Scorpio rising, the natal Moon is 21°53' Sagittarius and the natal Sun 6°49' Taurus. We draw a

HRH PRINCE WILLEM-ALEXANDER

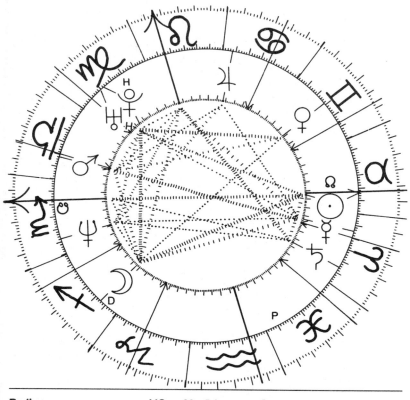

Radix

HRH PRINCE WILLEM-
ALEXANDER

Date: 27   4 1967
Time: 18 57   0   E O
Latitude: 52   5 N
Longitude: 5   8 E

Aspects: Radix/Radix   Orb: 8 0

MC	22	5	Leo		
ASC	7	55	Sco		
		Plac	—		
11.	24	54	Vir		
12.	19	23	Lib		
2.	6	15	Sag		
3.	12	27	Cap		
Node	7	8	Tau	6	
Part ft	22	59	Gem	8	

Sun	6	49	Tau		6
Moon	21	53	Sag		2
Mercury	22	0	Ari		6
Venus	15	42	Gem		8
Mars	20	17	Lib	R	12
Jupiter	26	33	Can		9
Saturn	6	42	Ari		5
Uranus	20	42	Vir	R	10
Neptune	23	26	Sco	R	1
Pluto	18	13	Vir	R	10
Perseph	5	24	Pis		4
Hermes	12	40	Vir		10
Demeter	26	55	Sag		2

MC Tri	Moo	0 12	MC Tri	Mer	0 5	MC Sxt	Mar	1 48	MC ses	Sat	0 23
MC ssx	Ura	1 23	MC Sqr	Nep	1 20	ASC Opp	Sun	1 6	ASC ssq	Moo	1 2
ASC qcx	Sat	1 13	ASC Opp	Nod	0 47	Sun ses	Moo	0 4	Sun ssx	Sat	0 7
Sun ses	Ura	1 8	Moo Tri	Mer	0 7	Moo Opp	Ven	6 11	Moo Sxt	Mar	1 36
Moo Sqr	Ura	1 12	Moo ssx	Nep	1 32	Moo Sqr	Plu	3 40	Mer Opp	Mar	1 43
Mer Sqr	Jup	4 33	Mer qcx	Ura	1 18	Mer qcx	Nep	1 26	Ven Tri	Mar	4 35
Ven Sqr	Ura	5 0	Ven Sqr	Plu	2 32	Mar Sqr	Jup	6 15	Mar ssx	Ura	0 24
Jup Tri	Nep	3 7	Sat ses	Nep	1 43	Ura Sxt	Nep	2 44	Ura Cnj	Plu	2 28
Nod Cnj	Sun	0 19	Nod ses	Moo	0 15	Nod ssx	Sat	0 26	Nod ses	Ura	1 27

line from the Sun to the same degree of the opposite sign and locate the Moon at the left-hand side at the ingoing arch, which means it is *waning*. The Moon is positioned below the horizontal Ascendant–Descendant axis, which means it is *below* the horizon. The scheme in Chapter 6 shows this to be the *4th order* of Bailey which says *'Moon/Descendant, shorter and backwards'*.

2. We find the distance between the Moon at 21°53' Sagittarius and the *Descendant* at 7°55' Taurus to be 135°, ignoring the minutes.

3. We divide this distance of 135° by 13° (the average daily motion of the Moon) = 10 degrees or days.

4. 10 days shorter than 273 days (the average time of pregnancy) = 263 days;

5. 263 days subtracted from the birthdate 27.4.1967 = 7.8.1966, which is the first possible regular date of conception. Another way of calculating is by subtracting a full year from the birthdate giving 27.4.1966; subtract 263 days (see 4) from 365 days = 102 days to be added to the date of 27.4.1966 to find the date of 7.8.1966.

6. According to the 4th order of Bailey, see the first paragraph, *'Moon radix is Ascendant or Descendant conception'*, we need to know the ST of the natal Moon 21°53' Sagittarius, and also (because according to the 4th order *'or Descendant conception'*) for the opposite point of 21°53' Gemini, which can be found in the tables of houses for *Baarn 52°N12'*. Both sidereal times have to be interpolated in order to be accurate.

Scheme for Calculating the 4th Order

Moon *below the horizon and waning*
Moon conception = Descendant or Ascendant radix
Moon Radix = Ascendant or Descendant conception

Distance between the Moon (20th Sagittarius)
and the *Descendant* (8th Taurus)
136°:13 =
10 days *shorter* than 273 days =
263 days before the birthdate 27.4.1967 =
7.8.1966

In the tables of houses for *52°N12' (Baarn)* we locate the

Interpolated ST of the Ascendant equal to the
position of the natal Moon

= 21°53' Sagittarius at ST approx. 13h 37m
and its opposite point 21°53' Gemini at ST aprox. 21h 12m

Because the birth was expected on 1 April, but actually took place on the 27th, it was approximately 28 days late, so we ignore this possibility of 263 days = 7.8.1966 and count backwards in time, in units of 14 days. The next date to be considered, 28 days before 7.8.1966 is *13.7.1966*, giving 291 days of pregnancy, which is more likely.

Here we have another problem because it is known the Royal couple between 2 July and 30 July were on a trip round the isles of the Greater Antilles, i.e. Curacao, Aruba or Bonaire, etc., or perhaps in Paramaribo (Surinam). Therefore this CC has to be calculated in a different way than before, in that the *ST of the rise of the natal Moon, which we took for Baarn, now has to be taken from the tables of houses for one of the following three mentioned latitudes.* According to Shanks' *International Atlas*:

Curacao   Willemstad, 12°N06', 68°W56',
           Standard Time since 1.1.1965 (LT +4 hrs is GMT)
           The difference between GMT and RLT is 68°W56' × 4m
           = 4h 36m.
Aruba   St John 12°N30', 68°W58',
           Standard Time is the same as for Curacao.
           The difference between GMT and RLT is 68°W58' × 4m
           = 4h 36m.
Surinam   Paramaribo, 5°N50', 55°W10',
           Standard Time since 1.10.1945 (= LT +3h 30m is GMT)
           The difference between GMT and RLT is 55°W10' × 4m
           = 3h 41m.

We have to be aware of the fact that these locations have *western* longitudes and therefore the GMT is *later* than RLT.

In the tables of houses for *Paramaribo (5°N50)* we locate the

interpolated ST of the Ascendant equal to the
position of the natal Moon
21°53' Sagittarius at ST approx. 11h 35m
and its opposite point 21°53' Gemini at ST approx. 23h 14m

Because the positions in the ephemeris we are using are calculated for *midnight*, the following calculations are slightly different to the other examples, which were calculated for 12h 00m at noon.

Possibility (1)
The CCC for *Paramaribo* is carried out as follows:
From the ephemeris we take the ST at *midnight (00h 00m am)* for
13.7.1966 and find in the tables of houses for *Paramaribo 5°N50'*
the ST of the Ascendant equal to the position of the natal Moon
and also for the second possibility of the same date, the ST of its
opposite point. The difference between the two sidereal times
supplies the RLT, as follows:

13.7.1966 midnight ST	19h 22m
RLT	− 7h 47m
ST 21°53' Sagittarius	11h 35m

We convert the RLT −7h 47m (which in fact is 16h 13m on
12.7.1966) into GMT by subtracting 3h 41m from it = GMT −4h
06m and we calculate the progression of the conception Moon in
GMT −4h 06m = −2°08' by using diurnal proportional
logarithms, to be found in the ephemeris:

RLT	−7h 47m (= 4h 13m pm on 12/7)		
Difference from GMT	− 3h 41m		
GMT	− 4h 06m	= Log.	7674
Daily motion of the Moon	12°28'	= Log.	+ 2845
Progression of the Moon		Log.	10519 = −2°08'

Checking the ephemeris for 13.7.1966, we take the position of the
Moon at midnight and adjust this position by subtracting from it
the calculated progression in −4h 06m at a daily motion of 12°28'
(which is the motion from 12 to 13 July), as follows:

Moon at 13 July at 00h 00m midnight	13°59' Taurus
Progression in −4h 06m	− 2°08'
Corrected Descendant radix	11°51' Taurus
Corrected Ascendant radix	11°51' Scorpio

Checking the tables of houses for *Utrecht (= 52°N05')*

Ascendant 11°51' Scorpio is rising at 52°N05' (Utrecht) at
approx. ST 10h 01m
approx. 22m later
than the official time
corrected LMT 20h 19m
corrected natal Moon 22°05' Sagittarius
corrected natal Part of Fortune 27°07' Gemini

The result of a birth 22m later than the official time can be
ignored.

Possibility (2)
The calculation of the second possibility of the *same* date, is as follows:

We take the same ST at midnight for 13 July but we will see we had better take the previous day, 12 July and for the second possibility we take the ST of the Ascendant equal to the *opposite* point of the Moon, 21°53' Gemini. The difference between the two sidereal times supplies the RLT, as follows:

12.7.1966 midnight 00h 00m ST	19h 18m
RLT	+3h 56m
ST 21°53' Gemini	23h 14m

We convert the RLT = +3h 56m into GMT by *adding* 3h 41m to it = +7h 37m and we calculate the progression of the conception Moon in GMT = +7h 37m, as follows:

RLT	+3h 56m		
Difference from GMT	+3h 41m		
GMT	+7h 37m	= Log.	4984
Daily motion of the Moon	12°28'	= Log.	+2845
Progression of the Moon		Log.	7829 = 3°57'

We take the position of the Moon at midnight and we adjust this position by adding to it the calculated progression in +7h 37m at a daily motion of 12°28' which is the motion between 12 and 13 July, as follows:

Moon 12 July at midnight 00h 00m am	1°31' Taurus
Progression in +7h 37m	+3°57'
Corrected Descendant	5°28' Taurus
Corrected Ascendant	5°28' Scorpio

Notice we have *added* the time difference between RLT and GMT.

Ascendant 5°28' Scorpio is rising at 52°N05' (Utrecht) at
approx. ST 9h 23m
approx. 13m earlier
than the official time
corrected LMT 19h 42m
corrected natal Moon 21°45' Sagittarius
corrected natal PF 20°24' Gemini

A birthtime 13m earlier also has to be ignored.

Possibility (3)
Now we will have a look at the possibility of a conception in *Willemstad*. The ST of the natal Moon for Willemstad shows a

difference of only 10m but the time difference between RLT and GMT is 55m more than for Paramaribo. A calculation set up for *Aruba* doesn't make much difference and can be ignored.
In the tables of houses for *Willemstad (12°N06')* we locate the

interpolated ST of the Ascendant equal to the
position of the natal Moon
21°53' Sagittarius at ST approx. 11h 45m
and its opposite point 21°53' Gemini at ST approx. 23h 04m

We take the same ST as before but now we take from the tables of houses for *Willemstad 12°N06'* the ST of the Ascendant equal to the position of the natal Moon at 21°53' Sagittarius and also for the second possibility of the same date, the ST of its opposite point, 21°53' Gemini, the difference between the two sidereal times supplies the RLT, as follows:

12.7.1966 midnight 00h 00m ST	19h 18m
RLT	+3h 46m
ST 21°53' Gemini	23h 04m

We convert the RLT +3h 46m to GMT by *adding* to it *4h 36m* instead of 3h 4m = +8h 22m and we calculate the progression of the conception Moon in GMT +8h 22m, as follows:

RLT	+3h 46m		
Difference from GMT	+4h 36m		
GMT	+8h 22m	= Log.	4577
Daily motion of the Moon	12°28'	= Log.	+2845
Progression of the Moon		Log.	7422 = +4°21'

We take the same position of the Moon at midnight 00h 00m am and as before we adjust this position by adding to it the calculated progression in +8h 22m at a daily motion of 12°28' which is the speed between 12 and 13 July = +4°21', as follows:

Moon at midnight 00h 00m am	1°31' Taurus
Progression in +8h 22m	+4°21'
Corrected Descendant radix	5°52' Taurus
Corrected Ascendant radix	5°52' Scorpio

Ascendant 5°52' Scorpio is rising at 52°N05' (Utrecht) at
ST approx. 9h 26m
approx. 10m earlier
than the official time
Corrected LMT 19h 47m
Corrected natal Moon 21°47' Sagittarius
Corrected natal PF 20°50' Gemini

We notice a difference of 32′ in length compared with the CC for Paramaribo.

Counting backwards another fortnight, we calculate the CC for 28.6.1966, which is 303 days of pregnancy and more likely than the previous CC of 291 days. But on this date, as far as we know, the Royal couple were still in Holland, at their home in castle 'Drakesteyn' in Baarn, near Utrecht. Of course, it is possible that they visited friends in Mexico at that time, but we don't have any information about this. Interestingly, a rough calculation set up for Mexico City leads straight away to the desired result of 7°31′ Scorpio, so this possibility is worth checking, see page 193.

The calculation of this conception date, set up for *Baarn (Holland)*, see at the beginning of this chapter for the positions, is as follows:

Possibility (4)
From the ephemeris we take the ST at 00h 00m midnight at 28.6.1966 and find in the tables of houses for *Baarn 52°N12′* the ST of the Ascendant equal to the position of the natal Moon and also for the second possibility of the same date, the ST of its opposite point. The difference between the two sidereal times supplies the RLT, as follows:

28.6.1966 (303 days) midnight ST	18h 22m
RLT	+2h 50m
ST 21°53′ Gemini	21h 12m

We convert the RLT +2h 50m into GMT by *subtracting* 20m from it = +2h 30m and calculate the progression of the conception Moon in GMT +2h 30m = +1°24′, as follows:

RLT	+2h 50m		
Difference from GMT	−0h 20m		
GMT	+2h 30m	= Log.	9823
Daily motion of the Moon	13°29′	= Log.	+2504
Progression of the Moon		Log.	12327 = 1°24′

Checking the ephemeris for 28.6.1966, we take the position of the Moon at midnight and we adjust this position by adding to it the progression in +2h 30m at a daily motion of 13°29′, which is the motion between 28 and 29 June = +1°24′, as follows:

Moon at noon 28.6.1966	7°22′ Scorpio
Progression in +2h 30m	+1°24′
Corrected Ascendant radix	8°46′ Scorpio

Ascendant *8°46′ Scorpio* is rising at 52°N05′ (Utrecht) at ST approx. 9h 42m

approx. 4m later
than the official time
corrected LMT 8h 01 pm
corrected natal Moon 21°55' Sagittarius
corrected PF 23°52' Gemini

This time, because we are postulating a conception in Baarn, we *subtracted* the time difference from GMT of 20m from RLT +2h 50m. The second option of the same date can be ignored.

Bailey states that a pregnancy of 303 days is not impossible although it has to be said, fairly rare. But now, not having found a CC exactly equal to the official time, we are forced to face an even longer period than 303 days, in this case, of 317 days. Ironically it will show exactly what we are looking for.

Possibility (5)
From the ephemeris we take the ST at midnight on 15.6.1966 (317 days) and as before we find in the tables of houses for *Baarn* (52°N12') the interpolated ST of the Ascendant equal to the position of the natal Moon and also for the second possibility of the same date, the ST of its opposite point. The difference between the two sidereal times supplies the RLT, as follows:

15.6.1966 midnight ST	17h 31m
RLT	+3h 41m
ST 21°53' Gemini	21h 12m

We convert the RLT into GMT by subtracting 20m from it = +3h 21m and we will calculate the progression of the conception Moon in GMT +3h 21m:

RLT	+3h 41m		
Difference from GMT	−0h 20m		
GMT	+3h 21m	= Log.	8552
Daily motion of the Moon	12°48'	= Log.	+2730
Progression of the Moon		Log.	11282 = +1°47'

Checking the ephemeris for 15.6.1966, we take the position of the Moon at midnight and we adjust this position by adding to it the progression in +3h 21m at a daily motion of 12°48', which is the motion between 15 and 16 June = +1°47', as follows:

Moon at noon 15.6.1966	6°02' Taurus
Progression in +3h 21m	+1°47'
Corrected Descendant radix	7°49' Taurus
Corrected Ascendant radix	7°49' Scorpio

Ascendant 7°49′ Scorpio is rising at 52°N05′ (Utrecht) at
ST approx. 9h 38m
which time is exactly the same as the official birthtime
= LMT 7h 57m pm
corrected natal Moon 21°53′ Sagittarius
corrected PF 22°53′ Gemini

As I have said before, a pregnancy of 317 days is far beyond any
limit and therefore unlikely. Also, the announcement of
birthtimes nowadays and in particular in the case of a Royal birth
has to be considered as accurate. The CC possibility of 8°47′
Scorpio for 303 days of pregnancy (28.6.1966) was 4 minutes later,
303 days is more likely than 317 and we ask, is it possible a
mistake was made and the birth really occurred at LMT 8h 01m
pm?

Summary of Possibilities

Date	No. days	CC		PF		ST	Time difference	☽
13/7	291	11°51′	♏	27°07′	♊	10h 01m	22′ later	22°05′ ♐
		5°28′	♏	20°24′	♊	9h 23m	15′ earlier	21°45′ ♐
		5°52′	♏	20°50′	♊	9h 26m	10′ earlier	21°47′ ♐
28/6	303	8°46′	♏	23°52′	♊	9h 42m	4′ later	21°55′ ♐
15/6	317	7°49′	♏	22°53′	♊	9h 38m		21°53′ ♐

As we have mentioned, it is quite possible that the parents, just
before they started their trip, should have visited friends in
Mexico. A conception correction for 28.6.1966, which gives an
acceptable pregnancy of 303 days, for Mexico City 19°N24′ and
99°W09′ (GMT 6h 36m 36s later), presents a corrected Ascendant
of 7°28′ Scorpio, only 1½ minutes earlier than the official
birthtime.

8th SCORPIO

*Janduz: 'A beautiful cock in a field is slowly flapping its wings.
In a circle around him some hens are pecking grain.
Further to the right an archer is shooting arrows at a flight of birds,
already far on the horizon.'*

Rudhyar: 'A high mountain lake is bathed in the full moonlight.'

9th SCORPIO

*Janduz: 'A poorly dressed child of about 10 sits on a log
and looks sadly, with pity, at a bird's nest fallen from a tree,
with two or three barely feathered young birds lying on the ground.
A kind of nimbus surrounds the head of the compassionate child.'*

Rudhyar: 'A dentist is repairing teeth ruined by civilised habits.'

Comparing the degree symbols of 8th and 9th Scorpio, and
checking out the natal chart, we find that the position of Neptune
in the 24th of Scorpio in the 1st house could perhaps be seen as
evidence for 9th Scorpio, but much more of 8th Scorpio is visible
when we look at the strong positions in Aries ('the cock and
hens') and in the cardinal cross, composed of Mercury in the 23rd
of Aries in a wide outgoing conjunction with Saturn in the 7th of
Aries, both planets opposition Mars, ruler of the Ascendant and
of Mercury in Aries, in 21st Libra. This in turn shapes an
activating outgoing square with aiming Jupiter ('the archer') in
27th Cancer. The Moon, ruler of Cancer, in 22nd Sagittarius, is in
mutual reception with Jupiter in Cancer ('the high mountain lake
in the full moonlight').

In the circuit we find the Sun in the 7th of Taurus, near to the
cusp of the 7th house, in conjunction with the north node in 8th
Taurus. The lower lines from the Sun in Taurus go to 16th Venus
in mobile Gemini in the 8th house of production and
transformation, in an outgoing, activating square with the higher
ruler of Taurus, Persephone, in 6th Pisces in the 4th house. In this
case the lower function of Taurus is activating the higher
function: the drive to establish a harmonious growth towards an
already prophesied future, by which I mean a religion (Pisces)
which aims for and reconnects (*re-ligare*, to bind) with the
prophetic (Persephone, Taurus) parts of the bible, revealing the
way humanity will develop. Venus forms ingoing, ripening,
squares with the mighty positions of Pluto, Hermes, and Uranus
in Virgo. These rare positions of the higher functions of Aries,
Gemini and Aquarius in Virgo, very important and significant for
the present maturing generation, are prominently found in the
10th house, and the inherent conditions are likely to be
substantial in the not too distant future. Venus in this case
takes a very important role because it is conjunct the Part of
Fortune. This has to be seen not only personally but also in a
collective sense as a spiritual growth towards the balanced
(Venus) establishment of purifying, cleansing (Virgo) impulses
(Pluto) and the strength (Pluto) to serve (Virgo) his country and
his people. One day his royal position could be encircled by

helpful angelic forces (Uranus) making a connecting link (Hermes) between heaven and earth in the struggle for a better and cleaner future, which turns out to be his life-task. Venus in the strengthening ingoing triangle with Mars in the 21st of Libra knows in which way it can be active in contributing towards a new environmental equilibrium, but being positioned in the 12th house is demanding a sacrificial willingness. The Moon in conjuction with Demeter, both in Sagittarius, supporting these demands, is the mirror of a soul force aiming for high purposes and ideals, inwardly seen, to achieve the massive cleaning-up of his country and the rest of the world, demanded by Virgo. In a world daily becoming more and more polluted and at this rate destined to become eventually uninhabitable, this is an almost superhuman task and in it he will be required to go 'from strength to strength'. This Prince, with the Sun in Taurus, supported by ingoing (strengthening) trines with the positions in Virgo in the 10th house, is very well equipped to succeed in his royal task.

From Gemini the energy is moving on to Mercury, the lower ruler of Gemini, in Aries, and to Hermes (the higher function of Gemini) in Virgo, constantly being recharged with new energy. The higher line from Taurus moves to Persephone in Pisces and to Neptune in Scorpio in the 1st house, connecting with Mars in Libra through which Venus is again activated. As a result of the tense oppositions between the three planets in Virgo and Persephone in Pisces, the Prince will have to call more and more on the co-operation of the Sun in Taurus as the overarching bridge, if he is to produce an understanding awareness and thus be enabled to lead his country through apocalyptic times, in which any future will seem to have faded away (the position of Persephone in Pisces), towards the promises of a biblically prophesied future (the meaning of Persephone, higher ruler of Taurus).

Jupiter, the lower function of Pisces, is positioned in Cancer, the sign which arches over the Netherlands. Through Jupiter, all the forces mobilised in this natal chart have to be aimed towards his Zebulonitic country, a small part of modern Israel, like arrows of idealism promising restoration and renewed growth in the dark and difficult times to come. We pray that the Lord will bless him richly and grant him strength in this gigantic task.

Bibliography

1 Solt, P. F. van, *De Regel van Hermes*, Dutch Astrological Society, 1938.
2 Janduz (J. Duzéa), *Les 360 degrés du Zodiac*, ed. Niclaus, Paris, 1939. republished 1975, Schors, Amsterdam, Holland.
3 Jones, Dr Marc Edmond, *Sabian Symbols in Astrology*, Shamballa, Col. USA, 1953.
4 Rudhyar, Dane, *The Astrology of Personality*, 1936; *An Astrological Mandala*, Random House, New York, 1973.
5 (a) Koppejan, Willem A., 'Gradenboek', 1956, (b) Dra. Helene W. van Woelderen Koppejan, *The Zodiac Image Handbook*, Element Books, 1990.
6 Sepharial (W. Gorn Old), articles in *Astrological Magazine*, approx. 1890, Foulsham London, reprinted London, 1962.
7 Bailey, E. H., D. A., F.A.S., *The Pre-Natal Epoch*, Foulsham, London, 1916. republished Samuel Weiser Inc., Maine, USA, 1974 (O.P.).
8 Thierens, Dr A. E., *Astrologische berekeningen*, Amsterdam, Holland, 1930, *Natural Philosophy*, Rider & Co., London.
9 Knegt, Leo, *Astrologie, Wetenschappelijke Techniek*, Amsterdam, 1928.
10 Dam, Drs Wim van, *Correctie van de geboorte horoscoop*, W. N. Schors, Amsterdam, Holland, 1980.
11 Gorter, Cornelis, *Astrologische Chronologie*, Couvreur, The Hague, 1939.
12 Hone, Margaret, *The Modern Textbook of Astrology*, Fowler, 1951.
13 Scheps, Niek, *Harps and Healing*, mss 1987.
14 Libra, C. Aquarius, *Astrologie*, L. J. Veens Uitg. Mij., Amsterdam, Netherlands.
15 Bouman, A., *Getalschrift*, Publ. Vanderstoep, Heinenoord, Netherlands, 1986.
16 Weinreb, Dr Friedrich, *Roots of the Bible*, Merlin Books, Braunton, 1986; Weinreb, *Leben im Diesseits und Jenseits*, Origo Verlag, Zürich, 1974; Bullinger, E. W., *Number in Scripture*, Lamp Press, London; 1952. Curtiss, H. A. and F. H., *The Key to the Universe*, Health Research, Mokelumne Hill California, USA, 1974; *The Key of Destiny*, Dutton and Comp., New York, 1919.
17 Steiner, Dr Rudolf, *Theosophy*, Publ. Anthroposophical Society.
18 Blavatsky, H. P., *The Key to Theosophy*, Publ. Theosophical Society.
19 Grotefend, H., Taschenbuch Zeitrechnung Mittelalter; Strubbe, Prof. Dr E. I. and Voet, Dr L., *Medieval Chronology*; Lietzmann, H., *Zeitrechnung Römischer Kaiserzeit*.

20 Picard, Max, *The Human Face*, Bijleveld, Utrecht, Netherlands, 1948.
21 Dali, Salvador, *La vie secreté de Salvador Dali*, ed. de la Table Ronde, 1967.
22 Avery, Jeanne, *The Rising Sign, your Astrological Mask*, Doubleday, New York, 1982.
23 Kamnitzer, Ernst, *Fragmente*, Wolfgang Jess Verlag, Dresden, 1929.
24 Dodd, Alfred, Fr. *Bacon's Personal Life-Story*, Rider & Company, London, 1986.
25 Arroyo, Stephen, *Astrology, Karma and Transformation*, CRCS Publications, Vancouver, 1978.
26 Ptolemy (a) 'Tetrabiblos' (trans. F. E. Robbins) Loeb Classical Library, Harvard University Press, Cambridge, Mass., USA., 1940, (b) *Centilogue* (trans. J. M. Ashmand), Foulsham, London.
27 The *Astrological Journal*, Winter 1972/3, pp. 26–32, 'Dutch Astrology' by E. I. K. Esser; Ephemeris of Persephone, Hermes and Demeter: ditto, Spring 1973, p. 41.
28 (a) Schulz, Gerhard, *Novalis*, Rowohlt, 1969, (b) van der Leeuw, Prof. G., *Novalis*, Hollandia, Baarn, Holland.
29 Leo, Alan, (a) *1001 Nativities*, International Publishing Co., Edinburgh, (b) *Casting the horoscope*, London.
30 Davidson, David and Aldersmith H., *The Great Pyramid*, Williams and Norgate, 1948.
31 (a) Schilfgaarde, Prof. Dr P. van, *Levenswegen*, Servire, The Hague, Netherlands, 1959; (b) Fr. Boll/C. Bezold, *Sternglaube und Sterndeutung*, p. 154, Teubner, Berlin, 1926; (c) A. Bouché-Leclercq, L'Astrologie grecque', Paris, 1899;
32 Uyldert, Mellie, *Astrologie I*, de Driehoek, Amsterdam, Holland, 1975.
33 (a) The Astrological Association *Newsletter*, November 1987;
(b) Filbey, John and Peter, *Astronomy for Astrologers*, Aquarian Press, 1984.
34 Fuller, Jean Overton, *Sir Francis Bacon*, East-West Publications, London, 1981.
35 Lilly, William, *Peace or No Peace*, 1643 II, p. 168.
36 Rawley, William, D. D., *Resuscitation*, 1657.
37 Novalis, *Spiritual Songs*, Mercury Press, Spring Valley, New York, USA, 1986.
38 Schoch, Karl, *Planetentafeln für Jedermann*, Berlin, Linser Verlag, 1927.
39 Schramm, R., *Kalendariographische und Chronologische Tafeln*, Leipzig, Hinrichs, 1908.
40 Neugebauer, Prof. P.V., *Astronomische Chronologie*, de Gruyter, Berlin, 1929.
41 Ram, Th. J. J., *Psychologische Astrologie*, Becht, Amsterdam, Holland, 1935.
42 Snijders, Ir. C. J., *Beginselen der Astrologie*, Becht, Amsterdam, Holland, 1940.
43 Cooper, J. C., *Encyclopedia of Traditional Symbols*, Thames & Hudson, London, 1978.

44 'Ganesha', *Esoteric Encyclopedia*, Theosophische Uitgeverij/Driehoek, Amsterdam.

45 Chandu, Jack F., *Time Changes in the World*, Ankh-Hermes, Deventer, 1985.

46 Wijk, W. E. van, *De Gregoriaansche kalender*, Martinus Nijhoff, The Hague, 1932.

47 Shanks, Thomas G., *The International Atlas*, ACS Publ., San Diego, USA., 1985.

48 Koppenstätter, Ed., *Zonen und Sommerzeiten*, Germany, 1937.

49 Dawkins, P., and Bokenham, Th., *The Virgin Ideal*, Francis Bacon Research Trust, Northampton, 1982.

50 Riess, E., *Philologus*, Supplementband 6, p. 358.

Index

sorrowful, 12th Gemini 101
Woodcraft Indians 169
world leader, 5th Aquarius 83,
170
worm (*tola'at*) 63

yin and yang 66

York, Princess of 129–36

Zeus 19
zodiacal circle 26
zodiacal pores 15
Zulus 151, 169